Speech, Writing, and Thought Presentation
in 19th-Century Narrative Fiction

OXFORD STUDIES IN THE HISTORY OF ENGLISH

The Early English Impersonal Construction
Ruth Möhlig-Falke

Information Structure and Syntactic Change in the History of English
Edited by Anneli Meurman-Solin, María José López-Couso, and Bettelou Los

Spreading Patterns
Hendrik De Smet

Constructions and Environments
Peter Petré

Middle English Verbs of Emotion and Impersonal Constructions
Ayumi Miura

Language Between Description and Prescription
Lieselotte Anderwald

Motion and the English Verb
Judith Huber

Categoriality in Language Change
Lauren Fonteyn

Speech, Writing, and Thought Presentation in 19th-Century Narrative Fiction: A Corpus-Assisted Approach
Beatrix Busse

Speech, Writing, and Thought Presentation in 19th-Century Narrative Fiction

A Corpus-Assisted Approach

BEATRIX BUSSE

OXFORD
UNIVERSITY PRESS

OXFORD
UNIVERSITY PRESS

Oxford University Press is a department of the University of Oxford. It furthers the University's objective of excellence in research, scholarship, and education by publishing worldwide. Oxford is a registered trade mark of Oxford University Press in the UK and certain other countries.

Published in the United States of America by Oxford University Press
198 Madison Avenue, New York, NY 10016, United States of America.

CIP data is on file at the Library of Congress
ISBN 978–0–19–021236–0

9 8 7 6 5 4 3 2 1

Printed by Integrated Books International, United States of America

CONTENTS

LIST OF TABLES AND FIGURES

Tables

Figures

ACKNOWLEDGMENTS

This book has a long history and I have many people to thank, for their support and the inspiration provided by their own work, as well as for the direct and indirect discussions I had with them about the topic of this book.

I particularly wish to thank Mick Short, who introduced me to the various ways in which the speech, thought, and writing of others can be presented. Without his wisdom and his support, nothing of this would have been possible. My gratitude goes to Terttu Nevalainen, Hallie Stebbins, and Meredith Keffer for accepting this monograph for publication in the series "Oxford Studies in the History of English" and for their patience with me. I would also like to thank the two anonymous reviewers of the manuscript for their constructive criticism and advice. Many thanks are due to the British Academy for their support of my research stay as British Academy Visiting Fellow at Lancaster University.

I also wish to thank the following colleagues and friends for their continuous support and their very helpful comments on my work. I hope I have mentioned them all: Joe Bray, Margaret Bridges, David Britain, Cathy Emmott, Monika Fludernik, Kellie Gonçalves, Gerhard Härle, Bernd Hirsch, Andreas H. Jucker, Annette Kern-Stähler, Ursula Kluwick-Kälin, Merja Kytö, Geoffrey Leech, Michaela Mahlberg, Tony McEnery, Dan McIntyre, Ruth Möhlig-Falke, Roçio Montoro, Marga Munkelt, Nadja Nesselhauf, Heinz-Joachim Neuhaus (†), Terttu Nevalainen, Nina Nørgaard, Jörg Peltzer, Paul Rayson, Virginia Richter, Elena Semino, Hilary Short, Mick Short, Jennifer Smith, Irma Taavitsainen, Michael Toolan, and Ingo H. Warnke.

I particularly wish to thank Ursula Kluwick-Kälin, Ruth Möhlig-Falke, Roçio Montoro, and Mick Short for their invaluable assessments of drafts of this book.

Finally, I wish to thank my family: my mum, my dad, who sadly passed away in October 2018, my sister Ina and her husband Norbert, and my uncle Toni. My deepest gratitude goes to my partner, Udo Gerdelmann.

Beatrix Busse, Heidelberg, July 2019

LIST OF ABBREVIATIONS

cat	speech, writing, or thought presentation category of the annotated stretch of text
CLAWS	Constituent Likelihood Automatic Word-Tagging System
CONCE	A Corpus of Nineteenth-Century English
div1	a boundary between individual text chunks
DS	direct speech
DW	direct writing
e	embedded discourse presentation
eIS	embedded indirect speech
eNRS	embedded narrator's representation of speech
FDS	free direct speech
FDW	free direct writing
FID	free indirect discourse
FIS	free indirect speech
FIT	free indirect thought
FIW	free indirect writing
h	hypothetical discourse presentation
i	inferred thought presentation
IS	indirect speech
IT	indirect thought
IW	indirect writing
N	narration
NI	internal narration
NRS	narrator's representation of speech
NRSA	narrator's presentation of a speech act
NRSAp	narrator's presentation of speech acts with topic ("p")
NRT	narrator's representation of thought

NRTA	narrator's presentation of a thought act
NRW	narrator's representation of writing
NT	narrator's presentation of / reference to thought
NV	narrator's presentation of voice
p	new paragraph
q	quotation phenomenon
sptag	denotes the respective speech, writing, and thought presentation categories
SW&TP	speech, writing, and thought presentation
w	words of the annotated text part
who	indicates the speaker

CHAPTER 1 | Introduction

1.1. *This Study and Its Aims*

It is difficult to imagine an example of a narrative that does not contain a reference to or a quotation of someone's speech, thoughts, or writing. These reports further a narrative, make it more interesting, natural, and vivid, ask the reader to engage with it, and, from a historical point of view, they also reflect cultural understandings of the modes of discourse presentation. To a large extent, the way we perceive a story depends upon the ways discourse is presented.

In the following passage from Elizabeth Gaskell's (2007 [1853]: 38) *Cranford*, the first-person narrator, Mary Smith, informs the reader about an invitation which Miss Matty and Miss Pole have received from Mr. Holbrook, Miss Matty's first, but unrequited love:

> I expected Miss Matty to jump at this invitation; but, no! Miss Pole and I had the greatest difficulty in persuading her to go. She thought it was improper; and was even half annoyed when we utterly ignored the idea of any impropriety in her going with two other ladies to see her old lover. (*Cranford* 2007 [1853]: 38)

The first sentence in this paragraph is from the narrator, whose thoughts are reported via indirect thought (IT). It is interesting to note that with first-person narration—here intradiegetic, with the narrator being a story participant (Bal 1997; Genette 1980; Rimmon-Kenan 2002 [1983]: 72)—the presentation of the narrator's thoughts tends to be achieved by dropping away the narratorial presence. Mary becomes the focalized consciousness, which is signaled by the reporting clause "I expected," which, in turn, introduces a stretch of IT "to jump at this invitation." Yet, the narrator always remains the controlling teller through internal focalization—although Cohn (1978: 144) makes the point that a "first-person narrator has less access to his own past psyche than the omniscient narrator of third-person fiction has to his characters," because she is all knowing.[1] The reported clause, which is IT, "to jump at this invitation" also contains an embedded reference to a writing act—that is, the "invitation"—which has been sent before. Then the narrative moves even closer to the

Speech, Writing, and Thought Presentation in 19th-Century Narrative Fiction. Beatrix Busse,
Oxford University Press (2020). © Oxford University Press.
DOI: 10.1093/oso/9780190212360.001.0001

focalized consciousness through the exclamative "but, no!," which is free indirect thought (FIT) and illustrates the narrator's surprise at and lack of understanding of Miss Matty's denial of the invitation. The narrative is modulated so that it is more removed from the narrator's thoughts and directed toward the characters', instead. Miss Pole's and Mary's verbal attempts at persuading Miss Matty to accept the invitation are rendered in the form of the narrator's report of a speech act in: "Miss Pole and I had the greatest difficulty in persuading her to go." The narrator does not mention the exact words of this persuasive attempt but just the speech act. Instead, for the length of a sentence, a turn is made to Miss Matty's words in free indirect speech (FIS) (and not thought), "She thought it was improper," which somewhat ridicules her adherence to social decorum, on the one hand, and her attempt at keeping up appearances, on the other. Following the presentation of Miss Matty's speech act in FIS is an inferred presentation of Miss Matty's feelings, "she was even half annoyed," and a presentation of Miss Pole's and Mary's report of a thought act in "we utterly ignored the idea," which also contains an embedded reference to Miss Matty's speech act in the "idea of any impropriety."

The analysis of these five sentences from *Cranford* shows that the portrayal of different forms of telling and showing the narrator's and characters' voices may come almost without any narration. Instead the modulations involve switches of perspective or point of view through the mode of discourse presentation and the respective categories, although it seems clear that the controlling voice of the "teller" (Simpson 1993) is always there; hence, Roman Jakobson's assessment that reported speech may be "a crucial stylistic and linguistic problem" (Jakobson 1971: 130). Discourse presentation is, generally speaking, a product of the author, that is, of the producer of the antecedent discourse—be it speech, thought, or writing—which is then reported in a special way and with a specific degree of faithfulness and verbatimness to the anterior discourse. For example, in his famous study, Vološinov (1973 [1929]: 118) claims for speech presentation that "[r]eported speech is speech within speech, utterance within utterance, and at the same time also speech about speech, utterance about utterance." Hence, at the intra-textual level, the narrator compiles the speech, thought, or writing of others by reporting the exact words or the content of what was said and presenting them in a specific mode of discourse presentation. Such discourse presentation is the intrusion of the voice of one speaker or writer in the discourse of another (Moore 2011: 2). Because of the different functions and effects that go hand in hand with the chosen mode, the narrator also becomes a translator and a figure who also commentates on the discourse of others.

This study offers a systematic investigation of speech, writing, and thought presentation[2] in a small corpus of 57,403 words from selected stretches of 19th-century narrative fiction. A systematic corpus-based approach to discourse[3] presentation has not yet been presented for 19th-century British English narrative fiction and, so far, scholars have only begun to show the importance of investigating systematically diachronic aspects within narratology and to draw our attention to the importance of cultural and historical contexts that reflect and construe historical patterns of discourse presentation (e.g., Fludernik 1993, 1996, 2003b; McIntyre and Walker 2011; Moore 2011; Marnette 2005 for historical French; Collins 2001 for historical Russian).

Frequently, within the linguistic framework, literature is not always seen as a reliable source for linguistic discoveries because of its artistic, fictional, and therefore special status. As a consequence, stylistics (Nørgaard et al., 2010; Short 1996; Simpson 2014)—that is, the linguistic analysis of mainly, but not exclusively, literary texts to explore the effects their wordings have on the reader—has been heavily criticized for its interdisciplinary character, its lack of a base in either linguistic or literary criticism, and the doubtful reliability of its main source of analysis, that is, literary texts. I would still like to follow Sinclair (2004: 51), who stresses: "no systematic apparatus can claim to describe a language if it does not embrace the literature also; and not as a freakish development, but as a natural specialization of categories which are required in other parts of the descriptive system."

There are various studies of discourse presentation in present-day English. These employ different approaches (for instance, Coulmas 1986a, 1986b; Holt and Clift 2007; Janssen and van der Wurff 1996; Vandelanotte 2009). Semino and Short (2004) develop the Leech and Short (1981/2007a) model further and investigate speech, writing, and thought presentation in an electronic corpus of 20th-century narrative fiction, newspaper reports, and autobiography. Their approach has been highly influential as the first corpus-based approach to analyze discourse presentation, and it has established the new scale of writing presentation. Semino and Short's (2004) work is also pioneering in its use of corpora and computerized methods to investigate nonfictional discourse. I use Semino and Short's (2004) approach, with modifications, on 19th-century texts in order to investigate the types, distribution, and functions of speech, writing, and thought presentation. The goal is to establish a description of discourse presentation in 19th-century English. I also compare the 19th- and 20th-century corpora in order to (a) discover diachronic changes and stability in the ways speech, writing, and thought are presented, and (b) test Semino and Short's (2004) model diachronically on historical data and on those cases whose categorization could be considered less straightforward. As such, the corpus approach is understood to be complementary to qualitative analyses. With additional recourse to studies by McHale (1978), Fludernik (1993, 1996), or Toolan (2001, 2007, 2009), Semino and Short's (2004) model has been chosen because it is based on the widely accepted model originally established by Leech and Short (1981/2007a). Further, their refined categorization enables the analyst to be as systematic and detailed as possible. In addition, a comparison with their 20th-century results is only possible if similar categories are used.

At this stage, certain issues need to be raised. It is important to highlight that, on the one hand, I am undertaking the analysis of discourse presentation in examples of narrative fiction which, naturally, illustrate older stages of the

English language; on the other hand, the fact that I have myself annotated a corpus also needs bearing in mind. Therefore, I have devoted some space (e.g., section 2.2 of Chapter 2, and Chapter 3) to outlining the methodologies and the challenges involved when (a) analyzing historical texts, and (b) applying corpus tools with a small corpus such as the one used here.

The first research question concerns the identification of the quantitative distribution of the different presentational modes on each scale of discourse presentation. This issue involves, for instance, such aspects as to whether direct speech (DS) is the most frequently occurring discourse presentation mode in general, and on the speech presentation scale in specific. It also addresses questions about the quantitative relationship between internal narration (NI) and narrator's presentation of thought (NT; Short 2007) on the thought presentation scale, and how forms of free indirect discourse function (FID) relate to each other, also as intoning dual or polyphonic voices. This is especially interesting because, for 19th-century novels, the claim is often made—based on intuitive observations—that they frequently contain FIS (Toolan 2001: 124).

From a quantitative and qualitative point of view, one goal is to investigate how the categories and functions of speech, writing, and thought presentation relate to one another in 19th-century texts and whether there is a continuity with Semino and Short's (2004) findings for 20th-century texts, or not. For example, in the Semino and Short (2004) corpus, the norm for speech presentation is DS, while that for thought presentation is NI followed by FIT (Semino and Short 2004: 114). Furthermore, the frequency and function of embedded, hypothetical, and inferred discourse presentation is interesting to note in quantitative and qualitative terms.

The quantitative identification of the modes of discourse presentation used in 19th-century narrative fiction also allows me to look into what Fludernik (1993: 281) has called the "direct discourse fallacy," that is, the constant equation of thought with speech or with thought being "inner speech" and the overestimation of the verbal component in thought (Palmer 2004: 71). This goes hand in hand with a sophisticated investigation of the prototypical practiced analytical focus to date on the seemingly more capturing categories, such as FIT or FIS, or the category of (free) direct thought. The systematic identification of the different scales and categories of speech, writing, and thought presentation cannot only satisfy the call for empirical evidence made by some scholars (e.g., Palmer 2004: 62), but can similarly account for the way the thought presentation scale needs to be seen within a general framework that encompasses context and consciousness in a purposeful, engaged, and socially minded way (Palmer 2010). Despite its datedness, I quote Palmer (2004) at length, because the claim still seems to be valid:

> Discussions about the relative frequency of the three modes will have only a limited value until careful empirical studies are done that use precise and universally agreed criteria for the modes [. . .]. Nevertheless, it is still worth making one or two general points while we await the empirical evidence. Fludernik's

> perspective on the issue is that, in the representation of consciousness, "direct discourse is the least common technique (except in the interior monologue of the twentieth-century novel), with a traditional preponderance of [thought report] and, in second place, free indirect discourse, which comes close to competing with [thought report] in late nineteenth- and early twentieth-century fiction" (1993: 291). I agree with her view that thought report is the most common mode, but I would dispute the weight that she gives to interior monologue. In my experience, what is called interior monologue often contains as much thought report as the other two modes, as well as a good deal of narratorial surface description of physical context. I would also dispute the weighting given to free indirect thought and would suggest that it can only be arrived at by classifying a good deal of colored thought report as free indirect thought. As I said, though, this can only be a very impressionistic discussion at this stage. (Palmer 2004: 62)

This quotation from Palmer (2004) illustrates that there is a need for empirical research to verify and falsify the highly valuable, yet "impressionistic" observations about discourse presentation modes in the history of English. In this study, I focus on all modes of discourse presentation and their respective functions, including those that are conventionally seen as closer to the narrator's end of the scales of discourse presentation, such as the narrator's presentation of a speech or thought act (NRSA/NRTA) or NV and NI.

What Palmer (2004: 62) describes for the discourse presentation categories can perhaps be compared to the attention that has been paid to the varieties of English in variationist sociolinguistics (Britain 2002), where it is often claimed that for a long time the emphasis has been placed on the major varieties of English (such as General American English, British English, and so on); possibly, this happened at the expense of the lesser known varieties, which are, however, equally revealing. For discourse presentation modes, as mentioned, so far the seemingly more interesting categories of FIS/FIT and direct speech (DS)/direct thought (DT) have been more frequently investigated. Yet, those categories in discourse presentation that summarize a speech or writing act, for instance, are of equal importance. And yet, there are still quite a few things to explore as regards the so-called more interesting or challenging categories of discourse presentation, such as the free direct forms of speech, thought, and writing as well as FIT and FIS, for example. Hence, the different modes of discourse presentation are seen in a continuum of equal importance.

Although Leech and Short (1981/2007a), Toolan (2001, 2006a, 2006b), Semino and Short (2004), and others have established general purposes of the respective types of speech, writing, and thought presentation, it is important to investigate their functions within the cultural, scientific, psychological, and social contexts of the 19th century as well. My aim in this book, therefore, is more encompassing than other studies have been on issues related to discourse presentation. My take on discourse presentation in 19th-century fiction explores, where possible, the close interaction between historical and social contexts at the time of writing and as represented in the novels under analysis.

Additionally, I also argue that the interplay between discourse presentation and point of view and the variety of contexts presented not only testifies to the advancement of narrative techniques, but is also a creative expression and reflection of 19th-century elaborations on vision, the psyche, Darwin's evolutionary theory, and the role of the artist. Besides, I discuss how the concept of "faithfulness" is also mentioned in contemporary 19th-century grammars. In sum, my approach to the analysis of discourse presentation attempts to fill some lacunae left by previous scholarly work.

A functional and contextual perspective to discourse presentation is strongly related to the effects of the various discourse presentation modes and how the reader perceives his or her alignment to the character and the contexts. Research on discourse presentation generally argues that, though the various speech and thought presentation categories are formally similar, their functionality is far from being also equivalent—in fact, they are sometimes claimed to have opposite effects. The use of free direct speech (FDS), for example, may transfer irony, whereas FIT, conventionally speaking, makes the reader feel very close to the mental world of the character and to his/her thoughts. The initially quoted example from *Cranford*, for instance, illustrates this manipulative to-and-fro. Thus, aspects such as characterization (Culpeper 2001; McIntyre 2014), that is, among others, the process by which readers comprehend characters and how vivid fictional personae are created, are also addressed in the study of discourse presentation categories.

Discussions and investigations of discourse presentation have also centered around the relationship between anterior discourse and the way this is reported faithfully or in a verbatim way (Fairclough 1988; Fludernik 1993; Sternberg 1982a; Short 1988, 2007, 2012; Tannen 1989). A distinction between speech presentation and speech summary has also been proposed by Short (2012), with a further suggestion that for the more summarizing categories a distinction be made between "proposition-domain summary" and "discourse-domain summary" (Short 2012: 24). Concepts of faithfulness and verbatimness of discourse presentation will be discussed in section 2.2 of Chapter 2. For reasons outlined in Chapter 2, this study exclusively draws on the speech, writing, and thought presentation scales for the quantitative analysis of the forms, types, and distribution of discourse presentation modes in 19th-century narrative fiction.

Another complex field of investigation is the relationship between discourse presentation and the micro- and macro-contexts of the novels as part of a corpus. Corpus techniques allow me to investigate whether it is possible to identify specific repetitive patterns, that is, collocations, clusters, units of meaning (Sinclair 2004: 24ff.), or lexico-grammatical phrases that are used to frame discourse presentation by means of narrative passages. Elements that further narrative progression, that is, those textual elements that highlight the reader's attention as to the continuation of the narrative, are called "diagnostic" (Toolan 2009: 16). In this study, the identification of diagnostic features is done by separating the different modes of speech, writing, and thought presentation from one another and comparing them with the language in CONCE, *A Corpus of Nineteenth-Century English*, compiled at the universities of Uppsala and Tampere (Kytö et al. 2000).[4] CONCE (Kytö et al. 2000) is a small corpus, made up of about 1 million words. It is divided into periods of several decades and takes account of 19th-century historical developments. It is genre-specific, containing texts from debates, trials, drama, fiction, letters, historical, and scientific monographs, and also includes a number of female authors (see Kytö et al. 2000; Kytö et al. 2006: 4ff.).

I pay special attention to collocations or collocational properties (Biber et al. 1999; Hoey 2005; Hoover, Culpeper, and O'Halloran 2014; Hori 2004; Hunston and Francis 2000; Mahlberg 2006, 2013; Sinclair 2004; Stubbs 2001, 2005; Toolan 2009). Corpus analytic methods to identify, trace, measure, and describe phrasal networks make use of software such as Scott's *WordSmith Tools* (2017) and Rayson's *Wmatrix* (2018) (although the results obtained from running corpora through these two pieces of software were further complemented by less automated searches). These tools serve to identify keywords, collocates, and clusters; crucially, they can also bring about a more fine-grained description of the lexico-grammatical features of discourse presentation stretches and accompanying narrative passages by highlighting language components such as modality, negation, or cohesive chains. It is then possible to suggest innovative ways that help us to automatically identify and describe the lexico-grammatical norms and conventions (and deviations) of the respective modes of discourse presentation. In other words, I will present lexico-grammatical patterns of discourse presentation that serve as a starting point for developing a tool to automatically identify discourse presentation modes.

In addition, the identification of lexico-grammatical patterns in 19th-century discourse presentation has methodological as well as theoretical consequences. The identification of theses stretches, I argue, contributes to explaining how readers identify discourse presentation modes and recognize modes of narrative progression (Toolan 2009). In this respect, the foreshadowing of a prospective discourse presentation mode and its summary—or what Sinclair (1991) has called textual prospection and encapsulation—is of vital importance. For example, the past tense form of the reporting verb *say* is an obvious and ubiquitous pointer toward introducing DS. Furthermore, what I will call paralinguistic narration is crucial to how modes of discourse presentation are introduced or marked. Paralinguistic narration includes references to body parts, such as eyes, mime, gesture and movement, and even descriptions of silence that co-occur in close co-textual proximity with and functionally interact with stretches of discourse presentation (Palmer 2010).

As I stated earlier, this book attempts to present a comprehensive account of 19th-century narrative fiction which involves addressing issues that go beyond the merely textual. One of those crucial matters is the portrayal of subjectivity; more specifically, I am interested in looking at how the linguistic projection of speech, writing, and thought presentation construes as well as reflects subjectivity. Subjectivity in this book is to be understood as the depiction of a character as an individual. Studies by Stephen Greenblatt (1980) and Terry Eagleton (1994) find the origins of subjectivity awareness, or the beginnings of the notion of "a subject," in Shakespeare's time, while others (Fludernik 2003a) trace the construction of subjectivity back to the Middle Ages. Since, in terms of English literary history, the 19th century is the age of the novel, the question of (the creation of) subjectivity carries a narratological-theoretical perspective, which can be investigated through systematic and detailed text-based analyses. Using a speech, writing, and thought presentation model can help illustrate the ways subjectivity is encoded in 19th-century narrative fiction. However, there are other linguistic markers of subjectivity such as, for instance, verbs of feeling or knowing, expressions of modality, or a combination of linguistic devices capable of projecting a variety of telling and focalizing perspectives (cf. the "reflector mode" identified by Simpson 1993). Therefore, the issue of "subjectivity" appears to be inextricably linked to the "narrator" figure (be it first person, third person omniscient, or limited narrator) and, consequently, to their role in the way discourse is presented. The conveyance of a story (and plot) through a narrator is accepted by narratological studies (cf. Stanzel 1981, 2002; Genette 1980, 1988; Chatman 1978, 2001), and although Banfield's (1982) *Unspeakable Sentences* questions the necessitative presence of a narrator, issues such as the angle from which a narrative is told, or who might be the focalized entity and who is the focalizer, still play a crucial role in how the discourse (be it speech, thought, or writing) of the characters is presented. Therefore, a further aim of this study is to relate the concept of subjectivity to a psycho-narratological investigation that attempts to discover how readers perceive discourse presentation, how it contributes to the meaning-inference process, and, finally, how this inference can be tested with the help of discourse presentation in 19th-century narrative fiction.

Fludernik's (2003a) notion of "diachronization" is another concern which I would like to consider in relation to speech, writing, and thought presentation in 19th-century narrative fiction. Linguistic approaches to discourse presentation tend to be undertaken by researchers working in, for instance, contemporary applied linguistics or critical discourse analysis (Caldas-Coulthard 1994). Work associated with discourse presentation (Banfield 1982; Fludernik 1993) generally shows, as mentioned, a lack of historical focus, and is not normally characterized by corpus methodologies either. Fludernik (2003a) rightly points out that there is a need to redress this lack and argues for a focus on the historical development of narrative form and function and for a theoretical take on these matters. This book is an attempt at dealing with this obvious gap. In addition, the pragmatic and sociolinguistic study of 19th-century English is also still neglected (see discussions in Görlach 1999 and Kytö et al. 2006) and is still biased, apart from a few notable exceptions (e.g., Kytö et al. 2006), toward dialectology or lexicology. Generally speaking, Late Modern English, and especially the English of the 19th century, has not been as extensively investigated as earlier periods of the English language, because often a similarity with 20th-century English is erroneously assumed. In its comparison with 20th-century results for speech, writing, and thought presentation gained by Semino and Short (2004), this study serves what Kytö et al. (2006: 3) have called the "need for analysing nineteenth-century English as a link between Present-day and earlier periods of English." Kytö et al. (2006: 3) mention internal reasons for the study of 19th-century English, such as the high proliferation of a variety of textual material, the possibility of studying gender parameters due to the high increase of literacy and female language users, the important sociopolitical and sociohistorical changes (and their impact on language usage, variation, as well as the development of varieties of English), the diversification of genres and the influential development of some of these genres, such as letters, the language of newspapers, academic prose, and the novel. Kytö et al.'s (2006) collection of case studies of 19th-century Standard English illustrates the tension between language stability and language change in this particular period. More interestingly, they emphasize the importance of paying as much attention to aspects of language continuity as to matters concerning language shifting:

> In diachronic studies, the focus is often on linguistic change. However, linguistic stability is also an essential object of study, as the possibility of tracing conditioning factors, both linguistic and extralinguistic, allows comparison of the situations that appear to encourage change with those which seem to promote stability. (Kytö et al. 2006: 9)

As far as this book is concerned, it thus seems vital that speech, writing, and thought presentation is equally viewed in light of those factors that might influence both stability and change. It is furthermore vital to assess whether it is possible to establish a norm or a standard.

Within a broader framework, this study addresses not only some of the neglected aspects of 19th-century English, but also of pragmatic[5] units of older stages of the English language, which have equally received too little attention (Jucker and Taavitsainen 2000: 67). In fact, pragmatic studies of 19th-century English are still rather scarce (Bailey 1996; Görlach 1999: 6; Beal 2004).[6] I argue that the investigation of speech, writing, and thought presentation can serve purposes that go beyond the narratological and stylistic. Looking at the linguistic devices implemented in 19th-century discourse presentation can bring to the fore issues related to the analysis of language in context, and especially, to the historical analysis of language in context as pursued by historical pragmatics. This study is, therefore, pragmaphilological and diachronic in orientation as it explores features of 19th-century speech, thought, and writing presentation to observe possible changes when compared to 20th-century texts.

In sum, I attempt to encompass what Brinton (2001) has defined as the tripartite division of the field of historical discourse analysis: historical discourse analysis proper, diachronically oriented discourse analysis, and discourse-oriented historical pragmatics. First, I deal with historical discourse analysis proper in the way I focus on particular stages of the use of speech, writing, and thought presentation in the English language. Second, I explain the discourse function of speech, writing, and thought presentation in the context of 19th-century fiction, which suggests that my approach is, indeed, diachronic and discoursal in nature. Finally, this study situates itself in the field of discourse-oriented historical pragmatics because it investigates not only changes in the use of speech, writing, and thought presentation, but also the motivations for it.

There are diachronic, synchronic, thematic, and narrative criteria behind my choice of data (see section 3.1 of Chapter 3 for a full description of the corpus). My corpus contains roughly 2,000-word chunks from 19th-century novels inclusive of Jane Austen's (1816) *Emma*, Benjamin Disraeli's (1826) *Vivian Grey*, Elizabeth Gaskell's (1854) *North and South*, and Oscar Wilde's (1891) *The Picture of Dorian Gray*, amounting to a small tagged corpus of 53,367 words. In the choice of narrative fiction, I take account of what Kytö et al. (2006: 11) have identified as one of the most important genres of the 19th century. This needs attention, too. My analysis of the roughly 2,000-word chunks of each novel chosen follows a corpus-based approach.

To conclude, this study aims to provide new insights into the nature of 19th-century narrative fiction which can be of use for corpus stylistics and text-linguistics, historical linguistics and pragmatics, as well as narratology and literary criticism. Although I am aware of the methodological caveats related to the size of the corpus and its representativeness, as well as the choice of excerpts from the texts, I attempt to circumvent those possible shortcomings by implementing a systematic, detailed, and coherent tagging of the corpus at hand. My approach is directly informed by New Historicism tenets insofar as the interpretation and evaluation process regards the reader's own position as valid. The analyst is able to recover and ascertain how meaning is created because he/she mediates in space between the historical time and the present construal (Fitzmaurice and Taavitsainen 2007b: 13).

Following this introduction, Chapter 2 presents as well as critically discusses Semino and Short's (2004) model of discourse presentation. It also discusses the particularity of the notion of faithfulness and discourse presentation in narrative fiction and presents a state-of-the-art overview of relevant research. It ends with a discussion of additional approaches related to the analysis of discourse presentation, which include Sinclair's concept of "trusting the text," and Toolan's (2009, 2016) concept of narrative progression. It ends with a summary of the main research questions of this study.

Chapter 3 deals with methodological aspects. It describes my corpus in detail, especially with respect to the parameters chosen to build it, the choice of texts, the annotation scheme, and the annotation procedure. It also discusses some methodological caveats related to the size of the corpus and the selection of texts.

Chapter 4 starts by introducing the quantitative findings concerning speech, writing, and thought presentation. The statistical distribution of the various categories is then compared to the 20th-century findings discussed in

Semino and Short (2004) in order to assess issues of language stability and change, as pointed out earlier. Furthermore, this chapter is also concerned with the contextualization of the results in a 19th-century sociocultural framework. A description of the various discourse presentation modes and their functions in 19th-century narrative fiction are the focus of Chapter 5. In addition, I will discuss the frequency, character, and combinations of ambiguous discourse presentation in my corpus. Subcategories of discourse presentation, such as hypothetical speech, writing, and thought presentation, are considerably recurrent in the 19th-century corpus. Furthermore, I describe and analyze repetitive lexico-grammatical patterns of the different modes of discourse presentation which have been retrieved with the help of assessing keywords, and collocational structures. These form the basis for my discussion of a procedure for the automatic identification of discourse presentation, which will be outlined in Chapter 6.

Chapter 7 investigates the crucial relationship between discourse presentation and narrative stretches in my corpus in the context of concepts of narrative progression and characterization. I focus on the function of reporting clauses as NRS, NRT, and NRW (narrator's presentation of writing), on what I will call paralinguistic narration, as well as the functions of description of silence, thought presentation, and visual narration.

The final Chapter 8 rounds this study off with a number of conclusive remarks and directions for future research.

1.2. *My Version of English Historical Linguistics*

In what follows, I address various aspects related to English historical linguistics in general and the analysis of discourse presentation in particular.[7] Crucially, I introduce my own notion of what I have termed New Historical Stylistics (Busse 2010b, 2014, 2015). I review historical linguistics in an ample sense to include concerns related to historical pragmatics and historical sociolinguistics, for instance, and, at the same time, to critically assess the methodological challenges and caveats involved when analyzing how the spoken and written words of others, as well as their thoughts, are presented in texts from the past.

In my own definition of New Historical Stylistics (Busse 2010b: 34), I state that New Historical Stylistics is "the application of the complex approaches, tools, methods, and theories from stylistics to historical (literary) texts." Keeping to answering the major stylistic question of "how and why a text means what it does," I aim at investigating diachronically changing or stable and/or foregrounded styles in historical (literary) texts, including, for instance, a focus on particular situations, genres, writers, and so on. At the same time, New Historical Stylistics embraces the synchronic investigation of historical (literary) texts from a stylistic perspective. In doing so, it applies an informed quantitative methodology and uses the analytical potential offered to us by (historical) corpus linguistics. This methodological framework is further enhanced and in interplay with a historically informed, systematic, and detailed micro-linguistically oriented qualitative analysis of the historical data under investigation.

When analyzing speech, writing, and thought presentation in 19th-century English and assessing its complex discoursal functions, one of the core questions that is identified by Fitzmaurice and Taavitsainen (2007b) and verbalized for historical pragmatics is still also of crucial relevance here:

> How do we, as historical pragmaticians, historical linguists, historical discourse analysts, or philologists, guarantee that the interpretations we offer of language forms and features in texts produced in periods distant from our own are valid? (Fitzmaurice and Taavitsainen 2007b: 11)

It is often deceptively assumed that 19th-century English is similar to present-day English because of their relatively close temporal proximity. This re-invocation of a rather simple, but essential and, at the same time, somewhat unmasking question is probably even more relevant in times of access to massive digitized linguistic data. Fitzmaurice and Taavitsainen (2007b), among others (see also Jucker and Taavitsainen 2000; Kohnen 2006a, 2006b), draw our attention to some methodological flaws in historical pragmatics when investigating older stages of the English language. Inspired by Fitzmaurice and Taavitsainen (2007b), but also broadening their work, I would like to raise again the question of what it means and what it may comprise to investigate historical stages of the English language in general, and in 19th-century discourse presentation in particular. I see innovative trends when combining traditional approaches and studies in historical linguistics with those approaches in modern linguistics that are as functionally oriented as, for example, (historical) pragmatics, (historical) sociolinguistics, and (historical) stylistics or corpus linguistics. These then need to be fused with the philological tradition in literary criticism or the (new) philology which stresses the importance of reading and interpretation. Any such attempt needs to see discourse analysis and interpretation as cultural practices going beyond the application of modern linguistic theories and methods alone. Furthermore, a weaker interpretation of Romaine's (1982b: 122) Uniformitarian Principle that "there is no reason for claiming that language did not vary in the same patterned ways in the past as it has been observed to do today" is equally paramount. All of the preceding would therefore demand a focus on the multifaceted and complex notion of context, an elastic and informed focus on interdisciplinarity, the interplay between the qualitative and the quantitative, between norms, conventions, and the innovative, between form and usage, authentic and edited data, vagueness, ambiguity and obscurity, and change as well as stability.

The combination of linguistic tools, methods, and approaches with discourse studies and philological approaches can further be explained and justified by the following premises which closely inform this book:

1) The interplay between form and meaning or semantics and pragmatics underscores the "linguistic description and interpretation" interface. A balance is necessary between the analysis of texts and the understanding of processes of and sources for interpretation and language interrelations (Leech 2008: 179). This balance between the text as a linguistic object—as a verbal icon—and what is outside of it needs close engagement. Leech (2008: 182) uses the image of Yeats's "widening gyre" with the text at its core. This interplay demands a combination of theory and practical application inclusive of a broad discoursal context as well as the textual one.

We do not have to be wholehearted integrational linguists in relation to the role of context—social, material, cultural, political, and linguistic—to realize that, ultimately, it is the context which determines functional import. The context is necessary to discern between the "marked/unmarked" nature of the linguistic phenomenon under investigation, to establish what changes and what remains constant, as well as to set the relationship between the conventional and the innovative (Fitzmaurice and Taavitsainen 2007b). Without contextual information we would not be able to understand that, in Shelley's ([1818] 2003) *Frankenstein*, we have at least three different or "nested" narrators, and the narratives they provide are presented, for example, in the form of a letter. Often, in interpreting texts we have to "range [. . .] so widely across the humanities and social sciences in order to place [a text] in its settings" (Leech 2008: 182). New Historicism certainly saw the meaning of a text in interaction with its contexts. Despite the criticism leveled at the traditional philological or literary critical approaches (e.g., New Criticism) and their focus on the aesthetic value of texts in their sociohistorical, cultural, and political contexts, these historically situated philological approaches (and their reconsiderations through theories from anthropology, history, or political history) are of equal value to the stance taken here (Fitzmaurice and Taavitsainen 2007b: 22–23). That is, in order to understand speech, writing, and thought presentation in 19th-century narrative fiction, it is useful to be aware of 19th-century discussions about, for example, vision and the psyche, the dominance of Darwin's evolutionary theory, and linguistic statements in 19th-century grammars. It is through this interplay and the "new philology" (Fitzmaurice and Taavitsainen 2007b: 22) that recent linguistic approaches and methods can be further enhanced.

The notion of context or background knowledge includes micro- and macrolinguistic as well as situational factors, such as the context of speaking, the power dimensions between addresser and addressee, the place and time of composition, the cultural and historical value systems, and so on. But it is also the complex task of explaining how texts mean and what they mean—which is even further complicated for historical data—that needs to be addressed. Although firmly rooted in linguistics, Leech (2008) laudably and knowledgeably suggests:

> There is a "division of labor," in making sense of any kind of text, between decoding the linguistic message, and interpreting it in terms of real-world

knowledge, pragmatics, sociocultural significance, and so on. This "division of labor" is crucial—for one task we use linguistic knowledge, and for the other we use cognitive capabilities not specific to language, such as inference and real-world knowledge—although the decoding and interpreting are closely interrelated activities. But we should not overestimate what the reader has to bring to the linguistic text, as contrasted with the meaning potential that is inherent in the text, by virtue of being in a particular language (Leech 2008: 191).

2) A sensitive and informed investigation of (historical) texts is in need of a basic reconsideration or, more positively speaking, a definition of what a text is. Rather than denoting anything that is outside in the world, here a text is seen as a linguistic object or a "manifestation of the use of language" (Leech 2008: 186).[8] This understanding of the notion of "text" goes back to its etymological origins meaning "weaving"; a text, thus, can be metaphorically understood as linguistic material which is "woven" into a large whole. If a text then is "a punctuated lineated word string in a particular language" (Leech 2008: 189), it has all the various levels of language coded with it. As such, it is a multilevel coding system. Therefore, at first, the text can be seen as itself meaningful or providing a common core.
3) Hallidayan notions (Halliday 1985, 1994; Halliday and Matthiessen 2004, 2014) such as his three meta- or macro-functions of language can also shed light on the interaction between textual analysis and interpretation. The textual function, which enables us to construct a text, builds on the ideational function, which enables us to talk about the world or convey a representation of reality. These then build onto the interpersonal function, which allows us to communicate with one another and to convey a discourse, which needs to be understood and interpreted by the addresser and the addressee.
4) In the interpretative process, the reader's task is to make sense of the text, and to reconstruct the communicative goals of the author on the basis of the textual evidence. This implies that readers need full awareness of contexts of production as well as of the language under investigation. A view of the text as an autonomous entity, however, has been questioned by different literary theoretical approaches (Greenblatt 1980, 1988). There is a variety of contextual information which guides our reading: generic knowledge, encyclopedic background knowledge and knowledge of schemas and scripts and belief systems, which may all lead to what Toolan (2009: 7) calls a "colouring by the reader." But our modern assumptions about a historical text can also easily lead us astray. Language change is inevitable. In addition, a text is plural in its meanings on the textual level, as difficult semantic choices demand a linguistic engagement that goes beyond dictionary consultation. In addition, the interpersonal level of interpretation, as well as the level of contextual implications, needs to be borne in mind, too. Interpreting older stages of the English language, the modern interpreter reconstructs the past. In this respect, the approach must be interdisciplinary (Nevalainen and Raumolin-Brunberg 2004), drawing on historical studies,

sociological investigations, and so on. Reality has to be seen as always determined by contexts, by the interpreter, and by the writer or historian (Berger and Luckmann 2000: 1–3, 24). As such, a faithful reconstruction of reality is impossible. Even more so, as analysts we are only capable of (re-)construing and (re)constructing our own interpretation of meanings and of historical reality. As Spiegel (1990: 75) argues, "since the historical text is not given but must be constructed, the historian of the text is a writer in his or her function of constituting the historical narrative, but a reader of the already materially extant text."

5) The methodology of investigating historical linguistic data is necessarily cyclic because due to the prerequisites just made we have to work—like in science—both deductively and inductively: from textual analysis to the formulation of hypotheses, and from the formulation of hypotheses to the linguistic/textual evidence or analysis.
6) A key concept in the analysis of historical data—and also in stylistics, as outlined in the following—is the concept or theory of foregrounding (Leech 2008). The notion of foregrounding lies at the intersection between the functional and the textual, because the linguistic code formally departs (by means of parallelism or deviation) from the linguistically or socially expected or from a linguistic as well as social norm; functionally speaking, it conveys a particular effect.[9] In the words of Douthwaite (2000):

> [C]ognitive psychology has demonstrated that habituation in perception and comprehension is a normal phenomenon in human life. Habituation routinizes life, it dulls the senses and the critical faculties. One way of combating habituation is to experience an entity in a novel fashion so that our attention is arrested, and our automatic mode of processing together with the standard response we produce to the familiar stimulus are impeded, slowed down, surprised even. This obliges us to examine the entity more closely and from a new perspective. As a result, we are challenged to place a new interpretation on reality. Impeding normal processing by showing the world in an unusual, unexpected or abnormal manner is termed defamiliarization. Thus, defamiliarization may be achieved by subverting the rules governing perception and behaviour. The linguistic technique employed in subverting the world in this manner is termed foregrounding. (Douthwaite 2000: 177)

Linguistically speaking, foregrounding can be achieved by means of (an overuse of) parallelism and deviation, and it is therefore closely connected with the interplay between form and function and quantitative and qualitative features. If we argue that foregrounded features will come to the attention of the reader, this also suggests that foregrounding invites us to move away from the text and into the realm of the reader's mind. As Leech and Short (1981/2007a) have shown, markedness of a textual passage, be it through lexical, syntactic, or other ways of deviation and parallelism, is not an indicator of the foregrounding of a textual phenomenon alone, because the reader still has to evaluate what is there. In addition, the concept of foregrounding also entails a norm and what can be called a norm, and how it can be measured. In the case of this study, great pains have been taken to construct a representative corpus as well as to compare it with a reference corpus of the 20th century. But even so, this is only one way of presenting speech, writing, and thought presentation, because only one genre is systematically investigated and the corpus is rather small. The concept of foregrounding is also essential to the way styles as well as stylistics have been described.

7) In the process of interpretation of historical (literary) data, I would like to stress the importance of the interplay between various methodological approaches and general analytical tools, such as a mixture of quantitative and qualitative investigations to avoid circularity; a pragmatic taxonomy to match an inventory of linguistic forms; mere "bean counting"; and a focus on individual and purely subjective and intuitive readings alone. Jonathan Gottschall (2008), in an article for *The Boston Globe*, makes a passionate demand for literary criticism to be able to explain human conditions, if only it were to embrace science and scientific methods. To some extent, this article downgrades the enormous achievements reached in literary criticism at times when computers were not available to support particular lines of argumentation and to verify interpretations by large amounts of data. Although Gottschall is right to argue that literary criticism needs to become more empirically grounded, his line of argumentation seems to somewhat forget that it is a grand(er) achievement to discover particular tendencies only by reading hundreds of texts. Unlike Gottschall, I firmly believe in the value of these "older" or, more positively phrased, "classical" literary and historical linguistic studies.

According to Fitzmaurice and Taavitsainen (2007b), discourse analysis and interpretation are cultural practices of traditions and histories. Corpora provide large amounts of data, but we need to be able to reproduce the conditions in which they were produced, otherwise what we provide is just a diagnosis of frequency and it is impossible to make our interpretations of historical data valid. However, there is no denying that new technologies and access to massive linguistic data that is digitized are influencing stylistics, modern historical linguistics, and diachronic stylistics. New advancements in technology offer us the possibility of exploring a wealth of more easily accessible data, allow us to engage with texts and literature in new ways, and generally influence the ways we investigate texts linguistically. Never have there been such "facilitated possibilities of searching, browsing, referencing and linking" (Toolan 2010: x). Through computerized text analysis, for example, we are now able to sort and systematically investigate much larger amounts of (historical) texts and corpora and to analyze such phenomena as repetition, foregrounding, and deviation on a much larger scale.

A more delicate and contextually based analysis is necessary, though, which deals with context and envisages the notion of "emergent grammar" or emergent styles (Fitzmaurice and Taavitsainen 2007b). Styles in historical texts are not always stable with respect to the form-to-function and function-to-form relationships; instead, these styles can be constantly modulated within a historical framework. What constitutes a writer's motivated choice may, in the course of time, be a norm and become highly frequent. Hence, it is valid to be more micro-linguistically/stylistically oriented and to investigate the styles of a genre, a person, or a situation and then evaluate these results against a reference corpus, which is historically based. In addition, Leech's (1985) distinction between deviation on a primary, secondary, and tertiary level needs to be seen in correlation with the effects of linguistic processes in historical contexts. Language norms, discourse-specific norms, and text-internal norms all play a role in evaluating stylistic change and stability within a historical dimension.

We also need to bear in mind that a bottom-up corpus linguistic approach is very much determined by and focused on lexis. Hence, complex discoursal frameworks cannot immediately be identified with the help of generally available programs for text analysis.

8) In times of big data, a sound knowledge or critical awareness of the corpora under investigation and the context in which these data and texts were produced are in order. This is especially relevant to a function-to-form investigation. Historical texts have been created within their sociohistorical, cultural and political surroundings, which can be analyzed from the philological perspective through theories borrowed from anthropology, history, and politics. Depending on which theory presents itself as relevant—the theory shapes and constrains the qualitative reading of the text as a communicative and contextual event. New Historicism and Greenblatt's (1988: 1) famous explanation of what "speaking with the dead" actually means see this interplay between a text and its material culture as indispensable for the interpretation process.
9) There is a need to use and construct representative data which is in line with the research goals outlined. The question of what constitutes representative data is not trivial because, again, it presupposes a sound and comprehensive knowledge of the linguistic period under investigation as well as of existing editions or copy texts of the language to be investigated. For example, investigating speech, writing, and thought presentation in 19th-century narrative fiction needs to encompass literary critical considerations such as genre, theme, and point of view and issues relating to corpus representativeness. Also, one should be aware of the fact that many of the 19th-century texts were serially published and often under a pseudonym.

10) The inclusion of contemporaneous sources (Nevalainen and Raumolin-Brunberg 2004) to our target texts cannot be underestimated. Although historical descriptions of or comments on a particular grammatical or linguistic phenomenon are frequently normative rather than descriptive, they nevertheless show us what was considered to be of importance and can give us vital clues to the purposes of usage. Therefore, I would even go further and argue that investigating contemporaneous sources alongside the target texts (in my case a selection of 19th-century fiction) serves to enhance modern (linguistic) theories and methods as well. Studying those sources may not serve as an interpretative program but as an interpretative aid.

11) The approaches used should be functional in that they focus on context as important parameters to determine meaning. An investigation of the relationship between language form and meaning needs to be enhanced by methods and terminology from historical pragmatics in order to discover both change and stability. This study performs a pragmaphilological approach (Jacobs and Jucker 1995) because in the attempt to investigate the character and function of discourse presentation of particular 19th-century novels, I perform a synchronic description of 19th-century discourse presentation. This study is, however, also situated within diachronic pragmatics and both a form-to-function and a function-to-form mapping. Yet, the distinctions between a function-to-form and a form-to-function mapping in diachronic pragmatics as well as a focus on historically synchronic pragmaphilological investigations are often interdependent and at times too complex to set apart from one another, especially because it is usually from a specific modern linguistic form or function that the analyst starts his/her explorations. Yet, there may be cases when the analyst needs to know about a particular function to discover linguistic realizations, and, in contrast, particular forms may have ambiguous functions in contexts. In the words of Traugott (2004b), onomasiological and semasiological changes are related to the interplay between structure and usage. For example, despite the fact that DS is as extensively used in 19th-century narrative fiction as it is in 20th-century fiction, the motivations for this, as well as the perception of this usage, might be different when situated within a contextual interpretation of 19th-century views of language.

12) One way of focusing on the text is the application of (historical) corpus linguistic findings to identify patterns of language usage. Since I have outlined a balance between form and function, between analysis and interpretation, the question is whether there are ways of proving linguistically, textually, stylistically, and statistically what is interpretatively significant about those features. Several pieces of software, such as *WordSmith Tools* (Scott 2017), have been recently adapted to account for the analysis of historical texts (see Archer 2009). Also, a major focus is on the development of statistical procedures to understand and manage non-randomness and statistical representativeness in corpus data (see Archer 2009). Although

a computer program tells us about the over- and under-representation of certain linguistic items in relation to a reference corpus, it will not tell us which features are foregrounded, which means that we still need to follow up those results with a close stylistic analysis that will help us determine how foregrounding is achieved. It is more likely that we can explain the special status of certain features as foregrounded because of the author's intentionality, rather than by some random or haphazard linguistic behavior.

13) I would like to claim that what I will call New Historical Stylistics is a useful method, tool and approach for historical investigations. Stylistics, seen as the application of linguistic theories and methods to mainly, but not exclusively, literary texts is functional, contextual, systematic, retrievable, and detailed, and as a discipline, it tries to find out how meaning is construed and what effects texts have on the addressee. Historically and/or diachronically speaking, stylistics is interested in the way styles change in historical contexts and is prototypically associated with rigorous linguistic analysis in combination with literary critical analysis in a historical dimension. In Leech's (2008: 1–2) words, it is an "interdiscipline" between linguistic description and literary interpretation, which leads to one of its central concepts—that of foregrounding. Stylistics deals with formal and functional concerns and it complements theoretical investigations with practical applications because "the proof of the pudding must be in the eating" (Leech 2008: 4). Leech states that by "choosing to take a text as a subject for stylistic analysis, we open ourselves to every possibility of establishing the nexus between form and interpretation in the text, and in this sense, of seeking its full communicative potential as a literary text" (Leech 2008: 4). In order to engage with the text and to find out how the text works, stylistics in its essence encourages and is reliant on linguistic analytic knowledge of an initially relatively theory-neutral kind.

Short (2007) stresses that the major difference between literary critics and stylisticians relates to the nature of textual understanding. Stylisticians believe that the range of textual understandings and effects (which depend on textual understanding) is rather small and therefore they counteract, for example, Fish's (1973, 1980) "interpretative communities."[10] Certainly, defining historical/diachronic stylistics or differentiating it from other historically oriented approaches might have to address the following questions:

- What is the status of New Historical Stylistics (Busse 2010b, 2015)?
- Is New Historical Stylistics a subcategory of Historical Linguistics, or does it represent a separate academic discipline?
- To what extent is New Historical Stylistics different from Historical Pragmatics and Historical Sociolinguistics?

Major differences result from the focus in New Historical Stylistics on (a) (changing or stable) style(s) and reasons for this styling, (b) literature mainly used as data of investigation, and (c) the reader and how he or she construes meaning in context. In addition, New Historical Stylistics is primarily characterized by an interdisciplinary perspective that includes, among others, literary criticism and theories as well as what Brinton (2001) has called a "diachronic(ally oriented) discourse perspective." The analytical usefulness and attraction of historical stylistics results from the fact that its methodology and foundations are based on general stylistics. It therefore includes linguistic approaches and theories beyond those used in, for instance, pragmatics or sociolinguistics.

14) Similar to (historical) stylistics and also corpus linguistics in general, investigations of older stages of the English language need to make transparent the procedures followed, the principles relied on for selecting the best possible data set, and the methods applied. The corpus of investigation in this study is rather small, is manually annotated, and focuses on narrative fiction alone. It might therefore face the charge of (a) self-reflexivity, as well as (b) not being fully corpus-linguistically oriented. Yet, in the choice of texts, linguistic, contextual, and literary-critical criteria have been applied to produce a representative corpus. Furthermore, the annotation has been cross-checked and, through the critical application of Semino and Short's (2004) model, it is possible to retrieve and falsify my analysis.

These somewhat programmatic assumptions are intended to further as well as to broaden the scope of historical linguistics and to set up a community of practices and practitioners who rely on their intuition but attempt to minimize subjectivity, who firmly believe in the importance of establishing frequencies, norms, and deviations, but who do not rely on numbers alone, who deserve the accolade of functionalist, but relate function and form to historical context(s), and who investigate changes, but also observe stability.

CHAPTER 2 | The Discourse Presentation Model So Far

IN THIS CHAPTER I DISCUSS in detail the Discourse Presentation Model I am using as the basis for the quantitative and qualitative analysis of the types, linguistic realizations, and functions of discourse presentation in 19th-century English narrative fiction. Although I refer to the original version devised by Leech and Short (1981/2007a), my focus is primarily on the Semino and Short (2004) reworking of that model, due mainly to comparability issues, but also because the latter elaborates further on some of the concerns described in the original, such as the claims to faithfulness or the capability for summary of the various discourse categories. I also elaborate on the additional categories Semino and Short (2004) have established and discuss why the concept of faithfulness should be retained for the analysis of discourse presentation. Following a description of the state of the art of research on (historical) discourse presentation and 19th-century English, I will discuss some of the theoretical underpinnings and the respective methodological framework that allow me to state why the linguistic realizations that characterize the different modes of discourse presentation are patterned in 19th-century narrative fiction.

2.1. *Presentation of Voices: Leech and Short's (1981/2007a) and Semino and Short's (2004) Models of Speech, Writing, and Thought Presentation*

2.1.1. Preliminaries

Leech and Short's Discourse Presentation Model (1981/2007a) has been extensively used and discussed by analysts of prose fiction (Fludernik 1993; Simpson 1993: 21–30; Toolan 2001: 136–140), but it has also been applied to non-literary texts (Caldas-Coulthard 1994; Jucker 2006a; Jucker and Berger 2014; McIntyre and Walker 2011; McKenzie 1987; Roeh and Nir 1990; Thompson 1996). In this book, I use the revised model proposed by Semino and Short (2004) in order

Speech, Writing, and Thought Presentation in 19th-Century Narrative Fiction. Beatrix Busse, Oxford University Press (2020). © Oxford University Press.
DOI: 10.1093/oso/9780190212360.001.0001

to compare my 19th-century fiction corpus to their results with regard to 20th-century discourse presentation. However, this is not to say that other valuable work within narratology or stylistics, for example work by Fludernik (1993), McHale (1978), and Pascal (1977), is not invoked when needed. Whereas one aim of Semino and Short's (2004: 9) examination is to test whether the model "could be applied sensibly, systematically and with insight to non-literary and non-fictional modes," my aim is to test whether it can be applied equally systematically and in detail to older stages of the English language, that is, to narrative fiction of the 19th century.

As originally described in Leech and Short (1981/2007a), the presentation of characters' speech, thought, or writing can materialize in a variety of modes which work on parallel formal scales but which, crucially, project distinctively different functional effects. Although thought presentation, as will be seen in the following, is, by definition, functionally different in terms of faithfulness claims, effects, and the construal of thought in linguistic form, as well as in terms of the possibility of summarizing thought, Short (2007) is correct to stress that it makes heuristic sense to display the three presentation modes on distinct parallel scales, as I also do in what follows.

Semino and Short (2004) elaborate on the original model by not only making a distinction between speech, thought, and writing presentation, but also by introducing new parallel categories on each scale which result from their analysis of a corpus of 20th-century narrative fiction, autobiography, and newspaper reports. Briefly, their new taxonomy includes the following categories: NV (narrator's representation of voice) on the speech presentation scale, NI (internal narration) on the thought presentation scale, and NW (narrator's representation of writing) on the writing presentation scale. (The categories will be further explained in the following sections.) The category of narration (N) is often situated on the left-hand sides of the scales for the respective categories and given in brackets, because although it is closely connected with NV and NRSA (narrator's presentation of a speech act)[1], it is not real speech presentation. Semino and Short (2004: 226), together with Short (2007), suggest that NI should be seen as another manifestation of the category of narration (as does Toolan 2001) and not as a category within the thought presentation scale. Finally, Short (2007) introduces the category of NT (narrator's presentation or reference to thought).

What follows is a full description of the various scales in formal and in functional terms. I also describe the set of criteria that Semino and Short (2004) have utilized for their reworking of the original model and on which my own analysis also relies.

2.1.2. Formal and Functional Differences between Direct and Indirect Discourse Presentation

In this section, I start by providing a general summary of the main formal differences between the two broad groupings of discourse presentation, that is, the syntactic, deictic, and orthographic markers used in either direct or indirect discourse. I then consider the functional effects projected by the use of direct forms versus more mediated, indirect categories.

As far as the category of speech presentation is concerned, reports of verbal activity may be direct or indirect, that is, they can either show or tell a character's words. Essentially, the core semantic difference between direct and indirect presentation lies in the verbatim presentation of characters' words versus the rephrasing of that semantic content in the words of the narrator or other characters. As such, the degree of involvement of the original speaker in the anterior discourse, and of the narrator in the posterior discourse presenting what is said, plays a crucial role. The distinction between showing and telling is signaled by clearly identifiable grammatical markers, although, as will be seen in the following, grammatical indicators are not the only criteria followed by Semino and Short (2004) in order to separate out the various categories in the three scales of discourse presentation. That is, formal linguistic features need to be borne in mind, but so do the propositional content that is being reported and the number of faithfulness claims with respect to the original.

As far as the actual linguistic markers distinguishing direct and indirect discourse presentation categories are concerned, indirect discourse is usually recognized because it remains in the same tense as the narrative that surrounds it, that is, the past tense, while direct discourse tends to be in the present tense. In indirect discourse, the grammar includes a complete adoption of the deictic orientation of the narrator, which means that first- and second-person identification are shifted to third-person deixis. Movement verbs are directionally less explicit in indirect discourse. Spatial and temporal deixis has to be adapted as well; for instance, *here* becomes *there*, and *tomorrow* is changed to *the next day*.

Orthographically speaking, indirect discourse usually dispenses with quotation marks (already in 19th-century discourse, quotation marks can be assumed to be the normative markers for direct discourse). The relationship between the reported and the reporting clause differs between direct discourse and indirect discourse. In indirect discourse, the relationship between reported and reporting clause is that of hypotaxis, while in direct discourse the syntactic relation is that of parataxis. Here, the framing clause can occur at the beginning, in the middle, or at the end of a reported clause, whereas in indirect discourse it usually occurs at the front. In indirect discourse, it is difficult to transfer "colourful idiosyncracies and dialectal qualities of the speech and thought of a character" (Toolan 2001: 127). Equally so, it is difficult to transfer imperatives, or interjections. Generally speaking, in indirect discourse, there is a loss of the character's vivid lexis. Thus, in "'Emma knows I never flatter her,' said Mr. Knightley" (*Emma* 1985 [1816]: 42), direct speech (DS) is not only marked by the use of quotation marks, but also by the use of the present tense and of the first-person singular as personal deictic orientation. The illocutionary force of this speech act is, however, difficult to determine due to the use of what is illustrated to be a very important strategy for all three modes of discourse presentation: the use of modality, which is often regarded as a means of turning a DS act into an indirect or hedged one (Bublitz 2001: 131; Fraser 1975; Taavitsainen and Jucker 2007: 112). Furthermore, the preceding example illustrates what can be considered double modality and evaluative devices in (a) "Emma knows" and (b) the adverb "never" coinciding with the verb "flatter," which, as a speech act verb, is normally used to utter an expressive (i.e., a compliment).

The formal differences between direct and indirect discourse categories, however, need to be viewed in relation to the wealth of diverse functional effects they project on the discourse presentation scale. For instance, one overall category, free indirect discourse (FID), has received a great deal of scholarly attention in the last 100 years, especially for its functional potential for combining the narrator's voice and character's voice. Because the two categories of free indirect thought (FIT) and free indirect speech (FIS), which are part of the overall label FID, are often not clearly separated from each other when mention is made of FID, there is a variety of approaches to FID which often only very generally highlight the array of effects it can project as well as the richness with which it endows narratives. Bakhtin (1981), McHale (1978), and Pascal (1977), for instance, have emphasized the "dual voice" effect emanating from the use of this category in general. Hamburger (1973) has emphasized the "unspeakability" of FID, while Banfield (1982) stresses the "unspeakability" issue for narrative sentences in general. For Banfield (1982), narration is unspeakable because, unlike discourse (which is both communicative and expressive), it does not contain a genuine addressee (nor any textual trace of it) nor a genuine expressivity-disclosing speaker (Toolan 2006a, 2006b). Stanzel (1981) stresses that FID, meaning FIT, typically accompanies internal character focalization. In terms of mimesis and diegesis, FID is mimetic diegesis, because it conveys aspects of a character's own words—hence its mimetic nature—although still filtered through the diegetic telling words of the narrator.

This wealth of possible approaches to the study of FID in particular, and speech, writing, and thought presentation in general, is due to the fact that the latter is a complex and high-level discoursal phenomenon. In order to capture this complexity and to do justice to the varied functional effects of these categories, Semino and Short (2004: 26) suggest a very specific type of corpus tagging. They argue that some standard tagging practices used in corpus linguistics cannot be applied to their 20th-century corpus in terms of process and product, because a considerable amount of contextual and pragmatic inferencing on the part of the analyst is necessary. They emphasize that their analytical interests cannot be met by automatic tagging, as contextual information is necessary to decide which type of discourse presentation is used. Furthermore, the investigation of speech, writing, and thought acts, that is, the investigation of embedded discourse, equally relies on a qualitative analysis and on pragmatic and contextual inferencing. This is especially so for free versions of discourse presentation (discussed in detail in the following), because reporting mechanisms, that is, a framing clause, including a reporting verb like *say* or *warn*, are conventionally nonexistent. Unlike Semino and Short (2004), though, I will show that it is still possible to identify certain repetitive linguistic patterns that can ensure a systematic identification of categories not based exclusively on the analyst's intuitions. As will be seen, this is especially important with relation to the free direct and direct discourse distinction, that is, free direct speech (FDS) versus direct speech (DS), on the one hand, and free direct writing (FDW) versus direct writing (DW), on the other.

In section 2.2 I also discuss the heavily contested concept of faithfulness, that is, the degree of accuracy with which anterior discourse, be it written or spoken, is reported; hence, my preference for the term *presentation* over *representation*. This concept is even more difficult to fulfill for thought presentation, resulting from the fact that we cannot witness other people's thoughts. For the interplay between discourse presentation on the one hand and what Short (2012) has termed "speech writing" and "thought summary," see section 5.4 in Chapter 5.

2.1.3. Reporting Signals

Before delving into a detailed analysis of the various categories, it is important to say a few words about those linguistic markers which can act as reporting signals. Reporting verbs usually occur in the direct and indirect scales and categories of discourse presentation, but not in the free versions.

In Semino and Short's (2004) model, reporting verbs are labeled separately as NRS (narrator's report of speech), NRT (narrator's report of thought) and NRW (narrator's report of writing), not only in order to facilitate their analysis (it helps with the new categories, especially with regard to word count and the adoption of the tags), but also because of the function of reporting verbs to evaluate or to describe the speech of others: "Strictly speaking, however, the reported clause is the IS [indirect speech] or DS [direct speech] string, while the reporting clause is the link between that report and the discourse in which the report is embedded" (Semino and Short 2004: 36). For them, reporting verbs "do not constitute part of the speech, writing, and thought presentation (SW&TP) scales themselves, but are effectively part of the narration which introduces adjacent discourse presentation categories" (Semino and Short 2004: 36). Despite the fact that reporting verbs are not seen as part of the SW&TP scales, they nevertheless fulfill crucial interplaying functions and reveal patterns of lexico-grammatical realizations which help us to develop algorithms for automatic annotation of discourse presentation and for accompanying reporting signals in close proximity (see also Mahlberg 2013). These functions will be outlined in section 7.1 of Chapter 7, which draws on existing studies in the field (Caldas-Coulthard 1988; Goossens 1990; Kissine 2010; Klamer 2000; Ruano San Segundo 2016; Rudzka-Ostyn 1988; Thompson 1996; Urban and Ruppenhofer 2001; Zwicky 1971).

2.1.4. Speech Presentation and the Categories on the Scale

What follows is a detailed description of the three broad discourse presentation groupings, namely speech, writing, and thought presentation. Speech presentation categories are normally described as functioning alongside the scale in Table 2.1 (Semino and Short 2004: 49).

The different speech presentation categories in Table 2.1 are distinguished from one another by (a) the formal (linguistic and orthographic) features involved in indirect and direct forms, (b) whether "the words and grammatical structures of the original utterance were presented, as well as its propositional form" (Semino and Short 2004: 9), and (c) the faithfulness claims between anterior and posterior discourse or, in other words, the rising degree of narrator involvement moving to the left-hand side and the character involvement moving to the right-hand side of the model.

NV is among the categories newly introduced by Semino and Short (2004: 43). It contains presentations of minimal speech, or verbal activity of the character, their manner or style, as reported by the narrator, but no mention of the actual content of the utterance itself. IS can also be a summary reference to speech events whose users represent a group of speakers. NV is different from NRSA to the extent that, in NRSA, the narrator informs the reader about the illocutionary force of the reported utterance.[2] An example of NV is "To her voluntary communications" (*Emma* 1985 [1816]: 262), where the reader is informed that speech has taken place. In Semino and Short's (2004) corpus, NV does not appear very frequently, but in terms of effect it can be said that it illustrates the point of view of a particular character and functions as an introductory statement to speech. It has a signaling function for what follows.[3]

NRSAs often consist of one clause where the speech report verb is followed by a noun phrase or a prepositional phrase indicating the topic. Hence, the speech act value is provided, but not the exact content. It is often used to summarize or to give background information. An example is "went on to express so much wonder at the notion of my being a gentleman" (*Great Expectations* 1999 [1860]: 109), where the speech act verb *express* is followed by a nominal group, "so much wonder at the notion." This example from *Great Expectations* is followed by an instance of IS: "Once more, I stammered with difficulty that I had no objection" (1999 [1860]: 109). The reporting clause "Once more, I stammered with difficulty" introduces the indirect reported clause "that I had no objection." Indirect stretches of speech presentation are often introduced by conjunctions such as *that*, *if*, or *whether* and a reporting clause conventionally

TABLE 2.1 The Speech Presentation Scale

NV	NRSA	IS	FIS	DS	FDS
Narrator's presentation of voice	Narrator's presentation of speech acts	Indirect speech	Free indirect speech	Direct speech	Free direct speech

Adapted from Semino and Short (2004: 49).

precedes the reported clause. As already discussed, the relationship between reporting and reported clause is that of hypotaxis.

According to Lubbock (1921; see also Short 2007; Toolan 2001), indirect discourse forms *tell* a character's words, while direct discourse presentations *show* them. Nevertheless, in comparison to NRSA, indirect speech (IS) seems closer to the character because it contains the speech act, the topic, and the propositional content, but not necessarily the precise words of the utterance. As such, it appears to be more faithful to the original, but it also foregrounds the act of reporting.

FIS carries linguistic features of DS and of IS. Other terms used are *erlebte Rede* or *style indirect libre* (Toolan 2001: 119). While the reporting clause of IS and the quotation mark of DS do not often occur with FIS, FIS may contain deictic features of both DS and IS. Therefore, its claims of faithfulness in relation to the words and structures used in the anterior discourse are not always clear, and FIS and FIT are not always easy to distinguish, often because they tend to share the linguistic feature of modality (Toolan 2001: 131). According to Semino and Short (2004: 13), FIS often creates ironic effects because it is perceived by the reader as distancing him/her from what the character said. Note an example from *Emma* where Mr. Woodhouse worries about a particular social event, a ball, being organized. His inference of Emma's disappointment is somewhat diminished by his pessimistic conviction that they should stay at home anyway: "and as for the ball, it was shocking to have dear Emma disappointed; *but they would all be safer at home*" (*Emma* 1985 [1816]: 264, my italics). Here the reporting clause is missing and the deictic orientation is that of reporting (past tense, change of pronouns, etc.).

DS and FDS are the modes of speech presentation in which a character's words are shown. DS consists of the reporting and the reported clauses, the latter signaled by quotation marks. DS is meant to bring with it a further faithfulness claim, as it reports verbatim the speech act value, the grammatical structure, and the words of the utterance as well as its propositional content. An example of this is found in the previously cited "'Emma knows I never flatter her,' said Mr. Knightley" (*Emma* 1985 [1816]: 42), where the reported clause is distinguished from the reporting clause ("said Mr. Knightley") by quotation marks. The effect of DS is that of vividness and dramatization, as the exact words of the character are given (Toolan 2001: 120). Toolan (2001: 129) points out that "the choice of direct speech reporting is also to accept a scenic slowing of pace, an enhanced focus on the specificity and detail of an interaction, and a greater pressure on the author to make such texts redeemingly interesting." Semino and Short (2004) concur with Leech and Short (1981/2007a) in singling out DS as the norm for speech presentation in their corpus of 20th-century narrative fiction.

Unlike DS, FDS must contain the direct reported clause (mostly in quotation marks), but it does not need to include the reporting clause. An example of FDS is taken from Charlotte Brontë's (1985 [1847]) *Jane Eyre* in which Mr. Rochester initiates the conversation and interrogates Jane:

> You have been resident in my house three months?
> Yes, sir.
> And you came from –?
> From Lowood school, in -shire. (*Jane Eyre* 1985 [1847]: 153–154)

FDS is said to be the most faithful category, as it presents the words of the character or the original with no obstruction from the narrator or the reporter. As most investigations of DS and FDS have differentiated between DS and FDS, Semino and Short (2004: 49) maintain that distinction in their tagging, although they see the difference between DS and FDS (and likewise between DW and FDW) as a variation of the same category. By following Short (1988), Semino and Short (2004) claim that there is no clear distinction between DS and FDS; instead, they argue that the latter is simply a subcategory of the broader discourse mode of DS, especially because no further faithfulness claim is added for FDS. This seems to be also valid for DW and FDW. In their analysis, Semino and Short (2004) have observed that, often, a stretch of direct speech presentation moves to free direct speech presentation. However, this presents further issues to be borne in mind for my own study, as the annotation process is made more difficult by the fluidity and malleability of both subcategories (if indeed they are to be understood as separate categories), and the danger of making arbitrary decisions therefore exists. Short (2007) suggests to include FDS in the category of DS to do away with these dangers. In this study, however, both phenomena are annotated separately for reasons that are discussed in the following chapters.

2.1.5. Writing Presentation and the Categories on the Scale

The writing presentation scale is realized in the following way and shown in Table 2.2.

Writing presentation, in which the anterior discourse or the original is a piece of written discourse, is similar in function to speech presentation. However, it is said to be stronger in relation to faithfulness claims because of the seemingly greater value of the written mode when compared to the spoken. In Semino and Short's (2004) corpus, writing presentation is more frequent in the news reports and (auto)biographies than in narrative fiction, and also the

TABLE 2.2 The Writing Presentation Scale

NW	NRWA	IW	FIW	DW	FDW
Narrator's presentation of writing	Narrator's presentation of writing acts	Indirect writing	Free indirect writing	Direct writing	Free direct writing

Adapted from Semino and Short (2004: 49).

quantitative distribution of the respective categories for writing presentation is different from those for the other discourse presentation scales (Semino and Short 2004: 48).

In writing presentation, similar options to those for speech presentation are suggested. Thus, NW includes those cases where the narrator reports that the character engages in an act of writing. NRWA is the most frequent category in Semino and Short's (2004: 105) corpus. It describes the written act, but no further reference is made to the content. Often a prepositional phrase that is followed by noun phrases occurs. An example would be the summary of the advertisement publicizing the search for Oliver Twist that Mr. Bumble discovers while reading the newspaper. Following a stretch of DW comes a stretch of NRWA writing presentation: "And then followed a full description of Oliver's dress, person, appearance, and disappearance: *with the name and address of Mr. Brownlow* at full length" (*Oliver Twist* 1993 [1837]: 122, my italics).

Indirect writing (IW) contains the writing act, the topic, and the propositional content, but not necessarily the precise written words of the anterior written piece. IW is usually introduced by a reporting clause or a reporting signal, as in the following example from *Emma*: "A letter arrived from Mr. Churchill to urge his nephew's instant return" (1985 [1816]: 263), in which "a letter arrived" serves as a reporting clause and "to urge his nephew's instant return" is the reported clause.

FIW may contain features of DW and IW. Often it does not contain the reporting clause, and the effects are similar to that of FIS insofar as the narrator exploits this mode in an ironic way. An instance of FIW can be found once more in *Emma*: "Mrs. Churchill was unwell" (1985 [1816]: 263) follows the information that "A letter arrived from Mr. Churchill to urge his nephew's instant return" (1985 [1816]: 263). The reader is made aware of the fact that this piece of information must have been given in the letter that was sent, hence, IW.

DW and FDW give a verbatim account of a written document, but often use the reporting clause to introduce it. Here is an example:

> The very first paragraph upon which Mr. Bumble's eye rested, was the following advertisement.
>
> *FIVE GUINEAS REWARD*
>
> Whereas a young boy, named Oliver Twist, absconded, or was enticed, on Thursday evening last, from his home, at Pentonville; and has not since been heard of. The above reward will be paid to any person who will give such information as will lead to the discovery of the said Oliver Twist, or tend to throw any light upon his previous history, in which the advertiser is, for many reasons, warmly interested. (*Oliver Twist* 1993 [1837]: 122)

The example is introduced by the reporting stretch "was the following advertisement," which is then followed by a rather long stretch of DW.

2.1.6. Thought Presentation and the Categories on the Scale

The thought presentation scale contains similar formal categories to the ones presented so far, but the functions of the parallel modes of thought presentation are critically different. This is due to three factors that differentiate thought from writing and speech presentation. When thought is presented, it is generally claimed that faithfulness cannot be observed because human beings do not have access to the thoughts of others. Therefore, the summary criterion cannot be applied because we cannot assume that there is an anterior thought act. In addition, it is difficult to determine whether, and if so how, thoughts are construed in linguistic form and, if we assume that thought belongs to cognition, it is impossible to assume and yet to clarify that all cognition is thought (Short 2007: 238). The thought presentation scale thus has to be understood in the following way:

> The result appears to be a series of "effect scales" that line up with one another and with the change taking place at the IT/FIT boundary. The possibility of summary is replaced with a set of effects relating to the extent of the narrator "interference" or reader "distancing" from the thoughts presented as we move along the thought presentation scale. (Short 2007: 233)

The thought presentation scale is presented in Table 2.3.

NI seems to be the most recurrent category in Semino and Short's (2004) corpus, followed by FIT and IT. In NI, the character is engaged in a specific act of thinking, but neither the propositional content involved nor the specific thought act is rendered. It is a report of mental or cognitive states and describes the character's cognitive or emotional experience. A character's inner state of mind is reported without real reference to his/her thoughts. NI can also describe a particular emotional reaction. In sum, NI encompasses all cases where a narrator reports a character's cognitive and emotional experience, without reporting a character's perceptions. An example would be the following reference to a mental state through the verb *puzzle*: "Seeing how puzzled Phillotson seemed, Jude said as cheerfully as he could [. . .]" (*Jude the Obscure* 1975 [1891]: 192). NI is formally parallel to NV on the speech presentation scale, as both have some intermediate position between the straightforward narration of actions and events.

TABLE 2.3 The Thought Presentation Scale

NI	NT	NRTA	IT	FIT	DT	FDT
Internal narration	Narrator's presentation of thought	Narrator's presentation of thought acts	Indirect thought	Free indirect thought	Direct thought	Free direct thought

Adapted from Semino and Short (2004: 49).

Different scholars have treated this phenomenon from different angles, and it is only recently that it has received greater attention. For instance, Simpson (1993: 24–25) alludes to the problem of attributing these phenomena of internal narration to discourse presentation as such; Cohn (1978) considers this phenomenon to be "psychonarration" (she also includes what Semino and Short [2004] label NRTA and IT as part of psychonarration); and Palmer (2004) argues that the depiction of conscience and consciousness is not always verbal, but can manifest itself in the mode of psychonarration (see also Fludernik 2009: 79–80).

Semino and Short (2004: 229) also consider including these phenomena under the heading of narration, as does Short (2007: 235–236), subsequently. They thus support Toolan (2001: 119, 143), who describes these presentations as "reports of mental or verbal activity which do not purport to be a character's articulated speech or thought." Toolan (2001: 119) considers these instances to be narration "[a]s long as those inward details remain matters of which the character is not consciously aware." Hence, by aligning NI with general narration, we can consider NI "as a statement that the narrator makes about the inner world of his or her characters" (Short 2007: 136). Furthermore, as already anticipated in Semino and Short (2004: 22), Short (2007: 236) introduces a new category, narrator's presentation of/reference to thought (NT), which aligns these instances more straightforwardly with the thought presentation equivalences of NV and NW and should, therefore, position this new category (NT) on the equivalent position to NW and NV of the thought presentation scale (Short 2007: 237). An example would be "he began to think" in "As he left the room, Lord Henry's heavy eyelids drooped, and he began to think" (*Picture of Dorian Gray* 1994 [1891]: 68).

NI is seen as part of narration, as Leech and Short (2007: 341–342) and Toolan (2001: 142) have done, that is, as the narration of internal states or events (parallel to the narration of external events). Hence, it is placed on the left-hand side of NT. As such, examples of NI do not present thoughts, but rather the narrator's statements of the internal world of the characters. Short (2007: 237) suggests that what Semino and Short (2004: 237) labeled as NI should be reexamined because these examples "appear to cover a wide range of different kinds of phenomena." Such a re-examination will be done in this study.

NRTA expresses the thought act, the topic, but does not attempt to duplicate the possible exact wording of the thought act (assuming, obviously, that such a deed would indeed be feasible at all). Similar to NRSA, the thoughts appear to be summarized, but as a summary cannot really take place with respect to thoughts and thought content, it is one of the most inexact categories. For instance, after Frank Churchill's departure, Emma's disappointment at his departure and at her seeming loneliness is summarized in NRTA: "and foresaw so great a loss to their little society from his absence" (*Emma* 1985 [1816]: 266).

IS includes the thought act, the topic, and the propositional content, but not necessarily the precise details or content of the thought act. When Emma engages in matchmaking between Mr. Elton and Harriet, the narrator presents

Emma's thought, introduced by the reporting stretch "she thought" in IS: "She thought it would be an excellent match; and only too palpably desirable, natural, and probable, for her to have much merit in planning it" (*Emma* [1816] 1985: 63).

FIT, which, unlike FIS, is extensively used in the 20th-century fictional corpus investigated by Semino and Short (2004: 13), is a very open category, because in terms of the words and grammar used as well as the syntactic, orthographic, and deictic distinctions employed, it contains features from DT and IT. An example from *Jane Eyre* presents Jane's thoughts when she observes Mr. Rochester:

> I knew my traveller with his broad and jetty eyebrows; his square forehead, made squarer by the horizontal sweep of his black hair. I recognized his decisive nose, more remarkable for character than beauty. (*Jane Eyre* [1847] 1985: 151)

As mentioned, plenty of work emanating from narratology, though not exclusively, has discussed issues related to the FIT category as subsumed within the more general umbrella term free indirect discourse (FID). Jefferson (1981: 42) generally considers FID to be a mixture of proper narrative or proper speech and thought. Toolan (2001: 135) points out that

> there are numerous ways of characterising FID, in fact: as substitutionary narration; as combined discourse; as a contamination, tainting or colouring of the narrative, as a dual voicing. My own preference is for viewing it as a strategy of (usually temporary or discontinuous) alignments, in words, values, perspectives of the narrator with the character. I favour the word "alignment" because it doesn't prescribe whether that closeness of narrator to character is going to be used for purposes of irony, empathy, as a vehicle for stream-of-consciousness or the clashing of two voices [. . .] the alignment is perceived, then the function (or "naturalization") is worked out by the reader. (Toolan 2001: 135)

Toolan's (2001: 35) term "alignment" is apt to describe the close relation between narrator and the character. One crucial disadvantage of using the term "free indirect discourse" (FID) is that, as mentioned, often a clear distinction is lacking between FIT and FIS, although they are clearly different in function. Moving from IT to FIT on the continuum—that is, to move toward the character—

> gives the character's expressivity and subjectivity fuller disclosure, pushing down the narrator into a less dominant role, carrying less scope for implicit editorial critique. And the assumption is that this option is taken typically where the narrator has no inclination to critique and ironize the represented thinking character; rather there is implicit narratological empathy with the character. (Toolan 2001: 138)

In sections 5.2.2.4 and 5.2.4.2 of Chapter 5 I will show that the quantitative distribution of FIS and FIT tags, as well as the number of words by which these tags are represented, are highly different and allow us to explain, for instance, why FID has received major attention in the literature, despite the fact that it is really FIT which—although represented by a moderate number of tags in the corpus—receives a higher number of words by which these tags are presented.

Finally, as far as the DT category is concerned, it often contains a reporting clause, and the reported clause is presented in quotation marks. FDT, in turn, only shows the direct thoughts of the character as thinker. Generally, recourse to more direct thought presentation indicates a more direct way into the character's mind and tends to also show the narrator's respect for the character's thinking process as the former is refraining from displaying any control over the thought world of the latter.

In classical narratological theory, for a long time the assumption has prevailed that the categories that are applied to fictional speech can be easily transferred to the presentation of fictional thought. Fludernik (1993: 281) has referred to this phenomenon as the "direct discourse fallacy," that is, the constant equation of thought with speech or with thought being "inner speech" and the overestimation of the verbal component in thought (Palmer 2004: 71). For example, Genette (1980: 178) claims that "[t]hought is indeed speech." Chatman (1978: 182) points out that the "most obvious and direct means of handling the thoughts of a character is to treat them as 'unspoken speech.'" Palmer (2004) criticizes that this approach does not do justice to the complex workings of the fictional mind and consciousness because it ignores the presentation of beliefs, intentions, purposes, and dispositions as thought reports (see also Cohn 1978: 12). Instead, he stresses that the mind is active and social, and that presentations of consciousness through a variety of discourse presentation modes, which characters are attributed with, have to be seen in interaction with those of other characters, with preceding discourses and so on (Palmer 2010). As such, the more diegetic forms of thought and also speech presentation are not privileged over the more mimetic and at times allegedly more "glamorous" (Palmer 2004: 57) forms of FIT, for example. Speech, thought, and writing presentation are equally important. Especially for thought reports, it is important to notice that they portray states of mind and contribute equally well, if not more effectively, than a description of a flow of consciousness to characterization. In addition, what is often labeled as "inner speech," that is, DT or FIT, and which often receives most attention because of its seeming similarity with speech, is too one-dimensional and, as we shall see, less frequent than the other modes. Therefore, it is very helpful to be able to use the delicate and robust system of scales as outlined by Leech and Short (1981/2007a) and Semino and Short (2004).

2.1.7. New Subcategories Introduced by Semino and Short (2004)

Next to the introduction of a new scale of discourse presentation, that of writing presentation, and one new category on all presentation scales, NI (internal narration), NV (narrator's presentation of voice), and NW (narrator's presentation of writing), some subcategories are briefly introduced by Semino and Short (2004). These "extra labels" are particularly necessary and useful because of the corpus linguistic methodology used by Semino and Short (2004). As they were interested in quantifying their data, this extra fine-tuning supports their methodological and systematic analysis. These new subcategories are:

a) narrator's representation of speech acts with topic ("p"): NRSAp;
b) quotation phenomena ("q" forms);
c) inferred thought presentation ("I");
d) hypothetical discourse presentation ("h");
e) embedded discourse presentation ("e").

To begin with narrator's representation of speech acts with topic (NRSAp), it has been mentioned that NRSA describes a discourse presentation category which gives the illocutionary force of an utterance but not an exact indication of content. Often the purpose is to summarize information. The press data section in Semino and Short's (2004: 52) corpus contains long stretches of highly amplified noun phrases—sometimes with embedded clauses. Although Waugh (1995: 160–161) suggests that, if propositional content is provided through longer stretches of information, these cases can be subsumed under the heading of IS, Semino and Short (2004: 53) introduce the subcategory label "p" for topic in NRSAp in order to be able to tag all cases of NRSA that contain explicit elaboration of the subject matter or topic (but where no separate reporting clause is given). An example of NRSAp would be "and complaining of the cold" taken from Dickens's *Oliver Twist* (1993 [1837]) where the topic "the cold" is mentioned following the speech act verb *complain*.

In Semino and Short's (2004: 54) corpus, especially in news reports, many direct references to what people have said—indicated by quotation marks—can be found. Due to the vivid effect this has on the reader and due to the fact that these quotations obviously increase the noteworthiness of what is said while brevity is retained, these occurrences were marked by the letter "q" for quotation. The presence of quotations affects parts of the report. This phenomenon has been studied mostly in relation to IS (Vološinov 1973). Clark and Gerrig (1990) talk about "incorporated quotations." Waugh (1995) describes this phenomenon as combining direct and indirect speech. Thompson (1996: 311–313) calls it "partial quotes." Quotation phenomena can also occur with narration, which Fludernik (1993: 127, 334) and others have labeled as "slipping" or "coloured narration."

Inferred thought presentation ("I") is introduced because there is a need "to make a distinction between cases where the thought presentation results from 'direct address' to the original on the one hand, and cases where no direct address was possible on the other" (Semino and Short 2004: 56). Especially the newspaper data contains thoughts attributed to a particular speaker, although the reporter has been privy to the alleged thoughts of some speaker.

The tagging procedure also accounts for examples of embeddedness. The prefix "e" is adopted to annotate cases of embedded discourse presentation.

For example, in a stretch from Gaskell's *Cranford* we find indirect thought (IT) presentation with at least two levels of embeddedness: "though she knew, and we knew, and she knew that we knew, and we knew that she knew that we knew, she had been busy all the morning making tea-bread and sponge-cakes" (Gaskell 2007 [1853]: 5). In their tagging system, Semino and Short (2004: 34) also add the attribute "level" to the speech act category in order to show the discoursal level. All of this tagging for embedded annotations makes them visible more readily in their electronic files. In their corpus, the deepest embedding involves three levels (Semino and Short 2004: 35, see also section 5.2.2.2 in Chapter 5).

Some cases of discourse presentation do not have anterior speech, thought, or writing, but are clearly presented as imaginary or hypothetical and can include "unrealised intentions and wishes, and predictions about the future" (Semino and Short 2004: 57). Hence, they are labeled as "h."

Another frequently occurring feature is that of narration identified as paralinguistic narration, which marks those cases that contain information about voice pitch or range, intonation, or body movement and that follow, precede, or come between various presentation modes. Section 7.2 of Chapter 7 will elaborate qualitatively on this phenomenon.

This chapter has outlined in detail the Semino and Short (2004) model of discourse presentation, which is based on Leech and Short (1981/2007a). The model is used to critically apply it to the quantitative and qualitative investigation of the types, linguistic realizations, and functions of discourse presentation in 19th-century English narrative fiction.

2.2. *The Notion of Faithfulness to an Anterior Discourse in Narrative Fiction*

The need for exploring the notion of faithfulness is not only expressed by Lord Henry in *The Picture of Dorian Gray* when he states, "Faithfulness! I must analyse it some day" (*The Picture of Dorian Gray* 1994 [1891]: 56). It is also highlighted as a crucial theoretical concept by various studies that investigate discourse presentation. Faithfulness addresses, as Moore (2011: 2) has nicely stated, the two allegiances of words—or perhaps even their duality, that is, their responsibility toward both the original context and the new frame—a to and fro between Plato's distinction of mimesis and diegesis. Hence, existing studies center around the relationship between the anterior discourse and that which is presented. Studies that focus on direct speech presentation (Tannen 1989) and on fictional dialogue (Sternberg 1982a; Fludernik 1993; Short 1988, 2012), for instance, have abandoned the notion of faithfulness, arguing that a faithful reproduction is neither possible nor necessary. This is one of the reasons why Tannen (1989: 101) prefers the term "constructed dialogue" over reported discourse. There may be condensed speech events (Fludernik 1993: 11), hypothetical speech events, or those that are told from memory. For Fludernik (1993), this is the discourse fallacy, which leads her to claim that the assumption of faithfulness in discourse reports needs to be abandoned altogether.

It is claimed that faithfulness does not apply to thought presentation, because it is impossible to have access to the thoughts of other people. To work with the notion of faithfulness in narrative fiction is challenging if faithfulness refers to the grammatically and lexically accurate reporting of other people's speech, thought, or writing. Because of its fictitious status in narrative fiction—which, as Searle once claimed, only pretends for the illocutionary act to take place—the utterance cannot be linked to a participant or an event in any real situation (Sinclair 1991: 58). Yet, despite this lack of bondedness to reality and the fact that thought cannot have an anterior discourse, other studies (Short, Semino, and Wynne 2002; Semino and Short 2004) argue for a context-sensitive approach that takes account of the variety and complexity of reported discourse and of the interrelationship between the effects of various modes of discourse presentation as well as the notion of mimicry and relatedness to a real situation. Baynham and Slembrouck (1999) reject the notion of faithfulness in their theory and analysis of what they call "speech representation," but also recognize the importance of contextual factors in the report/representation of the words of others.

Arguments against the notion of faithfulness in general and in narrative fiction in particular evolve around five main lines. Direct forms can, for instance, be used in cases where there is no such thing as a straightforward "original" that can be faithfully reproduced. This is the case (a) when there is hypothetical discourse, (b) when a person's nonverbal behavior is translated into a verbal form, (c) when the reporter spells out what is implied by someone else's speech, and (d) when what is reported relates to multiple originals. Second, it is possible that some words are omitted from DS, or DS can also be accompanied by some expressions which undermine the reliability of the quotation. Furthermore, many features of the original utterances are ultimately lost in any report (voice quality, accent, intonation) and due to the limited capacity of human memory it is not possible for speakers to reproduce previous utterances (Short, Semino, and Wynne 2002: 331–332).

Third, Tannen (1989) has also shown that DS reports in casual conversation are very unlikely to be accurate and are not normally even expected to be so. Fludernik (1993) and Sternberg (1982a, 1982b), along similar lines to Tannen, have argued that DS can be used when faithful reproduction is neither possible nor relevant. DS, for example, is then seen as a construction on the side of the narrator or reporter. It is worth noting, though, that Tannen (1989), on the one hand, and Fludernik (1993) and Sternberg (1982a, b), on the other, draw upon different sets of data. While the former concentrates exclusively on spoken data of informal conversation, Sternberg (1982a, 1982b) and Fludernik (1993) use fictional narratives and the results are often generalized. Clark and Gerrig (1990) address the issue of faithfulness from the perspective of the "philosophy of language," and they argue that direct quotations should be seen as demonstrations which are inevitably selective in terms of the aspect chosen from the original (see also Collins 2001).

This study opts for retaining the notion of faithfulness in relation to function in the investigation of discourse presentation in 19th-century narrative fiction. It is important to stress (following Short, Semino, and Wynne 2002) that contextual factors determine the degree to which the notion of faithfulness can be claimed. Hence, the approach to the notion of faithfulness should be "context-sensitive," because in some contexts, such as in DW or speech presentation in newspaper reports, faithfulness is retained. One would have to argue that a distinction be made between (a) verbatimness and (b) faithfulness, with faithfulness being a reproduction of the lexical items and grammatical structures of an original utterance, but not a reproduction of every single linguistic characteristic—which would be verbatimness (Short 2012).

Short (2012: 19) also suggests differentiating between (a) a discourse report, (b) discourse presentation, and (c) discourse representation. In other words, when (the content of) an utterance is reproduced, the question is whether the words are exactly reproduced or rather the sense of what is said. Judgment of both depends on context as well. It is obvious that for written language the expectations of the degree of faithfulness as well as verbatimness are higher than for spoken language. In discourse reports, a match between the anterior and the posterior discourse in deixis, grammar, and lexis is assumed for direct discourse; discourse presentation refers to the discourse that is presented; discourse representation assumes a discrepancy in deixis, grammar, and lexis between the anterior and the posterior discourse. This study of 19th-century narrative fiction uses the term *discourse presentation* and the concept of faithfulness "concentrates on those factors which are relevant in specifying as accurately as is feasible in context the precise communicative content of the discourse being reported" (Short, Semino, and Wynne 2002: 328). Hence, the notion of faithfulness is not in all aspects mimicry of an original locution but has to be understood as an approximation. This makes it a highly useful approach for the analysis of discourse presentation in narrative fiction, where an antecedent discourse does not exist.

For the present analysis, the concept of faithfulness (rather than that of verbatimness) is also necessary to explain the various categories of the different scales of discourse presentation. The following quote, taken from Short (2007: 231), illustrates the growing faithfulness claims for the speech presentation scale. The numbers on the left-hand side indicate the addition of the faithfulness claim, the acronyms on the right-hand side list the respective speech presentation category. This continuum of faithfulness claims would also be valid for the respective categories of writing presentation. These five steps include:

1) that speech/writing took place—NV/NW;
2 a) + the speech/writing act specified NRSA/NRWA;
3 a) + b) + the indication of the propositional content in IS/IW;

4 a) + b) + c) + features that are more difficult to pinpoint because it is so difficult to pinpoint whose words are used: that of the narrator or the character;
5 a) + b) + c) + words and structure used to express the content.

In terms of deictic, syntactic, and functional features, FIS can be described as having features of IS and DS, and it cannot be said whether claim 4 can actually be made. In IS, the addressee cannot really be sure which sentence was uttered (i.e., the mapping is undecidable). But in DS, the locutionary act need not be a depictive aspect of the quotation. You must say or imply that your wording is verbatim, as it is conventionally implied that it is. Hence, DS is not in all aspects mimicry of an original locution and it does not have to be. However, the writer claims a more faithful report of the original in DS than is the case for the other modes.

In addition, the notion of faithfulness construes the generally assumed effects of the various scales of discourse presentation. As the faithfulness claims for direct speech (DS) are assumed to be high, the actual effect that is attributed to it is that of a lively report of the anterior discourse. Therefore, faithfulness is related to such concepts as vividness and dramatization for direct modes of discourse presentation, but to distance or calmness for indirect ones. On the speech presentation scale, this also seems to match up with the showing and/or telling distinction. Also, the notions of summary and vividness can be seen as complementary, with summary being associated with NRSA. Summary can also take place through FIS (see the example from *Cranford* quoted at the opening of Chapter 1) or in FDS, but there is always vividness involved as well.

One of the main reasons why, for narrative fiction, a contextual approach to discourse presentation should be applied, which takes account of the complexity of the various modes of discourse presentation, is that the analyst should be able to explain the effects of the different modes. This is not to deny that narrative discourse is constructed and fictitious by nature, but rather to capture the various degrees of approximation to faithfulness. Here, it is important to stress that none of the discourse presentation scales—speech, writing, or thought presentation—is dominant. In other words, speech presentation cannot serve as a model for understanding the complexities of thought presentation. There cannot be an equation of speech with thought. What Fludernik has called "the direct discourse fallacy" (1993: 281) and the overestimation of the verbal component of thought may then also lead to an overestimation of the notion of faithfulness. In addition, discourse presentation is construed by the fact that what someone has said can be recorded and retained in language. Therefore, the presentation of speech and thought has more in common with the presentation of writing than tends to be acknowledged in the general literature on the topic.

To conclude, it is important to keep the concept of faithfulness for the analysis of 19th-century modes of discourse presentation in order to better understand their functions. Although accessing people's thoughts is an impossibility in real life (at least at the moment of writing this book), in narrative fiction we can do so, and it is on this level that the concept of faithfulness works. Readers are capable of processing characters' minds (Palmer 2004: 183–184), and the presentation of their minds in action, as if these minds were socially and contextually interconnected (Palmer 2010).

2.3. *"State-of-the-Art" Research on Speech, Writing, and Thought Presentation in 19th-Century English*

2.3.1. Studies Investigating Discourse Presentation

In this section, I briefly refer to work which has assessed the nature of discourse presentation from a variety of perspectives. In fact, from the final decades of the last century until today, scholars from a wide array of academic disciplines have provided thorough and sustained investigations on the nature of speech, writing, and thought presentation. The wealth of material stems, for instance, from literary theory (Pascal 1977), the "philosophy of language" (Clark and Gerrig 1990), applied linguistics (Thompson 1996; Mitchell 2014), conversation analysis (Caldas-Coulthard 1994; Holt 1999), psychology (Ravotas and Berkenkötter 1998), critical discourse analysis (Fairclough 1988), narratology and stylistics (Banfield 1973; Coulmas 1986a, 1986b; Fludernik 1993, 1996; Leech and Short 1981; McHale 1978; Young 2014; Weste 2014; Ikeo 2015) or other disciplines and perspectives (Collins 2009; Coulmas 1986a, 1986b; Holt and Clift 2007; Janssen and van der Wurff 1996; Marnette 2005; Vandelanotte 2009). Of course, grammarians have also addressed the concept of presenting other people's discourse. For example, Halliday (1985, 2014) uses the concept of projection to refer to the different modes of speech presentation. He distinguishes between *locution* and *idea*, with *locution* being the direct form of speech presentation and *idea* representing the "construction of meaning" (Halliday 1985: 193) where one element is dependent on another. Focusing on tense in what they call "represented speech," Vandelanotte and Davidse (2011) criticize that the complex temporal deictic centers—including the temporal reference point defined by the original speech act tense in DS and IS—have not been sufficiently addressed to capture the conceptual differences between so-called backshift (Comrie 1986) in linguistic studies. They outline that in DS there are two deictic centers (Coulmas 1986a, 1986b). DS is related to the speech event "which is constituted by the exchange between speaker and hearer and the temporal reference point defined by this exchange" (Vandelanotte and Davidse 2011: 237). The second deictic center is the speech event of which the narrator is part. IS is said to have only one deictic center, which is that of the narrator. Hence, all of the deictic elements shift to the narrator.

I would also like to mention the body of research that has recently achieved major attention in sociolinguistic research on varieties of Present-Day English: quotatives or quotative choices. These are frequently realized by constructions like "he said to me" and "she was like." *Be like* has been investigated from a sociolinguistic perspective with regard to age, gender, and regional variety of English. Another focus has been placed on the varying functions of *say*, indicators of various power structures between speaker and hearer, their potential for reinforcing the degree of faithfulness, or whether *say* is disappearing at the expense of *be like* (Macaulay 2001; Tagliamonte and Hudson 1999; Blackwell and Fox Tree 2012). From a historical perspective, *quoth* could be seen as an equivalent. It is impossible for me to do justice to such a rich take on discourse-presentation matters, so what follows is simply a succinct reference to the main tenets emerging from each general discipline that readers are invited to explore further.

On the narratology and stylistics realm, Fludernik's (1993) study still contains by far the widest range of examples from narrative fiction in German, French, and English, and it is probably one of the most comprehensive, impressive, and wide-ranging qualitative historical investigations into what she calls FID presentation. Her achievement is especially noteworthy as most studies of discourse presentation are not historically oriented.

Semino and Short's (2004) corpus-based approach and their methodological procedures are two of the reasons why their investigation essentially guides this study. Besides the various characteristics of Semino and Short's (2004) study that have already been discussed, they are also interested in investigating discourse presentation along the distinction *serious* versus *popular fiction*, assuming that there is distinction in the forms and frequencies of usage of different discourse presentation modes. Following Nash's (1990), Radway's (1984), and van Peer's (1986) claims that popular and serious narrative fiction can be identified by their distinctive use of different linguistic features, Semino and Short (2004) incorporate the serious versus popular distinction into their analysis of discourse presentation, despite the fact that the issue of what is to be understood as serious or popular writing is by no means a resolved matter.

Leech and Short (1981/2007a), as already discussed, present different categories of speech and thought presentation, but they also stress that the various categories of these scales have different effects. Leech and Short (1981/2007a) add a new category to the general taxonomy, that of narrative report of speech act (and the same category on the thought presentation scale). Furthermore, Leech and Short (1981/2007a) also propose a new position for the free direct category—FDS and FDT: instead of placing them between the free indirect and free direct categories on the scales, they position them toward the right-hand side of the scale, at the most extreme end. This ordering seems to have been accepted by most of the scholars working in the field, except for Person (1999: 1932).

Short (2007) focuses on thought presentation and presents some new laudable directions, which also deviate from Semino and Short (2004). Short (2007) argues that the notion of faithfulness is indispensable to explain the effects of the different scales of speech and writing presentation. Following Toolan (2001), he stresses that NI should be placed outside the thought presentation scale. Furthermore, he suggests treating embedded discourse within a cognitive stylistic framework rather than within the idea of levels (Short 2012).

The point of view taken in a narrative interacts with the ways discourse is presented. It is beyond the scope of this study to review all classic introductions to narratology and point of view, such as Bal (1997), Fludernik (1993, 1996), Genette (1972), and Stanzel (1981). Studies by Bally (1912a, 1912b), Banfield (1982), Fairclough (1988), Fludernik (1993), Fowler (1986), McHale (1978), Pascal (1977), Thompson (1994, 1996), Vološinov (1973), and Waugh (1995) have suggested forms and functions of discourse presentation that will be referred to in the following chapters. However, one issue that stands out from all of this research is the lack of studies that systematically analyze 19th-century narrative fiction from a corpus perspective.

Cohn (1978) grounded her work on what in the words of Semino and Short (2004) would be called thought presentation. Her examples are qualitatively discussed. McHale (1978) develops categories of discourse presentation and, prior to Leech and Short (1981/2007a), suggests that these categories represent a cline. He also stresses that free indirect forms are characteristic of the fictional (McHale 1978: 283).

Tannen (1989) focuses on direct speech presentation in casual conversation and illustrates that the assumption of faithfulness report is not realistic. Caldas-Coulthard (1988, 1994) suggests an insightful taxonomy of reporting verbs resulting from her analysis of speech presentation in press data. She chooses a critical-discourse-analysis perspective and also investigates how the voice of women is presented.

Toolan's work has consistently dealt with discourse presentation issues over the years. For instance, whereas Toolan (2001) and Toolan (2006b) discuss general linguistic aspects related to the construction of discourse (especially thought) presentation, Toolan (2007) takes on Sinclair's seminal paper "Trust the Text" (2004) and fruitfully elaborates on the notions discussed there. Toolan (2009) impressively illustrates diagnostic features of discourse presentation to further narrative progression. Toolan (2010) stresses the groundedness of the representation of speech and thought in written language and presents the different categories on the speech and thought presentation scale by literary examples. Toolan (2016) addresses speech presentation in relation to the function of repetition in narrative. He points out that what he calls "other-speaker" repetition in dialogic situations requires careful attention to what a previous speaker has said (Toolan 2016: 27). Reporting someone else's words in a direct way—which can also be seen under the important theme of repetition—"is difficult for an interlocutor to produce, unless they have attended closely to that other speaker's contribution" (Toolan 2016: 27). He also directs our attention to the fact that it can never be assumed that we fully understand one another. Hence, faithfulness must be seen as a relative concept. Further, faithfulness and verbatim report of what a previous speaker has said frequently occur in moments of uncertainty or in situations of (strategic) distancing.

Dixon and Bortulussi (1996) manipulate categories of discourse presentation in the story "Rope" by K. A. Porter in order to test how the narrator's position in it is constrained by dialogue style and how the reader constructs a mental representation of the narrator's knowledge. This interdisciplinary approach between literary criticism and psychology is also repeated and revised in their joint book *Psychonarratology* (Dixon and Bortulussi 2003). In the chapter on "Speech and Thought Presentation," it becomes obvious that although their research question is valid, particularly with respect to readers' perceptions of discourse presentation, the method they choose, the models they pretend to adopt, and the way they manipulate the story are neither coherent nor do they fit their research questions. Surprisingly, they do not quote or discuss Leech and Short (1981/2007a) or Semino and Short (2004). Further, their application of the speech and thought presentation categories is vague and they do not make a detailed distinction between the speech and thought scales. This weakens the effects they attribute to the categories, as well as how the readers are affected by them.

Further work which dips into the ample area of discourse presentation is that of Oostdijk (1990), de Haan (1996), and Thompson (1996). Oostdijk (1990) is useful for my own work insofar as it is one of the few attempts at developing automatic procedures for the identification of discourse presentation. De Haan (1996) investigates dialogue on seven popular fiction texts and focuses on sentence length, reporting verb types and associated syntactic patterns (on speech presentation in popular fiction, see also Montoro 2012). Thompson (1996) uses the *COBUILD Bank of English Corpus* to comprehensively analyze and interpret reporting strategies and, among others, establishes functions of (F)DS (Thompson 1996: 512–513).

A considerable body of studies deals with the role of reporting verbs that accompany discourse presentation modes (Caldas-Coulthard 1988; Goossens 1990; Kissine 2010; Klamer 2000; Rudzka-Ostyn 1988; Urban and Ruppenhofer 2001; Busse 2010b; Mahlberg 2013; Ruano San Segundo 2016). In these studies, the focus ranges from the lexico-grammatical realization of reporting verbs, their syntactic positions as well as their functions, over those that mark the narrator's stance, the degree of faithfulness of the given presentation, or that to help with characterization, to outlining the simultaneity of how what is said is accompanied by paralinguistic activities.

The number of studies that deal with historical (corpus-based) investigations of the forms and functions of discourse presentation in a variety of genres—including newspapers, witness depositions, narrative fiction, trial proceedings, medieval tracts, or royal language—has increased. Collins (2001) investigates discourse presentation in historical Russian. Marnette (2005) focuses on speech and thought presentation in historical French. She brings together theoretical frameworks that have often been treated separately and individually, such as those from stylistics, narratology, and linguistics. Her use of the French *théorie de l'énonciation* for the study of speech and thought presentation is highly complex. Evans (2017) explores the use of discourse presentation in Early Modern English royal language. Jucker (2006a) investigates speech reporting in newspapers of the late 17th and 18th centuries and draws on the *Zurich English Newspaper Corpus* (ZEN). McIntyre and Walker (2011) look at the presentation of speech, writing, and thought in Early Modern English prose fiction and news writing.[4]

In her elusive study, Moore (2011) analyzes ways and methods of quoting speech in different types of early, pre-Modern English texts. Apart from meticulously outlining the challenges and ways of editing and analyzing reported speech in medieval manuscripts, she presents a comprehensive model of historical lexical markers that signpost reported speech. Moore (2011) outlines, for example, internal perspective shifters, which include interjections, vocatives, or deictic pronouns, deictic markers of place and time, switches of tense, and other deictic markers (see also Wright 2000: 93–97). Speech-external linguistic structures include reporting clauses or even NV constructions. Moore (2011) considers politeness markers, which she sees as part of "conventional social interaction routines" (Moore 2011: 44), and also narrative interaction structures to carry the potential for marking direct speech. Following the identification of these diagnostic features, she moves on to analyze genre-specific markers in sermons, chronicles, and medieval literary texts. Interestingly, she claims that speech marking was less defined in medieval texts, which leads her to question modern concepts of faithfulness to an anterior discourse.

Lutzky (2015), using a corpus-based approach by drawing on the *Corpus of English Dialogues* (CED), investigates both quantitatively and qualitatively the use of direct speech quotations and the forms and functions by which these are introduced in witness depositions from the Early Modern English period.

Jucker and Berger's study of 2014 is a corpus-based investigation of discourse presentation in newspaper reports of the "home news" section from *The Times*, based on a small corpus of roughly 35,000 words, of which 5,000 words cover 30-year periods each, ranging from 1833 to 1998. Their study applies Semino and Short's (2004) model of discourse presentation with some modifications in the way they classify and quantify stretches of discourse presentation. Their focus is on speech presentation categories, as the other scales—thought and writing—are rare, except for IT. Instances of speech presentation are given per 10,000 words. It is difficult to compare their findings to my results because they do not provide a differentiation between the number of tags for speech presentation and the number of words by which these are represented. Interestingly, it is not the (F)DS categories that occur most frequently in their corpus, but the instances of (F)IS, with the year 1926 representing a peak. However, this might be because they counted consecutive paragraphs of FIS as individual instances. There does not seem to be too many instances of (F)DS in 19th-century news language, but the report of (F)DS is on the rise in the 20th century (Jucker and Berger 2014: 77).

Grund's (2017) historical corpus linguistic study focuses on what he calls "speech descriptors," that is, those features "other than the reporting expression and the represented speech that describe in some way what the original speech event was like" (Grund 2017: 43). Hence, he focuses on those features which, in my study, further enhance discourse presentation categories grammatically by means of adverbs, adjectives, prepositional clauses, participle constructions that modify the reporting clause, or NV, or NRTA. They may give information as to mime, tone, voice, gesture or body movement, express attitude, further modify how something is said, and so on. Grund draws on the corpus of *An Electronic Text Edition of Depositions 1560–1760* (Kytö, Walker, and Grund 2007), but his approach is text-driven. Unfortunately, he does not describe how he arrived at the different forms of reporting verbs, but immediately categorizes their function according to evaluation, emphasis, clarification, formulating hedging, and frequency (Grund 2017: 48). He outlines variation in the distribution of speech presentation—and hence, in the use of reporting verbs—as a result of the legal cases included in the corpus. For example, cases of theft and robbery contain less speech presentation. Structures that most frequently accompany speech presentation forms are propositional phrases, adjectives, and adjective phrases (Grund 2017: 51). It is also interesting to see that in some subgenres more adjectives occur: for example, in depositions from ecclesiastical courts, the nature of how something was said might have been more important. From a functional perspective, evaluation markers occur most frequently.

Reports of what other people have said and the various ways in which speech report can be given are also studied under the broad field of research of evidentiality (Bednarek 2006a, 2006b; Grund 2012) which, following a broad definition, describes the various ways that sources of information are given and how the reliability and probability of the information are evaluated—and accordingly, aspects of how authority, certainty, uncertainty, distance, or emphasis are expressed. Grund (2012) is among the few to investigate the forms of evidentiality markers and their respective functions from a historical perspective, using the witness depositions from the witch trials in Salem, 1692–1693. Following Aikhenvald's (2004) semantic taxonomy of evidentiality, he also includes quotatives, that is, information based on a report with or without a specific source, in his study. Direct and indirect speech as markers of evidentiality play a crucial role in the multilayered discourse structures of the Salem depositions. The reports are varied in a number of ways: (a) mode of presentation: as sets of statements, but also dialogues, predictions, questions and answers; (b) grammatical structures, ranging from verb phrases with *say* and *tell* including a *that*-clause being most dominant to verb phrases plus noun phrases. Quotatives with specific source account appear most frequently in the corpus. It comes as no surprise that quotative evidentials also take on a number of functions, which are crucial in relation to the role which language and the report thereof played in historical trials.

To conclude, this is but a rather succinct attempt at guiding the reader toward the considerable amount of work done on aspects related to discourse presentation. In what follows, I focus on issues more pertinent to my own study, namely research on 19th-century English.

2.3.2. Research of 19th-Century English and Other Relevant Studies

The syntactic, pragmatic, as well as sociolinguistic study of 19th-century English has been neglected or biased toward dialectology or lexicology, apart from a few notable exceptions (Görlach 1999: 1; cf. Kytö et al. 2006). Generally speaking, Late Modern English and the English of the 19th century have not been as extensively investigated as earlier periods of the English language and often, a similarity with 20th-century English is deceptively assumed especially for the English of the 19th century. Beal (2004: xi) notes that, until 2000, the 19th century was still seen as "last century" and therefore too close to be investigated linguistically with enough objective perspective. The following is a brief account of relevant linguistic research on issues specifically relating to the 19th century, viewed from a variety of perspectives.

General grammatical aspects have been investigated by a number of people, such as Arnaud (1973), Bailey (1996), Dekeyser (1975), Finegan (1998), Görlach (1999), Poutsma (1914–1929), Romaine (1998a, 1998b), and Smitterberg (2005).[5] Canonical 19th-century authors and their use of language have also received plenty of attention. Studies on Dickens and Austen are particularly abundant (see, e.g., Page 1973; Philipps 1970; Quirk 1961b, 1974; Sørensen 1985, 1989; Stokes 1991).[6] Recently, we have witnessed the publication of corpus-stylistic work that also focuses on 19th-century authors, despite the fact that they are not particularly diachronically oriented. Among them are Hori (2004), who investigates collocations in Dickens's language; Mahlberg (2007a, 2007b, 2013), who describes not only the intersections between stylistics and corpus linguistics but also illustrates how these can be fruitfully integrated to measure and describe, for example, key clusters of five-word sequences as pointers to local textual functions in Charles Dickens's novels (see also Mahlberg 2006); or Fischer-Starcke (2009), who also conducts keyword comparisons in Jane Austen's novels and illustrates how different reference corpora can result in different keyword clusters. Ruano San Segundo (2016) investigates the relationship between reporting verbs for DS and characterization in a corpus of Dickens's 14 major novels, which amount to roughly 3.8 million words. Using a corpus-based approach, he finds 17,021 tokens of reporting verbs for DS amounting to 130 types. It should be noted, however, that he leaves out the speech act verb *say* because of its ubiquity in the novels. Ruano San Segundo (2016: 120) has some interesting findings: for example, he confirms other literary critics' findings (Lambert 1981: 16–17) about Dickens showing a preference for reporting verbs like *replied* and *returned* for DS, while *answered* occurs not as frequently as expected. In three case studies of characters from three different Dickens's novels, he also illustrates reporting verbs for DS as a pattern-like contribution to characterization, certain verbs being used for specific characters. Finally, Biber and Finegan's (1997) study shows that the 19th century is of central importance for displaying increasing genre diversity in terms of linguistic makeup.

One of the most notable exceptions to the lack of attention given to 19th-century English is the collection of papers edited by Kytö, Rydén, and Smitterberg (2006). The volume is based on an investigation of "the standard language used in 19th-century South-Eastern England" (Kytö, Rydén, and Smitterberg 2006: 2). They stress the need for studying "stability and change"

(Kytö, Rydén, and Smitterberg 2006: 1) and for seeing the 19th century as a link between the past and the present. Internal reasons for studying 19th-century English are the rich and varied textual material and genres, the promising possibility of studying gender variability because of the number of female writers, the many important sociopolitical developments, and the fact that the 19th century is formative of the development of extraterritorial varieties. Despite this exception, as Kytö, Rudanko, and Smitterberg (2000) and also Denison (1998) have highlighted, the 19th century is fairly unexplored. Many papers in Kytö, Rydén, and Smitterberg (2006) use a corpus-based approach, although there are not many computerized and specialized corpora of the 1800s. The *ARCHER Corpus* (*A Representative Corpus of Historical English Registers*), for instance, covers the 19th century (though it lacks a specific focus), and the *Corpus of Late Modern English Prose*, covering the periods 1861–1919, contains mainly letters and journals. Many of the studies on 19th-century English in this collection are based on CONCE, the *Corpus of Nineteenth-Century English* compiled at the universities of Uppsala and Tampere, which is also used for comparison in the present study.[7]

A final note on the investigation of pragmatic units in 19th-century English is needed here. Largely owing to Jucker (1995) and Jacobs and Jucker (1995), the investigation of pragmatic phenomena through time has immensely grown in interest. Especially the investigation of the history of speech acts (Arnovick 1999; Jucker and Taavitsainen 2000; Kohnen 2000a, 2000b, 2006a, 2006b; Taavitsainen and Jucker 2007) has received major attention, as have other pragmatic units, such as discourse markers (Jucker 2002) and politeness (Watts 2002). A general awareness of "alternative histories of English" is shown in the collection of essays edited by Watts and Trudgill (2002). Skaffari et al. (2005) address the issue of genre and registers, and Fitzmaurice and Taavitsainen (2007b) that of methodology in historical pragmatics. Historical investigations into the pragmatic side of speech, writing, and thought presentation are, however, scarce. As Fitzmaurice and Taavitsainen (2007b: 11) argue: "the linguistic study of historical texts is complicated." They point out that the Uniformitarian Principle (Romaine 1982b: 122) cannot be easily adapted to historical pragmatics, because we have to differentiate between structure and use. Hence, the adoption of corpus linguistic tools and methods for historical pragmatics further complicates the investigation because the robustness of the method is stretched to approach pragmatic research questions.

2.4. *Additional Linguistic Frameworks and Models Necessary to the Analysis of Discourse Presentation in 19th-Century Narrative Fiction*

In Chapter 1 of this book, I suggested that a historically informed interpretation of texts also demands constant negotiation between text-based approaches and those that are oriented toward the reader. In order to guarantee this essential prerequisite, I propose in Chapter 2 to extend the framework for the analysis of 19th-century narrative fiction by a number of related theories and methodologies with a text- (section 2.4.1) and reader-centered focus (section 2.4.2).

2.4.1. Patterns in and of Discourse Presentation: Trusting the Text

In this chapter, I will argue that specific repetitive linguistic patterns may be constructive and reflective of specific modes of discourse presentation. I will state that similar to what happens in Present-Day English, collocational patterns or keywords exist not only in 19th-century English or appear in more than regular frequency, but also, and more importantly, that they are indicative of particular modes of 19th-century discourse presentation and can be used for semi-automatic annotation tools of discourse presentation. One of my theoretical underpinnings for this claim is Sinclair (2004), who elaborates on some radically progressive ideas about "trusting the text."

Sinclair (2004) claims that the process of reading (not re-reading) by the reader can be described as trusting the text "in a more particular way, trusting it to have been composed in such a way that what follows will answer or complete what has gone before" (Toolan 2007: 269). Sinclair (2004: 13) stresses that in the process of having read texts we have acquired experience and that therefore the use of a pronoun, for example, does not necessarily point back to the noun phrase it refers to but, more importantly, it takes us back to the previous sentences which are now part of our accumulated linguistic experience—which is in no way different from any other type of experience.

In cognitive stylistics, this phenomenon has been amply discussed, for instance in Contextual Frame Theory, as developed by Emmott (1997). Emmott (1997) refers to those pockets of accumulated cognitive experience which readers can bring up to the fore when necessary as "primed frames." Sinclair's take on the discoursal functioning of texts essentially underscores that we need to move away from considering texts to be "strings" of sentences somehow connected to one another. Instead, he emphasizes that when we read, what is important is what is taking place in the "current sentence" (Sinclair 2004: 13). The way Sinclair explains this discoursal understanding of texts is by means of two core principles: (a) *encapsulation* and (b) *prospection*. Encapsulation refers to the fact that "each new sentence encapsulates the previous one by an act of reference" (Sinclair 2004: 83) and, as such, constitutes the basic coherence of a text. Prospection may be seen as variation of this principle, or a "plane change" (Sinclair 2004), because "prospection occurs where the phrasing of a sentence leads the addressee to expect something specific in the next sentence" (Sinclair 2004: 88). It is therefore an essential structuring factor in conversation but also identifiable as a structural element in written texts. The interactive character of the sentence is therewith transferred to the next sentence. This is important in the reading process, although "awareness of previous words and phrases will die away sharply, though the traces, especially of something striking and memorable, may be retained with sufficient clarity to be reactivated" (Sinclair 2004: 91). Prospection can take place even if it gets interrupted by a sentence but is resumed through a specific signal (Sacks et al. 1978). Especially in written discourse, it is mandatory that prospection be coherently fulfilled. Much stylistic analysis has focused on retrospective analysis rather than on online processing, although this has recently been remedied by plenty of cognitive stylistics research where the reader is at the core.

For Sinclair, the underlying notion that the text is processed by the reader is the crucial aspect in explaining why discourse is dynamic. Prospection leads the reader to expect something in the next sentence (something is prospected rather than being interpreted retrospectively as referring anaphorically to what has already been said) and this carries key implications for the processing of discourse presentation. As examples of prospection, Sinclair (2004: 88) gives what he calls "quoted speech," that is, speech presentation, which—according to Sinclair (2004)—can be introduced to the reader or prospectively announced for the reader by phrases like "his message," or in "To quote the Prince of Wales again."

Corpus approaches can help us deal with all of the preceding issues by making it easier to bring to the fore keywords, collocations, disparities of topic and wording that may act as markers of prospection and encapsulation signposting discourse presentation. That is, corpus approaches (especially as dealt with in corpus linguistics, not so much in corpus stylistics)[8] focus more on overall patterns and less on the individual idiosyncrasies of a text under investigation. For example, Sinclair's (1991: 11) "idiom-principle" stresses that we use language in constructed or prefabricated phrases rather than in word-by-word combinations. Biber's et al. (1999) and Biber's et al. (2004) notion of "lexical bundles" is based on a corpus-based approach to multi-word units, which also illustrates the chunking tendencies in language usage. Further Hoey (2005), in a similar fashion to Sinclair (2004), discusses the way humans use language in terms of a complex linguistic weaving that is both quantitatively and qualitatively connected on all levels of language. Hoey (2005: 1) sets out from the lexico-grammatical interface and argues that a number of lexical items or words take on specific collocational patterns and that speakers may expect collocational patterns due to their primings (Toolan 2009: 16). Following the psycholinguistic notion of priming, Hoey (2005) argues that words tend to occur not only with specific other words, but also in specific sentence patterns, semantic and pragmatic roles, and even in particular text types.[9]

One crucial aim of this study is therefore to identify recurrent 19th-century lexico-grammatical patterns, that is, collocations or clusters which characterize a specific mode of speech, writing, or thought presentation—something that, to my knowledge, has not been attempted before. My aim is to analyze the keywords and various patterns identified by a computerized methodology in terms of the two principles suggested by Sinclair, that of encapsulation and prospection. Therefore, keywords and general patterns of modes of discourse presentation have to be seen within their co-text. This means that the meaning of a reporting stretch can only be fully identified if we observe collocational and colligational patterns within it, as well as what comes before a particular stretch of discourse presentation (i.e., what it "encapsulates") and what follows (i.e., "what it prospects").

I use the software package *WordSmith Tools* (Scott 2017) and exploit the keywords identification procedure to investigate whether there are any "disproportionately frequent words" (Toolan 2009: 31) or stretches in any of the different modes of speech, writing, or thought presentation. This is possible because, due to my manual annotation of the corpus under investigation, I am able to investigate individually all instances that have been coded, for instance, as IS, DS, FIT, or DT. Accordingly, all 22 different modes of discourse presentation and the respective stretches from the 19th-century corpus have been annotated. The different sub-corpora of the generated modes of discourse presentation will then be compared separately with the 19th-century CONCE corpus (see section 1.1 of Chapter 1). Thus, CONCE is used as reference corpus for comparison, to be able to establish frequencies of word-forms, keywords, and clusters in the respective stretches of discourse presentation types (speech, writing, and thought) annotated in my corpus.[10] For the analysis of stretches of discourse presentation, the identification of clusters is relevant because—similar to the corpus linguist's interest in identifying typical clusters for particular genres or text types—I will claim that modes of discourse presentation are marked by particular combinations of words that are disproportionately more frequent (compared to other corpora), although they are not the most frequent ones in a text. For example, stretches of NT or FIS contain relatively few words. These keywords and clusters will play crucial roles as pointers diagnostic of the different modes of discourse presentation because they have a signaling function. Further, I will show how these can be used as formal criteria to be useful for a computer tool that analyzes discourse presentation automatically and for which I will suggest first parameters to be programmed into respective algorithms.

In doing so, I draw on Toolan (2009, 2010), who identifies particular collocational patterns that further what he has called "narrative progression." Toolan (2009) shows how corpus linguistic methods help illuminate how narrative progression and narrativity are created. The assumption is that in narratives, in order to answer the question "What next?" readers are guided in their experience and expectations while reading, and that the core ingredients of narrativity (suspense, surprise, secrecy or gaps, mystery, tension, obscurity) are created as a result of implicit and explicit textual elements. The idea is that readers are guided not only by specific lexico-grammatical constructions and patterns in a narrative text but also by the way these are dispersed through the text (see also Sinclair 2004; Stubbs 2005; Emmott 1997; Toolan 2009: 15–25). As such, readers are prospectors, too, in the way they interpret the signals and judge the narrative of what has been told and is going to come. This approach to narrative progression allows Toolan to identify eight crucial features to which "high narrativity prospection" can be attributed, that is, features of texts which draw the reader's attention to the progression of the narrative. Among them are, for instance, sentences containing high frequency keyword character names, sentences with narrative-tense finite verbs in character-depicting action clauses, or opening sentences of narrative paragraphs (Toolan 2009, chapters 7 and 8). For discourse presentation—or more specifically for direct speech or indirect speech—a very obvious example would be the reporting verb *said*, used to introduce direct or indirect speech presentation. Chapter 4 will show that more complex and intuitively unexpected patterns can be revealed for NI, FIT, and so on.

The present investigation, therefore, takes inspiration from studies which assume that there is a more than regular connectedness between multi-word items; besides, my study also concurs with research that highlights that the statistical significance of certain overused items projects and constructs particular modes of discourse presentation and is directly responsible for the way readers infer meaning (see also Mahlberg 2006, 2007a, 2007b, 2013). Again, inspired by Toolan (2009: 29), I argue that the reader is capable of identifying, understanding, and processing the complex and various forms of discourse presentation, which are also often alternating, because there are some "diagnostic" lexical resources in the text that guide them. It is the aim of this book to identify these resources, to see to what extent they are specific of 19th-century discourse-presentation modes and to what extent the functions of these clusters can be compared to those identified for 20th-century narrative fiction. Thus, it is important to establish how these diagnostic lexical resources can encapsulate, prospect, or indicate a particular mode. However, it should be stressed here that, in a more stylistic vein (Nørgaard, Busse, and Montoro 2010), the identification of frequently occurring lexical patterns goes hand in hand with the stylistically foregrounded less frequent or occasional incidents or deviations from a norm, an aspect which I also address in the following sections.

2.4.2. Point of View, Discourse Presentation, and Bakhtin's (1981) Dialogism

I will conclude this chapter by briefly discussing certain stylistic, literary critical, and narratological aspects which have often been associated to discourse presentation. *Point of view* is at the top of the list of terms generally linked to the discussion of discourse presentation because of its connection with the notions of "voice," "perspective," or "angle." Point of view can be defined as an "angle of vision" (Wales 2001: 306) and it entails the presence of a conceptualizing character or focalizer. It is a filter of perspective through which the narrator, author, or even character presents events to the reader. Point of view and focalization have been discussed in narratology and stylistics.

Fowler (1996: 162) distinguishes between spatiotemporal, ideological, and psychological points of view. Spatiotemporal point of view refers to the ways in which a text is set in time and place. Ideological point of view describes a "system of beliefs, values, and categories by reference to which a person or a society comprehends the world" (Fowler 1996: 130). These can be transferred through the implied author, the narrator, or the author speaking through the characters. According to Fowler (1996: 166), the ideological point of view may be indicated linguistically by two strategies: one is modality, the other is psychological point of view. Modality can be realized by modal verbs, modal adverbs, and other constructions that express attitude, knowledge, prediction, or evaluation. Linguistic means which construe the worldview of an author, character, or narrator have been frequently discussed and they include, for instance, transitivity patterns, use of metaphor, as well as over- and under-lexicalization.

Psychological point of view concerns "the question of who is presented as the observer of the events of a narrative, whether the author or a participating character; and the various kinds of discourse associated with different relationships between narrator and character" (Fowler 1996: 169–170). In narratology this is a similar distinction to that between "who sees" and "who tells," that is, who focalizes.

Point of view is strongly connected with the position of the narrator and how the story is told. Both in stylistics and narratology, valuable typologies of narrator types have been suggested. Genette (1980), for example, draws on the famous Aristotelian distinction of mimesis and diegesis, that is, different ways of "showing" and "telling." His distinction between extradiegetic and intradiegetic narrators, describing narrators who are part of the story world (intradiegetic) and those that are not (extradiegetic), is enhanced by a further distinction between homodiegetic and heterodiegetic types of narrators. A narrator who does not participate in the story is called "heterodiegetic" (Genette: 1972: 255–256), whereas the one who takes part in it, at least in some manifestation of his "self," is "homodiegetic" (Genette 1972: 255–256; Rimmon-Kenan 2002 [1983]: 96).

Drawing on the notion of point of view and a series of linguistic markers associated with a variety of narrative voices, Fowler (1996) categorizes the various types of narration as types A, B, C, and D:

> Internal narration presents the perspective of an element from within the story, be it a character's consciousness (type A narration) or an omniscient narrator with access to characters' feelings, attitudes, and emotions (type B). External narration avoids claiming access to the characters' thoughts or feelings, nor does it make the narrator's thoughts and feelings explicit either (type C narration); the narrator's persona, however, might be underscored in relation to his/her knowledge of the actions and events of the story (type D), although still avoiding any evaluation or thought presentation. (Nørgaard, Busse and Montoro 2010: 126)

Fowler's (1996) model has been elaborated on by Simpson (1993) in his "modal grammar of point of view in narrative fiction." He combines insights from narratology and stylistics and, based on the question of who the narrator is, suggests two broad categories of narration "Category A" and "Category B." Category A refers to a first-person narrator who is also part of the story. Category B is a third-person "teller" who does not participate in the story. Broadly following the classic distinction between "seeing" and "telling," this Category B is then further subdivided into "Category B narratives in Narratorial Mode" and "Category B narratives in Reflector Mode." "Category B narratives in Narratorial Mode" describes narratives in which the teller does not intrude into the characters' consciousness but narrates from a floating position. "Category B narratives in Reflector Mode" describes stories which are narrated from the point of view of one of the characters who are made focalizers or reflectors.

In addition to the linguistic indicators already mentioned by Fowler (1996), Simpson (1993) introduces the concept of *shading*, which may be positive, negative, or neutral. Again, modality plays a crucial role here, because for Category A positive narratives we would find a concentration of *verba sentiendi* (verbs of feeling) (Uspensky 1973), evaluative adjectives and adverbs, and deontic modality. The negative shading of Category A would, in contrast, display epistemic and perception modalities. Category B in positive shading can contain not only instances of deontic and boulomaic modality, and evaluative adjectives and adverbs, but also FID.

What is of special relevance for my own study here is the fact that point of view and the respective types of narrator intersect with speech, writing, and thought presentation in intricate and meaningful ways. The ways in which characters' speech, thought, and writing are presented affect the angles from which a story is told and who appears to be the focalizer. Especially the modes of FIT or FIS are often said to be at the core of these points of intersection, because the reader gets the impression that characters and narrators speak simultaneously, especially in heterodiegetic third-person narratives.

To conclude, all of the preceding resonates with some classic notions discussed in literary criticism, especially the concept of *dialogism* proposed by Bakhtin (1981). For Bakhtin, there are two ways in which the word is oriented toward "alien words" (Bakhtin 1981: 282). One is that discourse is always oriented toward the word already uttered: The word is shaped in dialogic interaction with an alien word that is already in the object (Bakhtin 1981: 273–274). Another way of how language is oriented toward alien words is that words are also anticipatory and directed at the listener: "The word in living conversation is directly, blatantly oriented toward a future answer-word: it provokes an answer, anticipates it and structures itself in the answer-direction" (Bakhtin 1981: 280). These two ideas constitute the pillars of Bakhtin's notion of dialogism and reverberate the central aspect of discourse presentation, because it refers back or pretends to refer back to what has already been said, thought, or written. Discourse always encounters other discourses: "The style is at least two persons" (Bakhtin 1981: 280) and language is social because it is dialogic

(Palmer 2010) (which also seems to echo Sinclair's [2004] prospecting and encapsulating functions of language).

2.5. *Wrap-up and What Is Next*

In this chapter I have outlined the model of discourse presentation developed by Leech and Short (1981/2007a) and further extended by Semino and Short (2004). Prototypical formal as well as functional features characterize the different categories on each mode of speech, writing, and thought presentation. The discourse presentation model has been applied to a number of studies of discourse presentation in Present-Day English and other languages. More recently, corpus linguistic investigations have focused on specific aspects of discourse presentation. Leech and Short's (1981/2007a) model and the subsequent extension by Semino and Short (2004) has, however, rarely been applied to historical linguistic data.

I have outlined Sinclair's concepts of "trusting the text," prospection, and encapsulation to be of crucial importance in examining how readers are guided toward understanding that a stretch of discourse presentation actually functions as such. Toolan's (2009) concept of narrative progression goes hand in hand with the claim that a number of textual elements draw the reader's attention to the progression of the narrative and also to processes of characterization. Characterization is here understood as the individualization of the character (Culpeper 2001: 215). This is achieved by the choice of linguistic strategies that influence how a character's words can be interpreted and how certain impressions of characters are created.

With this framework in mind, the aims of this study can be summarized and sharpened as follows: The first aim is descriptive in that this study is a corpus-based investigation of speech, writing, and thought presentation in a corpus of 19th-century English narrative fiction. I use Semino and Short's (2004) approach on 19th-century English narrative fiction in order to analyze quantitatively and qualitatively the types, distribution of modes, and categories of discourse presentation and their functions.

Second, I suggest methodological and analytical processes to investigate discourse presentation in historical data and from a diachronic perspective. I also quantitatively and qualitatively compare my findings to Semino and Short's results for their 20th-century corpus investigation in order to further test the robustness of the model and to discover changing and stable trends in the ways characters' speech, writing, and thoughts are presented in narrative fiction.

Third, with the aim to develop a tool which allows for the automatic coding of discourse presentation, I shall investigate and present repetitive lexico-grammatical patterns (keywords, collocations, clusters, etc.) that are characteristic—both quantitatively and qualitatively—in the different categories of the different modes of speech, writing, and thought presentation.

Finally, I will pay special attention to the qualitative investigation of the meaning-making interplay between stretches of narration in close proximity to the various modes of discourse presentation in order to illustrate that interplay's potential for narrative progression, characterization, and its functioning as an additional resource for automatic identification of discourse presentation modes and categories.

CHAPTER 3 | Methodology

THIS CHAPTER FOCUSES ON the description of my corpus, on aspects related to the corpus-based approach I apply, and on the criteria I follow to ensure that the selection of my data and general methodology are as systematic and methodical an exercise as they can be. Furthermore, this chapter outlines the advantages and disadvantages of manually tagging discourse-presentation categories.

3.1. The Corpus and Its Scope

Already in the 1990s, Fludernik (1993: 9) explicitly rejected a corpus-based approach to the analysis of discourse presentation because both the compilation and the investigation of speech, writing, and thought presentation on the basis of a corpus held several caveats. She argued that corpus-based studies necessarily restricted themselves to one language, period, or nation—though corpus stylisticians today will certainly disagree with her on this particular issue, as multi-language or large diachronic corpora can now be more easily set up than used to be the case some 20 years ago. Fludernik (1993) also criticized that corpus-based studies tended to focus on statistical significance rather than on meaningful, albeit often fleeting and occasional, occurrences. More recent corpus stylistic studies have met this criticism by combining quantitative analysis with qualitative interpretation (see Busse 2010b; Mahlberg 2013). Fludernik's (1993) insightful observation that a corpus-based approach involves further methodological problems, such as the fact that occasionally it would have been necessary "to institute arbitrary definitions of the relevant categories" (Fludernik 1993: 9) is still relevant and also points to the fact that it is often necessary for a corpus stylistician to indulge in a rather large number of subcategories or even reduce the input of contextual information in order to gain statistically significant data—a point of criticism to which I will return in the following.

Speech, Writing, and Thought Presentation in 19th-Century Narrative Fiction. Beatrix Busse,
Oxford University Press (2020). © Oxford University Press.
DOI: 10.1093/oso/9780190212360.001.0001

At the other end of the analytical and critical scale, Sinclair (2004: 190) is skeptical of manual corpus tagging, when he states that "I would like to caution against the overuse of [. . .] the addition by hand of what are called 'tags'—to indicate aspects of formatting or analysis that are not apparent on the surface of the text." Tagging is a "perilous activity" (Sinclair 2004: 191) because the analyst then studies the tags rather than the language, and the text loses its integrity. Despite the obvious risks associated with manual annotation, Sinclair (2004: 190) acknowledges that "appropriate tagging can be a helpful procedure" even though tagged corpora cannot be used in the most orthodox corpus-driven sense (see later discussion). Yet, with a complex discoursal phenomenon such as discourse presentation, manual annotation is one way of being as systematic as possible for larger stretches of texts and of revealing some of the (repetitive) features that would otherwise be missed. Furthermore, it is only through sensible tagging and annotation schemes that some of the difficulties associated with discourse-presentation classification can be overcome; for example, FIT and FIS are notoriously difficult to separate, and often only ample contextual information can help where a concordance simply would not do. In addition, I argue that my methodology also avoids circularity, as it encourages further reassessment of the material. For instance, analyzing stretches of DS, NRW, or IT forces me to study instances of 19th-century English language in detail with respect to issues that go beyond techniques of discourse presentation. Moreover, the model itself may thus be tested, as those categories that were developed in relation to 20th-century English may need reworking with regard to older stages of the English language. Thus, my approach is also a tool to further refine the existing discourse presentation framework.

Semino and Short (2004) opt for a corpus-based approach because they want to test how easily (or not so easily) the Leech and Short (1981) model can accommodate text types other than those originally used, and how adequate the framework is when applied to larger stretches of texts. The annotation of my corpus follows Leech's (1993) seven maxims, among which is the claim that it should be possible to remove the annotation[1] so that the entire text comes back up as a unified whole. In addition, the systematic annotation of the text and the construction of an electronically tagged corpus prevent me from choosing simply "convenient" examples; in fact, manual annotation has highlighted phenomena (such as the relative infrequency of FIT) that would have been otherwise stayed unnoticed.

Research undertaken under the umbrella of corpus linguistics tends to fall on either of two different camps: *corpus-based* approaches versus *corpus-driven* approaches (Tognini-Bonelli 2001):

> The term *corpus-based* is used to refer to a methodology that avails itself of the corpus mainly to expound, test or exemplify theories and descriptions that were formulated before large corpora became available to inform language study. (Tognini-Bonelli 2001: 65)

According to the preceding definition, my own take on 19th-century discourse presentation is corpus-based, as I use corpora "to expound, test or exemplify" certain theories on discourse presentation that preceded the availability of the appropriate computer software or the existence of appropriate corpora. On the other hand, in a corpus-driven approach

> [t]he commitment of the linguist is to the integrity of the data as a whole, and descriptions aim to be comprehensive with respect to corpus evidence. The corpus, therefore, is seen as more than a repository of examples to back pre-existing theories or a probabilistic extension to an already well-defined system. The theoretical statements are fully consistent with, and reflect directly, the evidence provided by the corpus. (Tognini-Bonelli 2001: 84)

My analysis, therefore, cannot be considered to be corpus-driven because the texts have been tagged, which, in principle, has compromised "the integrity of the data." The debates surrounding the suitability of each approach are still recurrent among corpus linguists. For instance, according to Sinclair (2004), the corpus-driven approach is superior to the corpus-based approach because the data that are processed and analyzed are less contaminated.[2]

These debates become further complicated when the lack of appropriate software is an issue, as is my case here. As reliable software capable of automatically processing discourse presentation simply does not yet exist (in fact, one of the aims of this study is to help develop the basis that could eventually lead to the creation of such a software), I adopt a corpus-based approach inclusive of manual annotation and tagging.

The 19th-century discourse presentation corpus I use has been built by collecting selected sets of extracts from 19th-century novels that have been manually analyzed. In terms of the number of words normally used in corpus linguistics data, my corpus is rather small, as it consists of only 53,367 words. This presents a challenge with respect to the statistical significance of any values that my analysis brings up. Any statistical significance needs to be understood in the context of the small number of words manually annotated. Nevertheless, I argue that my analysis is still quantitatively sound, especially as it is aided by computer software which can implement comparisons with in-built corpora that have been pre-selected as representative of the text type I look at (that is, narrative fiction). As mentioned, recourse will be made to *WordSmith Tools* (Scott 2017) and *Wmatrix* (Rayson 2018) developed by Paul Rayson (http://ucrel.lancs.ac.uk/wmatrix.html; Rayson 2018).[3] The latter enables one to identify both statistically prominent parts of speech and semantic fields.[4] Admittedly, the assumption that word choice alone construes meaning stands on shaky grounds, especially with regard to approaches which no longer favor the separation of lexis and grammar, but stress their interplay in pattern grammar (Hunston and Francis 2000) or lexical priming (Hoey 2005), for instance. Yet, the application of statistical measurements thanks to software programs is intended as supportive for and thus stands in interaction with the qualitative analyses pursued. *WordSmith Tools* (Scott 2017) allow equally revealing comparative statistical procedures. On the basis of two different texts (or corpora), it is possible to measure and describe those keywords that are generated by the software and that are displayed on the basis of a keyness value (a log-likelihood value, for example).[5] For that purpose, keywords are produced from each text under investigation. Of course, this provokes issues of comparability, such as the selection of the right "comparator corpus" (Toolan 2009: 16–17; see also Scott 2009). According to Leech (2008: 167), the reference corpus or corpora should be of the same period as the text to be investigated in order to permit a synchronic investigation. Ideally, nonetheless, genre should also be taken into account; further, a comparison should be made between the target text and other genres. These varied attempts at seeing the target corpus in relation to a varied set of different corpora is what Leech calls a "scatter-gun approach" (2008: 167) and which opts for multiple comparisons with different reference corpora. Leech concludes that "slight differences of period, genre and so on among alternative reference corpora are unlikely to make substantive differences to the results" (Leech 2008: 167) because what is particularly characteristic about a text tends to show up irrespective of the corpora it is compared to. Because of its contemporaneous nature, I am using CONCE (Kytö et al. 2000) as the main reference corpus (see Chapter 2).[6]

As statistical analysis has advantages as well as disadvantages, both quantitative and qualitative results will be regarded as interdependent. In addition, the tagging has been pursued with regard to contextual information, which means that the narrative fiction to be annotated has been placed in context. It could be said that, ultimately, this tagging process relies on qualitative intuition and that both intuition and manual annotation are prone to mistakes. However, because the various categories are established according to well-defined criteria, my manual annotation has followed a systematic procedure which, additionally, has been partly checked and corrected by two experts in the field (Mick Short and Elena Semino from Lancaster University, GB).

My choice of texts is guided not only by diachronic criteria (I select examples from each decade of the 19th century), but also by generic, thematic, and gender-specific distinctions (that is, in relation to the authors of the novels) as well as by considerations of narrative point of view. Further criteria I followed in my choice of texts are: (a) literary approaches to the 19th-century canon and internal classification of electronic sources, and (b) independent opinions of three literary critics who advised me on the representative choice of novels from the 19th century. The distinction of "serious" versus "popular" narrative fiction, also incorporated in Semino and Short (2004), is notoriously complex to adopt in relation to 19th-century narrative fiction, because what we consider to be straightforwardly serious literature today, such as Charles Dickens's novels, was simultaneously regarded as serious *and* extremely popular in the 19th century.

Table 3.1 shows the corpus of narrative fiction from which text samples have been chosen.

As far as gender distinction is concerned, the 19th century offers a fruitful opportunity to investigate speech, writing, and thought presentation

TABLE 3.1 The Corpus of 19th-Century Narrative Fiction

PERIOD	AUTHOR	TITLE OF NOVEL	YEAR OF PUBLICATION	CHAPTER	NUMBER OF WORDS
1810–1820	Jane Austen	*Emma*	1816	Chapter 30	2,159
	Jane Austen	*Northanger Abbey*	1817	Chapter 17	2,465
	Mary Shelley	*Frankenstein or the Modern Prometheus*	1818	Chapter 7	2,757
	Sir Walter Scott	*Ivanhoe*	1819	Chapter 22	3,604
1820–1830	Benjamin Disraeli	*Vivian Grey*	1826	Chapter 3	2,283
1830–1840	Charles Dickens	*Oliver Twist*	1837	Chapter 17	3,206
1840–1850	Charlotte Brontë	*Jane Eyre*	1847	Chapter 13	2,341
	Emily Brontë	*Wuthering Heights*	1847	Chapter 24	1,786
	William M. Thackeray	*Vanity Fair*	1847	Chapter 30	2,538
	William M. Thackeray	*The Snobs of England (Book of Snobs)*	1846–1847	Chapter 25	2,412
1850–1860	Elizabeth Gaskell	*North and South*	1854	Chapter 12	1,987
	Elizabeth Gaskell	*Cranford*	1853	Chapter 4	4,219
	George Meredith	*The Ordeal of Richard Feverel*	1859	Vol. 2, Chapter 15	3,113
	Charles Kingsley	*Alton Locke*	1859	Chapter 13	2,498
1860–1870	Charles Dickens	*Great Expectations*	1860	Chapter 18	1,375
	Elizabeth Gaskell	*Cousin Phillis*	1863	Part 1, Chapter 1	3,165
	Wilkie Collins	*The Moonstone*	1868	Chapter 16	1,964
1870–1880	Mrs. Oliphant	*A Beleaguered City*	1879		3,008
	George Eliot	*Middlemarch*	1871–1872	Chapter 33	2,135
1880–1890	Robert L. Stevenson	*The Strange Case of Dr. Jekyll and Mr. Hyde*	1886	Chapter “Outside the Walls”	3,139
1890–1900	Oscar Wilde	*The Picture of Dorian Gray*	1890	Chapter 4	2,699
	Thomas Hardy	*Jude the Obscure*	1891	Chapter 7	2,550

in works published by both male and female authors. Hence, the corpus contains samples of a number of female writers, such as the Brontë sisters, Jane Austen, George Eliot, and Elizabeth Gaskell.[7] As regards the aim of investigating speech, writing, and thought presentation diachronically, roughly every decade of the 19th century is represented by either one or more than one novel. In terms of literary periods, the time span covered represents the Romantic and Victorian periods, which also allows us to consider correlating features of stability and change in relation to the important sociopolitical and sociohistorical developments of the 19th century. Generic criteria are captured by the inclusion of different subgenres of the novel in the 19th century, such as the Gothic novel (e.g., *Northanger Abbey, Frankenstein*), the sensational novel (e.g., *The Moonstone, Dr. Jekyll and Mr. Hyde*), the *bildungsroman* (e.g., *Jane Eyre, Great Expectations*), the novel of manners (e.g., *Middlemarch, Vanity Fair*), and the historical novel (*Ivanhoe*). Further, several novels deal with the social issues of the time, such as those of industrialization and urbanization as against a romanticized rural life, as we find for instance in Dickens's novels or in Gaskell's *North and South*. Literary scholars will find this classification unsatisfactory, but it is not my aim to present a thorough literary categorization of the selected novels (which is also partly disputed among literary scholars) but simply to show that a variety of different subgenres has been included.

Point of view was a relevant criterion in the choice of source texts containing first-person narrators (e.g., in *Wuthering Heights* or *Frankenstein*) and omniscient narrators (e.g., in *The Ordeal of Richard Feverel*). A further necessary criterion was the electronic availability of the text so that the SGML-conformant mark-up conventions could be applied more quickly. However, for every sample selected from either *Project Gutenberg* or the *Oxford Text Archive* the samples were proofread against accepted printed editions (see bibliography) of the respective novels.

I would by no means claim that my collection of extracts is in any way exhaustive, nor is it inclusive of enough data. On the contrary, I am aware of the limitations of my corpus (mainly because of its size), so my conclusions are always cautious. However, this should not detract from the fact that this is a first corpus-based attempt at discourse presentation analysis in 19th-century fiction. I can envisage that my work here can be complemented and extended in the future with the addition of further texts and text varieties, such as, for instance, Maria Edgeworth's *The Grateful Negro* (1802) or James Malcolm Rymer's *Varney, the Vampyre or, The Feast of Blood* (1845–1847), as well as other nonfictional text types like newspaper reports and autobiographies.

3.2. The Annotation Scheme

The annotation system follows Semino and Short (2004) and the formatting of the data uses a small set of SGML-conformant mark-up conventions to guarantee a firm basis for comparison. The following information is used to tag the beginning of every annotated file:

- "div1" is used to indicate boundaries between individual text chunks;
- "header" is used for bibliographical information and to include the list of speakers;
- "sptag" is used for the respective speech, writing, and thought presentation categories.

The header and headline of the annotation for the sample text of Austen's (1985 [1816]) *Emma* may serve as an example. It looks as follows:

<div1 type=fiction>

<header>

Name: Emma

Author: Jane Austen

Date: 1816

Publisher: Penguin

Chapter: 30

A Emma

B Mr. Knightley

C Mrs. Weston

D Mr. Weston

E others

F Frank Churchill

G The Churchills

H Mr. Woodhouse

</header>

<p>

Here, "<div1>" indicates the beginning of a sample from narrative fiction. The "<header>" introduces particular information about the sample text in terms of publication, publisher, and list of speakers, abbreviated by capital letters, which are alphabetically arranged.

The "<sptag>" tags, which, as in Semino and Short (2004: 29), precede the stretch of text to which the annotation belongs, contain the following three attributes:

1) The speech, writing, and thought presentation category of the annotated stretch of text ("cat");
2) an abbreviation indicating the speaker ("who");
3) the number of words of the annotated text part ("w").

The annotation of a stretch of text from Jane Austen's (1816) *Emma* then looks as follows:

</sptag>
<sptag cat=DS next=NRS who=A w=5>
"But you will come again,"
(*Emma* 1985 [1816]: 264)

The speech, writing, and thought presentation tags are surrounded by angle brackets. In the example given, the "sptag cat" is direct speech (DS), which means that the complete annotated stretch of text is direct speech. The value of the "who" attribute is "A" (the speaker of this stretch, who, in this case, is Emma). The stretch contains 5 words ("w"), and the speech act category that follows this stretch is narrator's report of speech (NRS), containing "said Emma." Word counts are computed in order to be able to analyze the length of discourse presentation categories in detail.

The tagset which I use is taken from Semino and Short (2004) (as outlined in Chapter 2), as well as some modified categorizations that have been made since then. Following Semino and Short (2004), reporting clauses were also tagged separately as NRS (narrator's report of speech), NRT (narrator's report of thought), or NRW (narrator's report of writing). As mentioned earlier, Semino and Short (2004) stress that

> [w]e also decided that reporting clauses should be tagged separately in order to facilitate their analysis and the study of the categories they "introduce." Otherwise, word counts for IS and DS, for example, would include not just the words of the relevant indirect and direct strings in the reported clause, but also the words involved in the reporting clauses. (Semino and Short 2004: 30)

Another reason for tagging the reporting clauses separately is one which is especially relevant to the analysis of the English language of the 19th century. In 19th-century English, there are various ways of indicating the reporting stretch and reporting clauses, which can vary in their grammatical structure, as Thompson (1996) and others (e.g., Jucker 2006) have observed.

In this study, signaling stretches will be annotated separately as well. The annotation procedure can be exemplified with another example from *Emma* (Austen 1985 [1816]: 266):

</sptag>
<sptag cat=DS who=A next=NRS w=3>
"I certainly must,"
</sptag>
<sptag cat=NRS who=A next=FDS-FDT w=2>
said she.

To sum up, the speech, writing, and thought presentation categories used are illustrated in Tables 3.2–3.4.

TABLE 3.2 Speech Presentation Categories

(NRS)	Narrator's Report of Speech (= Signaling Reporting Discourse, Reporting Clause of Speech, or Non-Clausal Equivalent)
N	Pure Narration
NV	Narrator's Presentation of Voice
NRSA	Narrator's Presentation of Speech Acts
IS	Indirect Speech
FIS	Free Indirect Speech
DS	Direct Speech
FDS	Free Direct Speech

TABLE 3.3 Thought Presentation Categories

(NRT)	Narrator's Report of Thought (= Signaling Reporting Discourse, Reporting Clause of Thought or Non-Clausal Equivalent)
N	Pure Narration
NI	Internal Narration
NT	Narrator's Presentation of Thought
NRTA	Narrator's Presentation of Thought Acts
IT	Indirect Thought
FIT	Free Indirect Thought
DT	Direct Thought
FDT	Free Direct Thought

TABLE 3.4 Writing Presentation Categories

(NRW)	Narrator's Report of Writing (= Signaling Reporting Discourse, Reporting Clause of Writing or Non-Clausal Equivalent)
N	Pure Narration
NW	Narrator's Presentation of Writing
NRWA	Narrator's Presentation of Writing Acts
IW	Indirect Writing
FIW	Free Indirect Writing
DW	Direct Writing
FDW	Free Direct Writing

3.3. The Annotation Procedure

Future analysts of discourse presentation may find it useful if the procedural steps of the functional mechanisms involved in the annotation are presented. In addition, it is the aim of this section to make the annotation procedure as transparent as possible in order (a) to show the contextual framework of each step taken and (b) to illustrate the complexity of discourse presentation.

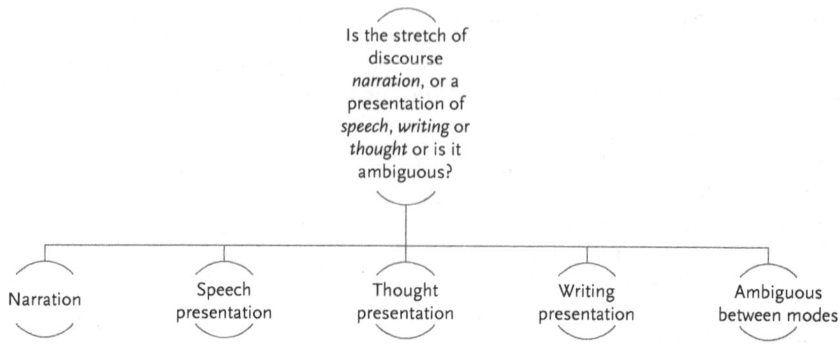

FIGURE 3.1. Steps one and two of the annotation process.

To determine the discourse presentation mode of a string of text, a five-step procedure is taken once the content of the passage to be annotated is clear and the characters participating are identified. This procedure aims at bringing to the fore the discourse presentation mode used, whether there are aspects of ambiguity to bear in mind, and the respective categories of discourse presentation that can be, consequently, identified. The annotation procedure is illustrated in Figures 3.1 and 3.2.

As shown in Figure 3.1, the first step includes the identification of whether the string of text is narration, speech presentation, thought presentation, or writing presentation. Step two is related to step one insofar as it aims at elucidating possible ambiguous cases. Once the scale of discourse presentation (or the ambiguity between two modes) has been established, the question arises of which category (or categories) of narration or of speech, writing, and thought presentation is to be used. This is step number three and is illustrated in Figure 3.2, depicting the categories for narration and the respective discourse presentation scales. For narration, these are N (pure narration), NI (internal narration, if, following Toolan [2001] and Short [2007], NI is seen as part of narration), and NRS, NRT, as well as NRW (which are the reporting signals and belong to narration). For speech and thought presentation, the respective categories mentioned in Chapter 2 are listed.

Step number four again asks for ambiguity between two categories. Once the annotation has been pursued, step five includes a possible re-annotation of the already tagged text for embedded discourse presentation.

To conclude, the annotation process involves a number of procedures. These include questions about whether the presentation of discourse is speech, thought, or writing, whether the presented stretches are narration, as well as which categories of speech, writing, and thought presentation are used, and whether these are ambiguous or embedded.

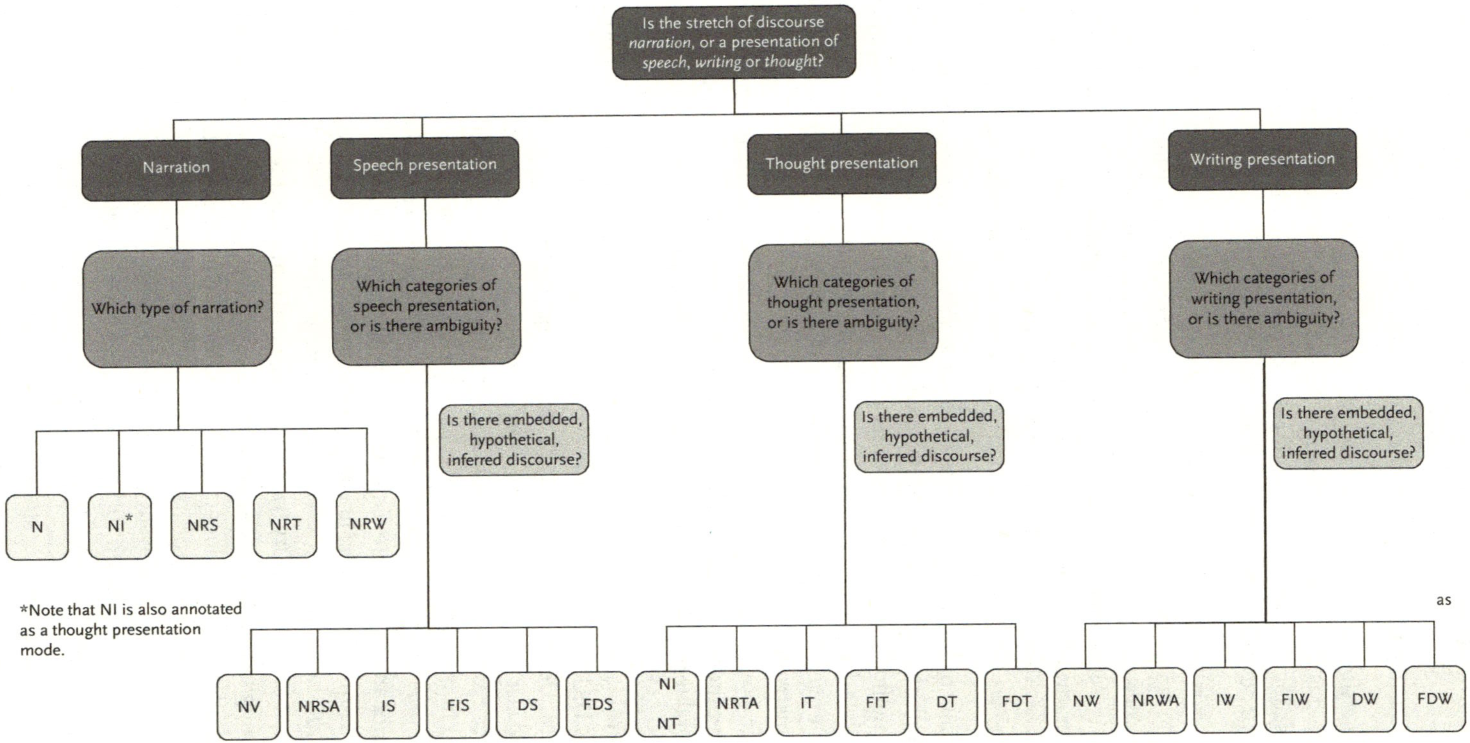

FIGURE 3.2. Steps three, four, and five of the annotation process.

3.4. *Methodological Caveats*

3.4.1. Corpus Construction and the Issues of Representativeness

The selection of narrative fiction based on the criteria mentioned in the preceding is followed by the choice of text samples from these novels. For narrative fiction, roughly 2,000-word extracts were chosen by Semino and Short (2004). They select the extracts in the following way:

> The extracts for inclusion in the corpus were sampled fairly randomly from within each publication. We did not seek out particular SW&TP features or kinds of writing, though we did try to ensure that we did not take all our extracts from, say, the beginnings or the ends of novels or autobiographies. Our extracts were not exactly 2,000 words long because we decided to opt, wherever possible, for relatively coherent sub-wholes (e.g. whole chapters, sections within chapters, or, at the very last, paragraph boundaries. (Semino and Short 2004: 23)

My small corpus of 22 text samples of at least 2,000-word chunks was manually annotated by one person following Semino and Short's (2004) model. Some methodological problems that relate to the choice of the corpus of language data from older stages of the English language, the choice of source texts, the overall size, the sample size, and the issue of representativeness need to be illustrated.

Biber (1990) states that 10-text subsamples from a particular genre accurately reproduce the characteristics of much larger samples from that genre in general terms. Biber (1990: 26) also notes that roughly 2,000-word chunks are reliable representatives of a particular text genre. It is important to discuss whether this number can be seen as representative of, for example, a novel by Charles Dickens. There is the danger of missing relevant data if these selected stretches are chosen randomly. This also brings up the issue of whether one chooses a coherent, continuous stretch or whether one chooses smaller stretches from the entire novel. The question also arises whether, with this method in mind, it is then only generally possible to say something about the distribution of types of speech, writing, and thought presentation as separate categories and to compare them as such. With regard to statistical significance, it is certainly problematic to compare the individual text chunks with one another, but the aim of this study is to get a larger variety of texts from different periods of the 19th century by considering the parameters mentioned earlier.

Although the choice of a sample which is representative of a particular novel (and therefore has to be longer than 2,000 words) or which serves the purpose of being representative of 19th-century narrative fiction entails different research questions, other issues are involved as well. A corpus-based approach enables me to investigate authentic data and make claims valid through large quantitative data. But there is a dilemma:

> The quantitative analysis of language use actually amounts to the study of the occurrence of linguistic forms within a context that is defined in terms of a set

of parameters that may have more to do with the design of the database than the production of language by speakers in the world. (Fitzmaurice and Taavitsainen 2007b: 27)

Hence, to what extent corpus-based analysis is apt to form a basis for the interpretation of functions, and whether it only focuses on frequencies of particular forms, are issues that need attention. In addition, the question arises as to how we include such practical matters as choice of editions of novels, or how we take account of the fact that some novels were serialized novels. A corpus approach can certainly provide the analyst with data to distinguish, for example, between norm and deviation, and hence between change and stability. But it is also worthwhile to ask how it is possible to include context in order to establish a balance between functional interpretation and the empirical status of analyses of frequency. For instance, as regards writing presentation, the hypoth esis is that writing presentation—especially the writing of letters—generally played a more influential role in 19th-century narrative fiction than in 20th-century fiction, because writing letters was an important means of communication in former times.

The relationship between narrative orientation (Toolan 2001: 68–69) and the choice of text samples is equally worth discussing. For example, similar to the several narrators in Brontë's (1847) *Wuthering Heights*, Shelley's (1818) *Frankenstein* is narrated by at least three first-person narrators. These are Mr. Waldon, who writes the letters to his sister, Victor Frankenstein, who is reported to tell his story to Mr. Waldon, and the Creature himself, who tells Frankenstein his story. Also, the discourse presentation in the novel is rather complex because it includes several embedded levels of discourse presentation. For example, Robert Waldon writes a letter to his sister in which he states that "I have resolved every night, when I'm not imperatively occupied, to record, as neatly as possible in his own words, what he has related during the day. This manuscript will doubtless afford you greatest pleasure" (Shelley [1818] 2003: 31). Leaving aside for the moment the difficulties in attributing the status of the manuscript as either writing representation with embedded discourse or as a new narrative, this quotation from the novel marks the necessity to account for the diversity of narrators (in order to detect either similarity or differences between them). Therefore, one might need to consider again the length of samples that is actually necessary to fully capture the whole essence of the novel and whether the narrative structure as well as the different points of view in novels like *Frankenstein* can be accounted for by the choice of chunks of that particular novel.

It must be stressed, however, that manual annotation of these word chunks is a way into the analysis of speech, writing, and thought presentation in 19th-century novels. It is certainly necessary to make fully transparent the procedure of choice, to illustrate which text chunks have been chosen, and to justify that choice. In addition, the role of context and its knowledge is essential in the manual annotation process. These methodological considerations also lead to literary discourse analysis and interpretation as a literary and cultural practice, as well as to the question of how these can be fruitfully interrelated with historical discourse analysis and corpus methods. I would like to repeat some of the arguments that have to be observed when a literary-critical approach and quantitative corpus-linguistic methods are fused. Literary discourse analysis, or what is called New Philology, emphasizes the historical, political, social as well as textual contexts of the writers, and stresses the role of the reader as offering an interpretation of the reading, a view taken on by New Historicists. For the interpretation, the reader functions as a mediator between the context of the text and that of the present creation, but is informed about the various contexts of the text: "[W]hereas corpus based linguistic discourse analysis is supported by the strength of quantitative analysis, literary discourse analysis is powered by the persuasive force of rhetoric" (Fitzmaurice and Taavitsainen 2007b: 24).

3.4.2. The Complexities of Annotating Discourse Presentation: An Example

Many stretches of discourse are ambiguous. This fact relates to the ways in which speech, writing, and thought are presented, and to the means the narrator uses in order to create ambiguity. The following extract from chapter 30 in *Emma* illustrates the complexity of the tagging process:

> (1) One thing only was wanting to make the prospect of the ball completely satisfactory to Emma—its being fixed for a day within the granted term of Frank Churchill's stay in Surry; for, in spite of Mr. Weston's confidence, she could not think it so very impossible that the Churchills might not allow their nephew to remain a day beyond his fortnight. (2) But this was not judged feasible. (3) The preparations must take their time, nothing could be properly ready till the third week were entered on, and for a few days they must be planning, proceeding and hoping in uncertainty—at the risk—in her opinion, the great risk, of its being all in vain. (*Emma* 1985 [1816]: 262)

It should be stressed in advance that the tagging process should systematically account for ambiguous cases. This introductory passage can be ambiguously read as either beginning with a presentation of Emma's thoughts or as a summary of a conversation (with the Westons, Frank Churchill, and her father), which is reported. The reader is led toward thinking that s/he reads Emma's thoughts in FIT or is confronted with the narrator telling the reader what her state is through NI in sentence 1: "One thing only was wanting to make the prospect of the ball completely satisfactory to Emma—its being fixed for a day within the granted term of Frank Churchill's stay in Surry." "Mr. Weston's confidence" can be read as embedded NI. We are either informed about Emma's thoughts in NI or, if read as FIT, Emma's wants are disclosed through the use of modality—"was wanting"—a sign of free indirect discourse (FID) in general (Toolan 2001: 131). So, the deictic shifts that need to take place while the reader is processing this stretch can be of a different kind, and it is through this that the ambiguity is created.

The sentence "she could not think it so very impossible that the Churchills might not allow their nephew to remain a day beyond his fortnight" can be read as consisting of NRT in "she could not think" and IT in "it so very impossible that the Churchills might not allow their nephew to remain a day beyond his fortnight." This last stretch of text also contains an embedded NRS (that is hypothetical) and IS in "that the Churchills might not allow" (eNRS) and "their nephew to remain a day beyond his fortnight" (eIS).

Sentence 2, "But this was not judged feasible," then seems to switch away from Emma's thoughts to the speech of others. The sentence is FIS because the reporting clause is missing and the passive sentence implies that it was uttered in response to something Emma has said. This sentence may accordingly provide the reader with a first clue as to the scale of discourse presentation that is used in sentence 1: It can also be read as either N-FIS, indicating that it summarizes Emma's publicly uttered opinions about the ball and Frank Churchill's presence, her inferences about Churchill's reactions to Frank extending his stay, and how the other interlocutors receive her hesitations in his actual participation in the ball.

The status of sentence 3 as FIS reinforces this view because it refers back to sentence 2, and again it abounds in the use of modality through the use of the auxiliary *must*. It also consists of a paratactically connected list of sentences and the enumeration of the non-finite verbs of "planning, proceeding and hoping" (a frequently occurring strategy of enumeration in Austen to ridicule the seriousness with which her characters consider these matters). The ironic voice of the narrator, who summarizes the report through FIS, is diegetic. The final words of this sentence, "at the risk—in her opinion, the great risk, of its being all in vain," contain a repetition of the prepositional phrase "at the risk"; these words are also modified by an evaluative adjective "great" and thus support the playful and colorful mixture of Emma's idiosyncratic voice and the narrator's voice. The stretch "in her opinion" diegetically foregrounds Emma's skeptical insistence on her belief that Frank Churchill might have to cancel the ball.

This playful ambiguity between the scale of discourse that is presented—speech or thought which is free and indirect—leads to an interpretative difference through the alignment (Toolan 2001: 135) with the character and the "dual voice." If it is read as thought presentation in the beginning, the reader feels closer to Emma and her thoughts and probably sympathizes with her. If it is read as FIS—that is, assuming that she presented her thoughts to her interlocutors—we could be witnessing a sort of transference of ironic effect from the narrator and onto the reader. However, the fact that this initial paragraph can be read as FIS or FIT—with completely different effects depending on how the attentive reader perceives it—illustrates the playful way in which the narrator manipulates the reader. It can be assumed, however, that the casual reader in the initial online process of reading does not fully discover this ambiguity.

In the annotation process, ambiguous cases will be accounted for in the speech act category tag ("<sptag cat>"). For example, a stretch that is ambiguous between narration and FIT would be categorized as "<sptag cat= N-FIT>." An example would be:

> </sptag>
> <sptag cat=N-FIT who=A next=FIS w=24>
> but if this reflected at all upon his impatience, his sorrowful look and total want of spirits when he did come might redeem him.
> (*Emma* 1985 [1816]: 264)

To conclude, this section has outlined the complex annotation procedures of discourse presentation. In future studies, it would be highly fruitful to test the importance of a difference between online- and post-processed reception of discourse presentation by the reader; so far, reader-oriented approaches to how ambiguous cases of discourse presentation modes are processed and what happens in the reading process have not been addressed.

CHAPTER 4

Types, Distribution, and Lexico-Grammatical Realization of Discourse Presentation Categories and Their Functional Implications

CHAPTERS 4 AND 5 ARE the core of this study. They present the analyses of speech, writing, and thought presentation practices identified in the corpus of 19th-century narrative fiction from both a quantitative and a qualitative angle. The aim is to assess, analyze, and interpret the types, linguistic realizations, and functions of the categories for each mode of discourse presentation. Further, I will compare my findings with those described in Semino and Short (2004) for their corpus of 20th-century narrative fiction. One focus will be on the investigation of the quantitative distribution of the number of tags for the different categories of discourse presentation on each mode. These will be computed as raw figures and by means of percentages. I will also analyze the number of words by which the respective tags of discourse presentation are realized in order to give a systematic account of the representative number of words in general, but also about the mean length of the allocated tags. Charting (statistically) foregrounded keywords, collocations, and clusters helps to identify lexico-grammatical patterning of the individual categories of the discourse presentation modes. One method to achieve this will be the comparison of stretches of discourse presentation and their lexical realization in my corpus with 19th-century linguistic data compiled in the *Corpus of Nineteenth-Century English* (Kytö et al. 2000) (CONCE), which is a one-million-word corpus, containing debates, trials, drama, fiction, letters, historical and scientific monographs. Following the quantitative distribution of the tagged stretches of discourse presentation is the analysis of the functions of the categories of discourse presentation on each mode.

4.1. *General Quantitative Observations*

Table 4.1 and Figure 4.1 show the percentages for the three modes of discourse presentation and for narration, computed by the number of tags that present

Speech, Writing, and Thought Presentation in 19th-Century Narrative Fiction. Beatrix Busse,
Oxford University Press (2020). © Oxford University Press.
DOI: 10.1093/oso/9780190212360.001.0001

TABLE 4.1 Percentages of Narration Tags and of Discourse Presentation Tags with NI, NV, and NW as Part of Discourse Presentation in the 19th-Century Corpus

DISCOURSE PRESENTATION / NARRATION / OTHER MODES		NUMBER OF TAGS (PERCENTAGES)	NUMBER OF TAGS (RAW FIGURES)
Speech	Discourse Presentation	37.04%	1,860
Thought		21.43%	1,076
Writing		2.39%	120
Narration		35.17%	1,766
Other		3.98%	200
Total		100%	5,022

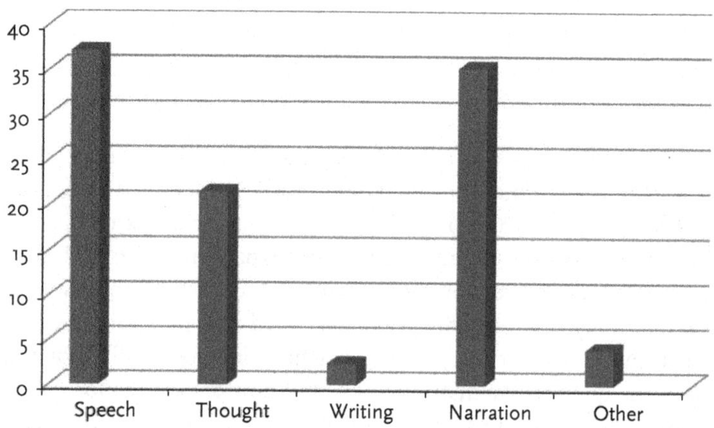

FIGURE 4.1. Percentages of occurrences of narration tags and of speech, writing, and thought presentation and other tags in the 19th-century corpus (NV, NI, NW as part of discourse presentation).

the various categories of the different modes of discourse presentation. The term *tag* refers here to the identification of stretches of discourse presentation, which can be a specific mode on either the speech, thought, or writing scale. This meaning of *tag* has to be differentiated from Genette's meaning of tag which is elaborated on. Stretches of narration are tagged separately (and include all occurrences of reporting clauses) in order to be able to compare discourse presentation with narration. The interplay between stretches of discourse presentation and narration is, as discussed before, crucial for determining their individual and mutually dependent functionalities in 19th-century writing. Table 4.1 and Figure 4.1 also include the results for ambiguous annotations of discourse presentation, which are summarized under the term "other."

In the 19th-century corpus, the total number of tags (including those tags identifying narration) amount to 5,022; 64.8% of these tags are tags for

TABLE 4.2 Figures for Narration and Discourse Presentation Categories with NI Tags Counted as Part of Narration in the 19th-Century Corpus

DISCOURSE PRESENTATION / NARRATION / OTHER MODES		NUMBER OF TAGS (PERCENTAGES)	NUMBER OF TAGS (RAW FIGURES)
Speech	Discourse Presentation	37.04%	1,860
Thought	Discourse Presentation	17.53%	881
Writing	Discourse Presentation	2.39%	120
Narration		39.07%	1,961
Other		3.98%	200
Total		100%	5,022

discourse presentation categories, and 35.17% are narration tags. In terms of frequency, there are large imbalances among the three modes of discourse presentation. The tags for speech presentation are by far the most frequently used, as Table 4.1 reveals; 37.04% of all tags are speech presentation tags, while 21.4% of all tags are thought presentation, and 2.4% are writing presentation tags.

As Table 4.2 illustrates, the results change slightly if we follow Short (2007) and consider NI to be part of narration.

If NI is counted as part of narration, the pattern changes, because 39.07% are narration tags and 60.9% are computed as tags for discourse presentation categories, that is, there is a variation of 3.9% of cases that shift between discourse presentation and narration depending on the classification of internal narration (NI). The number of thought presentation tags decreases at the expense of those tags identified as narration, which then surpass the percentage rate of speech presentation tags (39.07% for the former and 37.04% for the latter). Despite this, the tags for the speech presentation categories still occur twice as often as those for the thought presentation categories.

These tagging results for 19th-century narrative fiction confirm Toolan's (2001, 2006a, 2006b) and Short's (2007) claims concerning the need to investigate the category of NI further. Following these results, I would argue that in the 19th century, narrative techniques and discourse presentation strategies are more fully, or simply differently, accomplished than they have actually been given credit for. This can be claimed because all modes of the different discourse presentation scales appear in my corpus. Further, the systematic annotation of discourse presentation in 19th-century narrative fiction reveals that free indirect speech (FIS) and free indirect thought (FIT) differ markedly in frequency, and this possibly reflects a difference in function as well. It follows from this that these two modes of speech and thought presentation should not simply be summarized under the one broad, undifferentiated label of "free indirect discourse" (FID).

In order to investigate and contextualize further the initial results of my quantitative analysis, I implement a comparison between the figures summarized earlier and Semino and Short's (2004) figures for the 20th century. Certainly, as mentioned in Chapter 2, the comparison is not without its flaws because, for instance, the distinction made in Semino and Short (2004) between serious and popular narrative fiction cannot be easily mirrored in my 19th-century selection of novels. However, the comparison helps to get a broad overview of tendencies of stability and change in the use of discourse presentation. The comparison between the figures for the two corpora is established by computing individually for each corpus the raw numbers of discourse presentation tags and their respective percentages. The distribution of discourse presentation and narration categories (alongside the ambiguous cases) in the two centuries under investigation is displayed in Table 4.3 and Figure 4.2. Both the table and the figure display the percentages in my 19th-century corpus compared to Semino and Short's 20th-century corpus.

TABLE 4.3 Percentages of Discourse Presentation Tags (NI as Part of Discourse Presentation) in 19th- and 20th-Century Narrative Fiction Compared

DISCOURSE PRESENTATION / NARRATION / OTHER MODES		PERCENTAGES OF TAGS IN 19TH-CENTURY CORPUS	PERCENTAGES OF TAGS IN 20TH-CENTURY CORPUS (SEMINO AND SHORT 2004)
Speech	Discourse Presentation	37.04%	50.06%
Thought	Discourse Presentation	21.43%	24.4%
Writing	Discourse Presentation	2.39%	1.65%
Narration		35.17%	20.99%
Other		3.98%	2.9%
Total		100%	100%

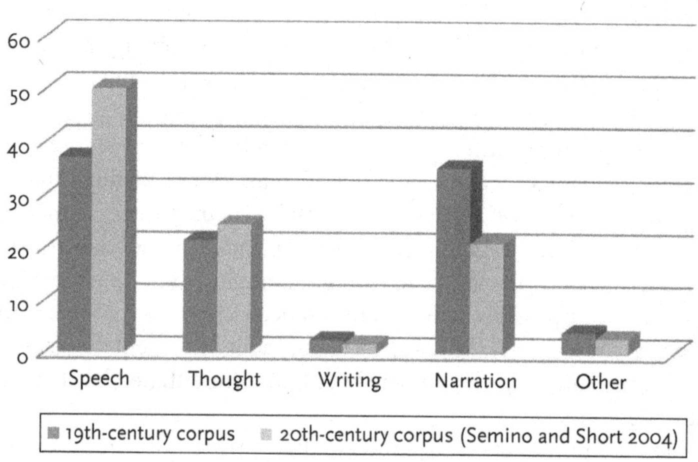

FIGURE 4.2. Percentages of tags of speech, writing, and thought presentation in the 19th- and 20th-century corpora.

One difference particularly stands out between the two corpora: The number of narration tags has decreased over time between the 19th-century and the 20th-century data (that is, if NI is counted as discourse presentation). It seems as if the higher number of narration tags in the 19th century may have given way to tags for speech presentation in the 20th-century data. In other words, there seems to be a reverse tendency between narration use, on the one hand, and speech and thought presentation categories, on the other, when 19th-century and 20th-century narrative fiction are compared. While narration use is clearly over-represented in the 19th century (35.17% vs. 20.99%), the latter set (that is, both speech and thought presentation categories taken together) are preferred in 20th-century writing (50.06% and 24.4% for speech and thought presentation in the 20th century, as against 37.04% and 21.43% for the same categories in the 19th century). Writing presentation, in turn, is only slightly favored in 19th-century novels (2.39% vs. 1.65%). The distribution of the rank scale of the three modes of discourse presentation is thus similar for 19th-century and 20th-century narrative fiction—with speech presentation tags being most frequently found in the two corpora. Therefore, it seems that it is discourse presentation tags that are more frequently found in the 20th-century narrative fiction sequences, whereas narration and, to a lesser degree, writing presentation tags feature mainly the 19th-century corpus of narrative fiction.

An even more detailed picture emerges when relating the number of tags for discourse presentation and narration to the number of words in each tag. Before I present the results of the length of each stretch by the number of words, I would like to outline how, in my corpus, I arrived at computing the percentages for the number of words that encode the different categories of speech, writing, and thought presentation. For the general figures presented in Table 4.4, I first counted the number of words encoding the different tags individually. I was then able to compute percentages by relating the number of words used for each mode (speech, writing, or thought) to the overall number of words being used for either discourse presentation or narration. For example, for speech presentation, 21,019 words are used in the respective categories

TABLE 4.4 Percentages of Words under the Respective Categories of the Speech, Writing, and Thought Scales (NI, NV, NW as Part of Discourse Presentation) in the 19th- and 20th-Century Corpora

DISCOURSE PRESENTATION / NARRATION / OTHER MODES	PERCENTAGES OF WORDS REPRESENTING THE TAGS IN 19TH-CENTURY CORPUS	PERCENTAGES OF WORDS REPRESENTING THE TAGS IN 20TH-CENTURY CORPUS (SEMINO AND SHORT 2004)
Speech	36.6% (21,019)	31.59%
Thought	21.5% (12,341)	19.20%
Writing	2.4% (1,378)	0.63%
Narration and Other	39.5% (22,665)	45.04%

TABLE 4.5 Percentages of Words under the Speech, Writing, and Thought Tags (NI as Part of Narration) in the 19th- and 20th-Century Corpora

DISCOURSE PRESENTATION / NARRATION / OTHER MODES	PERCENTAGES OF WORDS REPRESENTING THE TAGS IN THE 19TH-CENTURY CORPUS	PERCENTAGES OF WORDS REPRESENTING THE TAGS IN THE 20TH-CENTURY CORPUS (SEMINO AND SHORT 2004)
Speech	36.6% (21,019)	31.59%
Thought	18.9% (10,850)	19.20%
Writing	2.4% (1,378)	0.63%
Narration and Other	42.1% (24,156)	45.04%

of the speech presentation scale. This amounts to 36.6% of all words tagged in the corpus as either discourse presentation. The overall mean length for a stretch of speech, writing, or thought presentation will be discussed in section 4.4 for each category separately.

Tables 4.4 and 4.5 illustrate a number of crucial findings that need closer inspection. First of all, these tables show that even if NI is classified as narration, the percentage of the number of words used in the narration tags always surpasses the percentage of the words used in any of the other discourse presentation categories both in the 19th- and 20th-century texts; that is, narration contains the largest number of words both in the 19th- and 20th-century narrative fiction corpora. Note, however, that Semino and Short (2004) do not provide the reader with the raw figures for the number of words which represent the scales and modes of discourse presentation.

Second, these figures show some interesting findings when viewed in relation to the temporal axis. As Table 4.3 illustrates, narration tags occur more frequently in the 19th-century than in the 20th-century texts (35.17% vs. 20.99%). And yet, in the 20th-century corpus the percentage of the number of words that present narration tags is higher than in the 19th-century corpus (39.5/42.1% vs. 45.04% in the 20th-century corpus). This seems to suggest that the fewer tags presenting narration in the 20th-century corpus (i.e., the fewer occurrences of narration) are made up for by the increase in the number of words allocated to the narrators when they do make their presence felt.

A third issue that arises from these figures concerns speech presentation. Although there are by far fewer speech presentation tags in the 19th-century corpus compared to the 20th-century data (37.04% vs. 50.06%; see Table 4.3), the 19th-century speech presentation tags include ~5% more words (i.e., 36.6% in the 19th century [21,019 words] as against 31.59% in Semino and Short [2004] for the 20th century; see Table 4.4). That is, when 19th-century characters' speech is presented, it seems that what they say is presented in a more verbose way than in 20th-century narrative fiction. We shall see in the following that this holds true especially for DS and FDS in both corpora.

Fourth, as far as the thought presentation mode is concerned, it appears that the total number of words used to present thought in the 19th-century corpus is higher (12,341 words, i.e., 21.5%) when NI is computed as part of the thought presentation scale (19.2% for the 20th-century corpus). If the NI category is considered part of discourse presentation (see Table 4.4) it is slightly lower in the 19th-century corpus (10,850 words, i.e., 18.9%) than in the 20th-century corpus. Finally, writing presentation is more frequent not only in terms of the number of tags used in the 19th-century corpus (2.39% vs. 1.65%; see Table 4.3), but also in terms of the number of words encoding writing presentation in such tags (1,378 words, i.e., 2.4% for the 19th century vs. 0.63% for the 20th century).

To conclude, these figures thus bring to the fore a series of specific formal and functional as well as distributional patterns of 19th-century discourse presentation. For instance, although there are fewer tags of discourse presentation modes on all scales and in both centuries when compared to the narration tags, the 19th century displays a preference for longer discourse presentation stretches in terms of the number of words being used. This might be one reason why we, as readers, feel that discourse presentation in the 19th-century corpus is prevalent. Further, another effect of the larger number of words used in the discourse presentation modes might be a demonstration of how communication in general and the human mind in particular worked in the 19th century (see Chapter 7), which in turn heightens the pragmatic potential of those stretches of discourse presentation.

4.2. *The Different Scales of Discourse Presentation and Their Modes: Quantification of Tags and Number of Words by Which These Are Represented*

4.2.1. Number of Tags

I continue my analysis of discourse presentation by looking at the distribution of tags for the various categories separately, both in terms of raw figures and percentages. These results will be compared to those from Semino and Short (2004) for their 20th-century corpus of narrative fiction. Furthermore, I shall investigate the number of words (raw figures and percentages of all words used) by which the individual tags for the different categories are realized. I will then also calculate the mean length of words for each category on each mode of discourse presentation, that is, I will analyze the average length of a stretch of tags for DS, NRTA, and so on. This is done by dividing the number of words that represent, for instance, DS stretches altogether through the number of tags by which DS is represented in the corpus.

Table 4.6 shows that on the speech presentation scale, DS is the most frequently tagged category (see Table 4.6 and Figure 4.3).

DS tags also come on first position in the 20th-century fictional sub-corpus tagged by Semino and Short (2004: 67). For the writing presentation scale

TABLE 4.6 Percentages and Raw Figures of Tags for the Speech Presentation Scales in the 19th-Century Corpus

SPEECH PRESENTATION MODE	NV	NRSA	IS	FIS	DS	FDS	TOTAL
Pure	111	190	75	38	637	406	1,457
Embedded	34	150	83	3	21	7	298
Hypothetical	4	11	3	0	3	0	21
Hypothetical / inferred	0	1	0	0	0	0	1
Embedded / hypothetical	9	52	13	0	2	0	76
Inferred	1	2	1	0	0	0	4
Embedded / inferred	1	2	0	0	0	0	3
Total	160	408	175	41	663	413	1,860
Percentages	3.2%	8.1%	3.5%	0.8%	13.2%	8.2%	37%

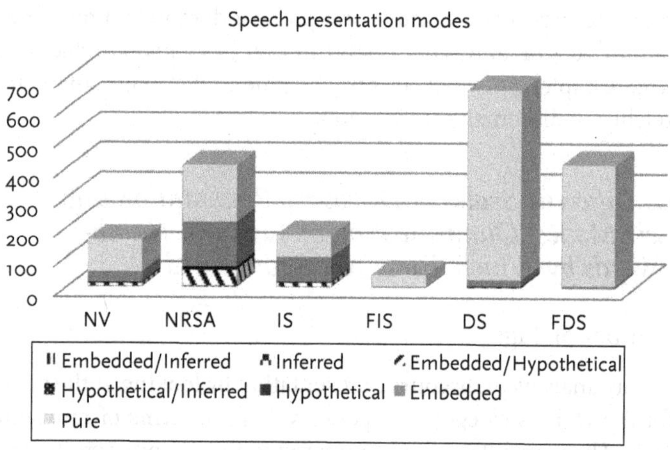

FIGURE 4.3. Number of occurrences of speech presentation tags by raw figures in the 19th-century corpus.

(see Table 4.7 and Figure 4.4), narrator's presentation of writing (NW) is most frequently tagged in my corpus. This is different in Semino and Short (2004: 100), where the (F)DW categories occur most frequently (despite an also overall low frequency of writing presentation tags in both corpora).

As regards thought presentation, my corpus shows a preference for narrator's report of thought act (NRTA) instances (see Table 4.8 and Figure 4.5). Semino and Short (2004: 117) identify internal narration (NI) as the most frequently tagged category in their 20th-century corpus, followed by FIT.

TABLE 4.7 Percentages and Raw Figures of Tags for the Writing Presentation Scales in the 19th-Century Corpus

WRITING PRESENTATION MODE	NW	NRWA	IW	FIW	DW	FDW	TOTAL
Pure	26	17	9	9	21	0	82
Embedded	11	10	5	1	1	0	28
Hypothetical	0	0	0	0	0	0	0
Hypothetical / inferred	0	0	0	0	0	0	0
Embedded / hypothetical	2	6	2	0	0	0	10
Inferred	0	0	0	0	0	0	0
Embedded / inferred	0	0	0	0	0	0	0
Total	39	33	16	10	22	0	120
Percentages	0.8%	0.7%	0.3%	0.2%	0.4%	0.0%	2.4%

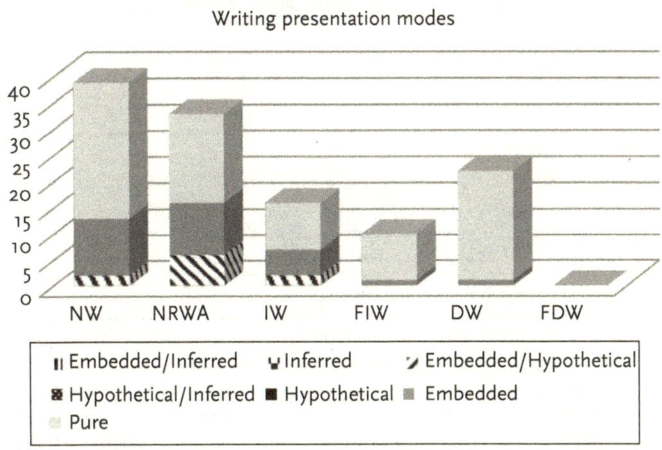

FIGURE 4.4. Number of occurrences of writing presentation tags by raw figures in the 19th-century corpus.

Going back to the speech presentation scale (see Table 4.6 and Figure 4.3), the high numbers of tags for the direct categories DS and FDS in my corpus stand out (13.2% [663 tags] and 8.2% [413 tags], respectively). With 8.1% (408 tags) of all tags, NRSA is on the third position of the number of tags used on the speech presentation scale in 19th-century narrative fiction, followed by IS (3.5%, 175 tags) and NV (3.2%, 160 tags). FIS is represented by the fewest tags: 41 tags, amounting to 0.8%. Hence, in addition to a focus on DS presentation in 19th-century fiction, which may be either reported or free, there is a preference for those categories of speech presentation that summarize speech

TABLE 4.8 Percentages and Raw Figures of Tags for the Thought Presentation Scales in the 19th-Century Corpus

THOUGHT PRESENTATION MODE	NI	NT	NRTA	IT	FIT	DT	FDT	TOTAL
Pure	157	32	221	184	187	18	3	802
Embedded	26	0	83	45	0	2	0	156
Hypothetical	5	1	10	7	0	0	0	23
Hypothetical / inferred	0	1	2	1	0	1	0	5
Embedded / hypothetical	3	1	19	9	0	0	0	32
Inferred	0	1	22	9	0	0	0	32
Embedded / inferred	4	0	11	11	0	0	0	26
Total	195	36	368	266	187	21	3	1,076
Percentages	3.9%	0.7%	7.3%	5.3%	3.7%	0.4%	0.1%	21.4%

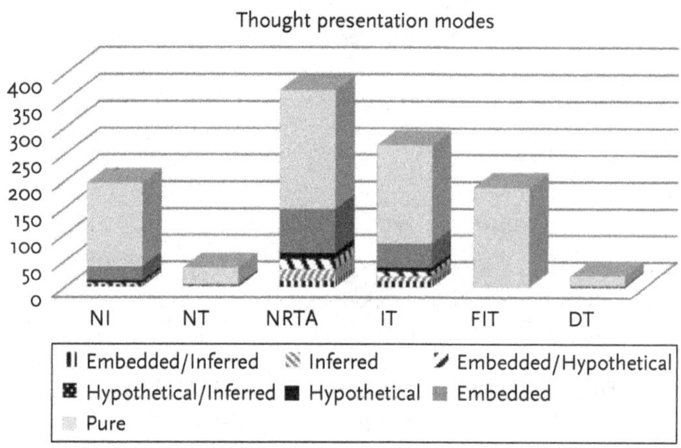

FIGURE 4.5. Number of occurrences of thought presentation tags by raw figures in the 19th-century corpus.

acts or events. Strikingly, FIS is not among the most frequent categories in the corpus. This result on the one hand justifies differentiating between FIS and FID, rather than conflating the two under "free indirect discourse" (see earlier discussions in sections 2.1.2 and 2.1.6 of Chapter 2). On the other hand, it shows that the category of FIS is not as prominently employed in 19th-century narrative fiction as is often assumed.

The distribution of speech presentation categories is similar in the 20th-century fictional sub-corpus, even though one could perhaps argue that proportionally speaking, (F)DS categories occur even more frequently in the 20th-century corpus than in the 19th-century corpus. Hence, the high overall number of speech presentation tags in the 20th-century corpus (see Table 4.3).

NRSA receives 251 tags (8.1%), IS 117 tags (3.5%), NV 111 tags (3.2%), and FIS 57 tags (0.8%) in Semino and Short (2004: 67).

For the writing presentation scale (see Table 4.7 and Figure 4.4), the distribution of tags looks different. Due to the very low frequency of instances of writing presentation in my corpus, the following description of my findings should be taken with caution. In terms of raw numbers of tags and percentages, the direct categories DW and FDW do not occur frequently when compared with the direct categories DS and FDS for speech presentation. And yet, on the writing presentation scale, DW is the third-most frequent category after NW and NRWA and thus deserves some attention.

The presentation of writing is mostly achieved by those strategies that summarize writing acts or writing events: NW (0.8%, 39 tags) and NRWA (0.7%, 33 tags). IW, FIW, and FDW are extremely rare or nonexistent. While writing presentation occurs also in the 20th-century fictional sub-corpus (Semino and Short 2004: 100), the two sub-corpora show a slightly different distribution of writing presentation tags. In the 20th-century sub-corpus, NRWA occurs most frequently (29 tags), followed by (F)DW (19 tags). Tags for NW, IW, and FIW are rare.

Tags for thought presentation are generally considerably fewer than those attributed to speech presentation (roughly 13% fewer tags; see Table 4.8 and Figure 4.5). The categories that allow us direct access to a character's thought, DT and FDT, are extremely rare in my 19th-century corpus. Although the number of tags for DT and FDT are higher in Semino and Short's (2004: 117) corpus than in my 19th-century data, the two categories are also the least frequent ones for thought presentation in the 20th-century fictional sub-corpus. In other words, while the distribution of DS and FDS is highest on the speech presentation scale in both corpora, the corresponding categories on the thought presentation scale are very rare.

As already mentioned, the strategies of thought presentation that summarize a thought act or a thinking process are the most frequent categories in my 19th-century corpus: NRTA has 368 tags (i.e., 7.3%), while IT has 266 tags (i.e., 5.3%). The presentation of mental processes, tagged by NI, comes third with 195 tags (i.e., 3.9%). In Semino and Short's (2004: 117) 20th-century fictional sub-corpus, NI occurs most frequently (with 409 tags); IT (133 tags) is on third position, and NRTA (88 tags) comes on fourth position. Hence, it can be said that the categories that are positioned closer to the narrator's end of the scale appear more frequently in both corpora, although the number of tags and the corresponding rank-scales differ. In 20th-century thought presentation, the presentation of mental states dominates, whereas in the 19th century it is the summary of a mental act in NRTA.

FIT, as that category of thought presentation which has so far received most attention in the literature, comes on fourth position in my 19th-century corpus, with 187 tags (i.e., 3.7%). This quantitative result allows us to put the scholarly focus on this category into perspective for the 19th century. The 19th-century result for FIT tags can be better understood when compared to the

20th-century result by Semino and Short (2004: 117): With 227 tags, FIT comes on second position in their fictional sub-corpus. We may tentatively conclude from these results for FIT that a development toward a more complex portrayal of characters' psyche and their mental processes seems to be taking place diachronically.

The direct modes of thought presentation (FDT, DT) are also more prominent in the 20th century than in the 19th century—which might equally suggest a development in the frequency in which a character's thoughts are presented directly. And yet, both corpora show a predominance of more conscious styling of a character's mental worlds by means of summarizing categories, such as NRTA or even NI, which allow the narrator to guide that portrayal.

4.2.2. Number of Words

I now consider the whole taxonomies for discourse presentation and narration in relation to the number of words used to encode tags for each of the individual categories. Speech presentation in 19th-century narrative fiction is realized not only by most of the tags, but also by most of the words in the corpus (36.6%; 21,019 words in total). Thought presentation comes on second position of the overall number of tags, and the same can be observed for the overall number of words (21.5%; 12,341 words in total). Writing presentation is represented by a very low number of tags as well as words (2.4%; 1,378 words in total).

For speech presentation, the rank scheme for the number of words that represent the different categories corresponds to the already presented rank-scale for the tags. By far, most of the words for discourse presentation in the corpus occur in DS (11.4%; 7,111 words in total) and FDS (12.0%; 7,465 words in total; see Table 4.9). But while there are more tags for DS than for FDS, there are more words for FDS than for DS, which shows that the free direct category of discourse presentation is more verbose and may be seen as an adherence to the notion of faithfulness by the narrator in representing the words of characters in exactly the way they have been uttered.

The summarizing categories for speech presentation NRSA and IS, which are more toward the narrator's end of the scale, also come second and third with regard to the number of words (NRSA: 4.8%, 2,999 words; IS: 3.0%, 1,857 words). The margin of percentages of tags between NRSA and IS is significantly higher than the margin between the number of words that represent these categories, with IS having fewer words. However, we will see in the following that the mean length of words in IS is longer than that of NRSA.

NV, as the summary of a speech report, is on fifth position with regard to the number of words by which the tags are represented (i.e., 1,050 words in total that represent 1.7% of all words). FIS amounts to only 537 words in total (i.e., 0.9% of all words), which shows that FIS is represented not only by a small number of tags but also by the fewest amount of words. This would go against some of the qualitative claims made with regard to speech presentation and

TABLE 4.9 Percentages and Raw Number of Words Presenting Speech Presentation Categories in the 19th-Century Corpus

SPEECH PRESENTATION MODE	NV	NRSA	IS	FIS	DS	FDS	TOTAL
Pure	754	1,523	724	499	6,989	7,330	17,819
Embedded	266	985	889	38	91	135	2,404
Hypothetical	28	69	65	0	14	0	176
Hypothetical / Inferred	0	8	0	0	0	0	8
Embedded / Hypothetical	0	396	169	0	17	0	582
Inferred	2	11	10	0	0	0	23
Embedded / Inferred	0	7	0	0	0	0	7
Total	1,050	2,999	1,857	537	7,111	7,465	21,019
Percentages	1.7%	4.8%	3.0%	0.9%	11.4%	12%	33.8%

the 19th century, which tend to highlight FIS as prototypical in the 19th-century novel (Toolan 2001). My corpus appears to refute these claims, as FIS is the category with the fewest tags (see Table 4.6) and also the smallest number of total words (Table 4.9).[1]

As mentioned, the writing presentation scale is only represented by a small number of tags. The same holds true for the overall number of words. It is worth mentioning, however, that although DW is represented by only a few of the tags for writing presentation in my corpus (see Table 4.7 where DW is on third position with regard to the number of tags), it nevertheless has most of the words (474 words, i.e., 0.8% of the total of words; see Table 4.10). It may thus be concluded that if DS occurs, it is rather verbose.

The summarizing categories NRWA, NW, and IW come on second and third positions of the number of words for the writing presentation scale. FIW occurs with only a small number of words. Sending letters or reporting that notes have been sent from one person to another are typical 19th-century means of communication and exchange of information.

To take stock, we have seen that it is possible to compare the results gained for discourse presentation in 19th- and 20th-century narrative fiction, despite the small size of my 19th-century corpus. The quantitative distribution of tags, as well as the high number of words for speech presentation, especially for DS and FDS, is similar in both corpora. Both in 19th- and 20th-century narrative fiction, writing presentation is rare. Tags for thought presentation categories occur second most frequently overall. In both corpora, the two summarizing categories of thought presentation NRTA and IT, and NI, which presents a character's mental state, occur most frequently (see Table 4.8). FIT comes on position two on the 20th-century rank scale of tags for thought presentation;

TABLE 4.10 Percentages and Raw Number of Words Presenting Writing Presentation Categories in the 19th-Century Corpus

WRITING PRESENTATION MODES	NW	NRWA	IW	FIW	DW	FDW	TOTAL
Pure	185	180	121	94	470	0	1,050
Embedded	70	61	34	8	4	0	177
Hypothetical	0	0	0	0	0	0	0
Hypothetical / Inferred	0	0	0	0	0	0	0
Embedded / Hypothetical	22	52	77	0	0	0	151
Inferred	0	0	0	0	0	0	0
Embedded / Inferred	0	0	0	0	0	0	0
Total	277	293	232	102	474	0	1,378
Percentages	0.4%	0.5%	0.4%	0.2%	0.8%	0.0%	2.2%

in the 19th-century corpus it is on position four. In both corpora, however, it is presented by a high number of words (see Table 4.11).

The quantitative investigation given here, also called for by Palmer (2004, 2010) within his framework of the "social mind in action" in narrative fiction (Palmer 2004: 62), is crucial in order to systematically measure and describe the variety of scales of discourse presentation and switches from one "text-world" to the next (Werth 1999; Gavins 2007). Unlike in everyday interaction, where we do not have access to the thoughts of others, we are actually capable of doing so in a variety of ways in narrative fiction. As the discussed figures show, Palmer (2004: 53) is right to question the bias toward a verbal norm, that is, a focus on speech presentation in general, which is usually favored by researchers of discourse presentation when attempting to describe how the fictional mind works. Approaches to thought presentation like Chatman's (1978), who notes that the "most obvious and direct means of handling the thoughts of a character is to treat them as 'unspoken speech'" (Chatman 1978: 182), do not always account properly for the thought presentation categories in their full complexity. Palmer, in contrast, stresses the importance of what he calls "thought report" (Palmer 2004: 57), that is, summaries of states of mind, mood, desires, emotions, sensations, visual images, attention, memory, and latent mental states, which describe thought in terms of motives, intentions, behavior, and action. Again, as shown in Table 4.8, the most direct thought presentation categories—direct thought (DT) and free direct thought (FDT)—are not as frequent in my corpus as those categories which are more oriented toward the narrator, such as NI, NT, and NRTA, and which, by definition, summarize a character's state of mind. Therefore, Margolin's (2000) claim that "modern Western literary narrative [. . .] has a clear preference for the rich,

TABLE 4.11 Percentages and Raw Number of Words Presenting Thought Presentation Categories in the 19th-Century Corpus

THOUGHT PRESENTATION MODE	NI	NT	NRTA	IT	FIT	DT	FDT	TOTAL
Pure	1,182	322	2,450	1,687	4,187	120	29	9,977
Embedded	224	0	636	320	0	15	0	1,195
Hypothetical	52	12	75	93	0	0	0	232
Hypothetical / Inferred	0	6	26	4	0	24	0	60
Embedded / Hypothetical	15	10	197	84	0	0	0	306
Inferred	0	4	220	93	0	0	0	317
Embedded / Inferred	18	0	149	87	0	0	0	254
Total	1,491	354	3,753	2,368	4,187	159	29	12,341
Percentages	2.4%	0.6%	6.0%	3.8%	6.7%	0.3%	0%	19.8%

detailed and 'unmediated' presentation of individual human inner life on all levels of consciousness" (2000: 606) needs to be questioned, too. My 19th-century data certainly show that characters' minds do not simply consist of a private passive flow of consciousness, as thought report and summary take on a crucial role in linking "individual mental functioning to its social context" (Palmer 2004: 76).

Fludernik (1993), in her description of the presentation of consciousness, is partly right to stress that "direct discourse is the least common technique, with a traditional preponderance of [thought report] and, in second place, free indirect discourse, which comes close to competing with [thought report] in late nineteenth- and early-twentieth-century fiction" (Fludernik 1993: 291). Her observations about free indirect discourse, however, do not seem to find full support in my corpus. While tags for FIT are more frequent in it than those for FIS, FIT is still in fourth place on the thought presentation scale, preceded by those categories that are more situated at the narrator's end of the thought presentation scale, such as IT, NI, and NRTA. However, FIT is represented by most of the words on the thought presentation scale. These findings again show that a clear distinction has to be made between FIS and FIT and that the categories closer to the narrator's end of the scale, which present a report of a character's thinking process, are more prominent than the direct thought presentation categories in 19th-century narrative fiction.

I would like to push my analysis further by presenting the relation between the number of tags and the number of words used for the different modes of discourse presentation in a different layout that depicts a focus on the (almost) parallel scales, except for NT, and that also displays the mean length of words used to represent it. This design has been chosen in order to be able to compare to what extent the categories are similar or different in terms of the quantification of tags and numbers of words. Hence, Table 4.12 is sorted according to the number of tags for each category on each scale (percentages and raw figures), the number of words (percentages and raw figures), and the mean length of words for each category on each scale. The mean length of words for each category is computed by dividing the number of words that represent the particular category altogether by the number of tags for each category; thus, for instance, the mean length of stretches of DS are computed by dividing the number of words for all of the DS stretches through the number of tags.

To begin with and to recapitulate some general observations, the direct speech presentation categories are tagged most frequently in both corpora, with DS being the most prominent category, followed by FDS. NRTA follows DS and FDS in the 19th-century corpus. In the 20th-century corpus it is NI. Despite the fact that the overall number of tags for these categories is considerably lower than those for (F)DS, the summarizing of characters' mental processes seems to play a crucial role in both corpora.

The rank scale for the overall number of words that present the different discourse presentation categories in my corpus looks slightly different, because it is not NRSA that follows FDS (12% of all words) and DS (11.4% of all words) on the third position, but FIT (6.7% of all words). As regards the average length of tags, most of the words—that is, the largest mean length—occur for FIT (21.54 words per tag), astride DW (21.54 words per tag) and followed by FDS (18.07 words per tag). In the 20th-century corpus, the largest mean length also occurs in FIT (25.83 words per tag), followed by FIS (18.63 words per tag), and DT (14.03 words per tag).

Let us look at the distribution of tags, as well as the number of words that represent them, by moving from the categories that are more on the narrator's end of the scale to those that present the discourse of the character more directly. To begin with the narrator's end of the speech, writing, and thought presentation scales and the categories that report a speech, writing, or thought event, it can be said that there are slightly more tags for NI (3.9%) than for NV (3.2%). NW is rare (0.8%). In both corpora, however, there are more tags that summarize mental processes (NI) than there are tags that present that speech has taken place (NV). Perhaps this result can be correlated with the fact that there is a dominance of DS and FDS in both corpora, which makes NV less necessary. In turn, the lower number of (F)DT categories in both corpora can be correlated to the higher numbers of tags for NI and NRTA.

Stretches of NI are also represented by more words in the 19th-century corpus (2.4% of all words, 1,491 words in total; see Table 4.12), than for NV (1.7% of all words, 1,050 words in total). The mean length of words for NI (7.64 words per tag) is almost one word longer than that for NV (6.56 words per tag). Whether this is a significant result is difficult to judge from a quantitative point of view. Given the constant focus in the literature on this topic on speech presentation modes, it is perhaps surprising that the summarizing category

TABLE 4.12 Quantification of Discourse Presentation Categories in the 19th-Century Corpus, Including a Comparison with the 20th-Century Corpus (Semino and Short 2004)

DISCOURSE PRESENTATION CATEGORY	TAGS—RAW FIGURES, 19TH-CENTURY CORPUS	TAGS—PERCENTAGES, 19TH-CENTURY CORPUS	WORDS REPRESENTING TAGS—RAW FIGURES, 19TH-CENTURY CORPUS	WORDS REPRESENTING TAGS—PERCENTAGES, 19TH-CENTURY CORPUS	MEAN LENGTH OF WORDS, 19TH-CENTURY CORPUS	TAGS—RAW FIGURES, 20TH-CENTURY CORPUS (SEMINO AND SHORT 2004)	MEAN LENGTH OF WORDS, 20TH-CENTURY CORPUS (SEMINO AND SHORT 2004)
NV	160	3.2%	1,050	1.7%	6.56	111	7.58
NW	39	0.8%	277	0.4%	7.10	10	5.70
NI	195	3.9%	1,491	2.4%	7.64	409	13.40
NT	36	0.7%	354	0.6%	9.80		
NRSA	408	8.1%	2,999	4.8%	7.35	251	11.87
NRWA	33	0.7%	293	0.5%	8.87	29	11.75
NRTA	368	7.3%	3,753	6.0%	8.90	60	9.41
IS	175	3.5%	1,857	3.0%	10.71	117	11.74
IW	16	0.3%	232	0.4%	14.5	5	17.00
IT	266	5.3%	2,368	3.8%	8.90	85	11.94
FIS	41	0.8%	537	0.9%	13.09	57	18.63
FIW	10	0.2%	102	0.2%	10.02	4	10.40
FIT	187	3.7%	4,187	6.7%	22.39	227	25.83
DS	663	13.2%	7,111	11.4%	10.72	832	12.45
DW	22	0.4%	474	0.8%	21.54	11	7.52
DT	21	0.4%	159	0.3%	7.57	19	14.03
FDS	413	8.2%	7,465	12.0%	18.07	737	12.45
FDW	0	0%	0	0%	0	8	7.52
FDT	3	0.1%	29	0.01%	9.66	58	14.03

of NI on the thought presentation scale is on average realized by more words than the similar category—although having a different function—on the speech presentation scale. Stretches of NI in the 20th-century corpus have by far a longer mean length (13.40 words per tag) than those in the 19th century.

With a tag-percentage of 8.1% for NRSA and 7.3% for NRTA, NRSA occurs more frequently in my corpus than NRTA. The number of words by which these tags are represented are, however, lower for NRSA (4.8%) than for NRTA (6%). The mean length of words is higher in stretches of NRTA (8.90 words per tag) when compared to NRSA (7.35 words per tag). Again, NRWA is closer to NRTA than to NRSA in terms of the mean length of words, although it is generally assumed that writing presentation categories are closer to speech presentation categories. Hence, it is striking that for the summarizing categories, the mean length of a tag is longer for NI and NRTA than for NV and NRSA and also more words are used, despite the fact that the number of tags for NRSA precedes those for NRTA. Although it should be stressed that tags for NT are rather few in the corpus, as are the overall numbers of words by which they are presented, it is also striking that the average length of the stretches of NT surpasses that of NI and NRSA.

Tags for indirect reports—that is, those stretches of discourse presentation that are accompanied by a reporting clause—occur more frequently as IT (5.3%) than as IS (3.5%). Again, tags for IW are rare (0.7%). Overall, there are more words to present IT (3.8%) than IS (3.0%), but the mean length for each stretch is longer for IS (10.71 words per tag) than for IT (8.90 words per tag). Strikingly, the average length for stretches of words presenting IW with 14.50 words per tag surpasses those for both IT and IS. But note the low number of tags and words altogether for this category of writing presentation (only 16 tags and 232 words in total).

The free indirect categories of speech, writing, and thought presentation show both a peculiar number of overall tags and of overall words for each category. Tags for FIT (3.7%) by far outnumber those for FIS (0.8%) and FIW (0.2%). This finds an even more pronounced expression in the number of overall words presenting these categories. With FIT on position three of the rank scale concerning the number of words, words that present FIT in my corpus amount to 6.7% and a mean length of 22.39 words per tag. For FIS this is 0.9% of all words and a mean length of 13.09 words per tag. Words for FIW make up 0.2% of all words with a mean length of 10.02 words per tag. With this result, tags for FIT have the longest average length per tag in my corpus, surpassing even the figures for DW (21.54 words per tag) and FDS (18.07 words per tag). This is striking and impressively illustrates why FIS has to be separated both structurally and functionally from FIT. The prominent effect of FIT is thus due to the number of words by which the tags are represented, rather than to the mere occurrences of FIT tags.

Direct discourse—either free or with a reporting clause—is very prominently realized in my corpus when it comes to DS and FDS. These two are by far the most frequent speech presentation categories, and they are also presented by the highest number of words overall. There are more tags for DS (13.2%, 663 tags) than there are for FDS (8.2%, 413 tags), but FDS stretches are represented by more words (12%) than DS stretches (11.4%). This also leads to a higher average number of words that present FDS, with 18.07 words per tag for FDS, as opposed to 10.72 words per tag for DS. Note that the tags for DW and FDW, as well as the number of words, are generally rather low, whereas the mean length of individual stretches of DW with 21.54 words per tag is the second highest average length in the corpus overall.

To conclude, criticizing the hierarchical component inherent in the discourse presentation model, I discussed in Chapter 2 that the effects of particular categories of thought presentation are different from those of speech presentation (Leech and Short 1981: 342–348; see also Fludernik 1993, who introduces a very elaborate model consisting of over 30 elements that take account of the distinction between speech and thought presentation modes). From a quantitative point of view, the scales of speech and thought presentation in 19th-century narrative fiction are differently distributed: Thought presentation tags that present a summary of states of mind are more frequent than those categories on the thought presentation scale that are closer to the character, whereas unmediated DS tags closer to the character are more often the norm on the speech presentation scale in my 19th-century corpus. These results could give quantitative evidence to what Fludernik (1993: 281) has termed the "direct discourse fallacy," according to which a character's direct discourse should never simply be accepted as fully reliable because the narrator's mediation is always a distortion (irrespective of whether reporting tags introducing speech are present or not). Fludernik (1993) sees "narrative discourse as a uniform one-levelled linguistic entity which by its deictic evocation of alterity [. . .] projects a level of language which is not actually there but is implied and manufactured by a kind of linguistic hallucination" (Fludernik 1993: 453).

CHAPTER 5 | Scales and Modes of Discourse Presentation and Their Functions

THIS CHAPTER REPRESENTS THE analysis of the functions of the respective scales and modes of discourse presentation in 19th-century narrative fiction. Particular lexico-grammatical realizations of the various modes of discourse presentation, which emerge from the analysis of their keywords, for example, are correlated to their functional import. The chapter begins with a section on subjectivity. It then moves on with a description of the functions of each mode on the speech, writing, and thought presentation scale.

5.1. *A Note on Subjectivity*

As stated before, this book attempts to present a comprehensive account of 19th-century narrative fiction which involves addressing issues that go beyond the merely textual. The results presented here thus also show the portrayal of subjectivity through the elaborate use of discourse presentation modes. The linguistic projection of speech, writing, and thought presentation construes as well as reflects subjectivity to be understood as the depiction of the character as an individual. Studies by Stephen Greenblatt (1980) and Terry Eagleton (1994) find the origins of subjectivity awareness, or the beginnings of the notion of "a subject," in Shakespeare's time, while others (e.g., Fludernik 2003a) trace the construction of subjectivity back to the Middle Ages. As in terms of English literary history, the 19th century is the age of the novel, the issue of (the creation) of subjectivity carries a narratological-theoretical weight, which this systematic and detailed quantitative investigation of the types and distributions of discourse presentation categories has shown. Using a speech, writing, and thought presentation model can help illustrate how subjectivity is encoded in 19th-century narrative fiction.

I have stated from the beginning of this book that my approach to the analysis of discourse presentation in 19th-century fiction is multidisciplinary and encompasses a variety of perspectives. It is no surprise, therefore, that I am

Speech, Writing, and Thought Presentation in 19th-Century Narrative Fiction. Beatrix Busse,
Oxford University Press (2020). © Oxford University Press.
DOI: 10.1093/oso/9780190212360.001.0001

interested in correlating my quantitative findings with the sociocultural context of the 19th century; that is, I view the results of my quantitative analysis in terms of (a) 19th-century preoccupations with the English language in relation to the increase of literacy and education; (b) the rising interest in research on the area of psychological consciousness, including the effects of optical inventions, and the way literature reacted to this; and (c) the influence of Darwin's evolutionary theory and the debates around it. The spread of literacy and education, for instance, finds a direct reflection on the leveling of speech forms (Görlach 1999: 4). Furthermore, the 19th century also witnessed a strong philological interest in the origins of language which is thus related to all facets of human speech and thought. Therefore it comes as no surprise that 19th-century novelists' awareness of the role of language is construed and reflected in this complex interplay between the various forms of discourse presentation and narration. At the beginning of the 19th century, Wordsworth's demand for authentic language "really used by men" (Wordsworth 1992 [1798]: 59) in his "Preface" to the *Lyrical Ballads* illustrates the 19th-century preoccupation with the social functions of language, but also the key role of speech in depicting human interaction.

Furthermore, in the prefaces of 19th-century grammars the function of the English language to be "this land's great highway of thought and speech" (Alford 1866: 2) is generally highlighted. Other discussed topics embrace the use of punctuation in the presentation of direct speech (DS), listings of reporting verbs, the distinction between direct speech (DS) and indirect speech (IS), and the notion of faithfulness to an original, which receives special attention and shows the 19th-century engagement with presenting communication in its entire complexity. Further, the bias toward speech, on the one hand, and faithfulness, on the other, precedes some of the discussions about the discourse fallacy related to speech presentation that narratologists and literary critics have entertained about one century later. To begin with issues of punctuation, Goold Brown (1860), for example, in *The Institutes of English Grammar, Methodically Arranged*, observes that a "quotation or observation, when it is introduced by a verb, (as *say, reply* and the like,) is generally separated from the rest of the sentence by a comma; as 'The book of nature,' said he, 'is open before thee'" (Brown 1860: 246). The focus on the separation between the quotation and its introduction by a verb implies an awareness of the different syntactic and functional status of the reported and the reporting clause. Note how Brown uses the reporting verbs *say* and *reply*—two verbs which have also been identified to be particularly frequent in my corpus, as will be illustrated in the following.

Further, 19th-century grammarians are occupied by typographical issues. Brown (1860), again, describes what he calls "abrupt pauses": "A sudden interruption or transition should be marked with a dash," or "to mark a considerable pause, greater than the structure of the sentence or the points inserted" (Brown 1860: 248). Interestingly, he also mentions the use of interjections in DS (Brown 1860: 249). These two phenomena have also been highlighted to be of considerable importance for both DS and thought presentation.

This focus on speech also brings us back to the concept of faithfulness to an anterior discourse in speech presentation. Henry Alford (1866) in *A Plea for the Queen's English* enthusiastically remarks that it is necessary to "render the words accurately, and all is clear" (Alford 1866: 167). This statement is embedded in a discussion about the use of tenses in translation. Henry Sweet (1891–1898), in turn, deals with reporting speech in relation to repetition, which immediately entails a kind of inbuilt assumption that the report needs to be faithful, "when we repeat a statement made by another person" (Henry Sweet 1891–1898: 106). He also uses the term *narration* alongside the concept of *repetition* to stress that there is a need to be faithful to an anterior discourse because the term narration entails a rhetorical component in which it is part of an oration that considers the facts (OED entry "narration," 2.a.):

> We can quote his very words, as in *John said, "I am sorry."* Here the speaker makes his own statement, namely, that John said something, and then lets John, as it were, make his own statement in his own words, so that the whole sentence contains two separate statements of facts. This way of repeating statements is called direct narration. When the speaker repeats what was said to him in his own words we have indirect narration, as in *John said (that) he was sorry*. Here John's being sorry is not stated by John himself at all. Nor is it stated as a fact even by the speaker, who mentions it only as an idea suggested to him by some one else. Hence the subject of all indirect narration is a statement not of facts but of thoughts. (Sweet 1891–1898: 107)

This quotation illustrates why, in 19th-century fiction, direct discourse and also direct thought (DT) tend to be writers' preferred choice, as it is assumed that only direct modes of discourse presentation can be faithful to the original. What Sweet (1891–1898) calls "direct narration" is DS with a reporting clause and the reported clause in DS being indicated by quotation marks. Interestingly, Sweet separates the presentation of facts in speech and in thought. He also stresses the difference between the reporting clause, which is the narrator's and the words "said" to him, and points out that both are factual, which is rather surprising because often the reporting clause is only seen as a kind of introductory element for the reported stretch (Sweet 1891–1898: 106). Therefore, Sweet is aware of the narrator's voice as an intrusion and the fact that, syntactically speaking, there is a relation of parataxis between them.

The claim that indirect narration is a statement of thoughts needs to be put into perspective as well, because it implies the important observation that, with indirect reporting, we move further toward the narrator. Therefore, what is reported can no longer be a description of facts because it contains the reporter's "coloring" of a formerly made statement. Sweet (1891–1898) describes projection (that is, indirect statements) as report of "thoughts." However, he moves on to stress that "the mere statement of an occurrence as a thought and not as a fact need not necessarily throw any doubt on the truth of the statement" (Sweet 1891–1898: 109). He also notes that IS serves to shorten the proposition by not including the exact words but just the speech act:

> Thus, when I repeat a statement made to me by someone else, and repeat it in an indirect instead of direct narration, I may do so because I doubt the truth of the statement, but I may also do so merely because I do not remember the exact words of the statement, or because I want to shorten it. Nevertheless, in some cases thought-statement does almost necessarily imply that the statement is false. (Sweet 1891–1898: 109)

Brown (1860) adds to the preceding reflections by pointing out that IS is needed to introduce indirect questions which, consequently, "lose the quality and sign of interrogation" (Brown 1860: 249) because they are reported; the verb used for reporting is "mentioned but not put directly as a question" (Brown 1860: 249). In this respect, the notion of the mimetic, faithful function of discourse presentation cannot be underestimated within the context of 19th-century discourse about language. And it is in literature that this function can be fruitfully exploited. In *Literary Criticism*, George Eliot criticizes some of the "Silly Novels by Lady Novelists" because the female characters depicted are often presented as rather unrealistic images of ideal womanhood. Yet, she highlights the role of speech: "In her recorded conversations, she [i.e., the female character] is amazingly eloquent and in her unrecorded conversations amazingly witty" (Eliot: 1856, quoted in Görlach 1999: 224).

The rising interest in psychology illustrated, for example, in pre-Freudian physiological psychology (Zwierlein 2005: 3) and in works such as Spencer's (1855) *Principles of Psychology*, or Lewes's (1874–1879) *Problems of Life and Mind*, also finds an explicit and implicit inclusion in literature with the discussion of issues of consciousness, agency, cognitive processes, and depiction of the mind. For example, Eliot (1986 [1871–1872]) talks about the famous "web of connection" in *Middlemarch* and expresses the social nature of a human being, which also affects the mind: "There is no creature whose inward being is so strong that it is not greatly determined by what lies outside" (Eliot 1986 [1871–1872]: 784–785). In Eliot's (1998 [1876]) *Daniel Deronda*, it is stressed that the mysteries of the human psyche—like the mysteries in the sciences (Zwierlein 2005: 5)—are still to be explored: "There is a great deal of unmapped country within us which would have to be taken into account in the explanation of our guts and storms" (*Daniel Deronda* 1998 [1876]: 235). Like Eliot, Oscar Wilde also generally muses about the potential of literature for presenting human thought and consciousness, but, at the same time, concedes that

> [h]e who would stir us now by criticism, must either give us an entirely new background, or reveal to us the soul of man in its innermost workings. [. . .] People sometimes say that fiction is getting too morbid. As far as psychology is concerned, it has never been morbid enough. We have merely touched the surface of the soul, that is all. In one single ivory cell of the brain there are stored away things more marvellous and more terrible than even they have dreamed of, who, [. . .] have sought to track the soul into its most secret places, and to make life confess its dearest sins. Still, there is a limit even to the number of untried backgrounds, and it is possible that a further development of the habit of

introspection may prove fatal to that creative faculty to which it seeks to supply fresh material. [. . .] There are always new attitudes for the mind, and new points of view. (Wilde 1997 [1881]: 145)

Wilde criticizes that "introspection" has not been sufficiently embraced by authors and artists, although "there are always new attitudes for the mind, and new points of view" (Wilde 1997 [1881]: 145). Despite these acknowledged deficiencies in the portrayal of the human psyche, discourse-presentation strategies in general and those forms of thought presentation identified in my corpus, in particular, give apt linguistic testimony of the 19th-century preoccupation with these topics and help to construe the discourse about these issues.

The interface of discourse presentation strategies and narrative passages also bear witness to authorial efforts to present the mind of characters; these efforts are ultimately directed at readers so that they can create their own mental worlds. This interplay is especially prominent in some of the stretches of narrator's report of speech (NRS), for instance, where the speaker's or hearer's eyes play a crucial role as a marker of stance (Biber et al. 1999: 967; Mahlberg 2013; and section 7.3 in Chapter 7 of this book). This interplay marks an additional attitudinal comment on the side of the narrator. For example, in Dickens's (1993 [1837]) *Oliver Twist*, eye movement is frequently interconnected with either a presentation of speech or of the focalized state of mind, as in: "When Mr. Bumble had laughed a little while, his eyes again encountered the cocked hat; and he became grave" (*Oliver Twist* 1993 [1837]: 120). Mr. Bumble's look at his hat recalls him to his occupation: He has to continue his business without delay. Young Dick's confrontation with Mr. Bumble provides another example: He "stood trembling beneath Mr. Bumble's glance; not daring to lift his eyes from the floor; and dreading even to hear the beadle's voice" (*Oliver Twist* 1993 [1837]: 120). Here the narratological camera moves between Mr. Bumble as the focalized element and the young boy Dick. Paralinguistic reference to his facial expression and his eye movement are a narratological means of describing the boy's fear; that is, thanks to the description of Mr. Bumble's physical traits (in this case his glance), the reader has more immediate access to the young boy's state of mind.

Henry James's (1975 [1908]) concept of the "house of fiction," outlined in his *Preface* to the "second edition" of *A Portrait of a Lady*, may also serve as a theoretical description of the interplay between the mind, language, and emotions, and their subsequent verbal manifestations. James sees the novel as a literary form which can range "through all the differences of the individual relation to its general subject matter, all the varieties of outlook on life" (James 1975 [1908]: 7). The famous image of a "house of fiction," which he uses to portray the complexity of life, is described in the following way:

> The house of fiction has in short not one window, but a million—a number of possible windows not to be reckoned, rather; every one of which has been pierced, or is still pierceable, in its vast front, by the need of the individual vision and by the pressure of the individual will. These apertures of dissimilar

shape and size, hang so, all together, over the human scene that we might have expected of them a greater sameness of report than we find. They are but windows at the best, mere holes in a dead wall, disconnected, perched aloft; they are not hinged doors opening straight upon life. But they have this mark of their own that at each of them stands a figure with a pair of eyes, or at least with a field glass, which forms, again and again, for observation a unique instrument, insuring to the person making use of it an impression distinct from every other. He and his neighbours are watching the same show, but one seeing more where the other sees less, one seeing black where the other sees white, one seeing big where the other sees small [. . .]. The spreading field, the human field, is "the choice of subject"; [. . .] but they are, singly or together, as nothing without the posted presence of the watcher—without, in other words, the consciousness of the artist. (James 1975 [1908]: 7)

In a similar fashion as Thomas De Quincey (1845), who outlined his notion of the human brain functioning as a palimpsest, James describes how the various facets of the human condition can both be seen in the "house of fiction" as well as described by the author or narrator, who uses—with his eyes and his consciousness—the various and multi-shaped windows to watch what is happening. James's reference to the watchers' eyes as well as to the "artist's consciousness" clearly alludes to the presentation of discourse in its interplay with narration as one linguistic means of achieving the variety of shapes of these windows, of the presentation of the multi-layered voices, and of characterization.

Richter (2009) sees narrating in 19th-century novels as an evolutionary adaptation and as a creation of a room for the imagination in order to preserve what Darwin and his theory of natural selection had destroyed in *The Origin of Species* (1859). Darwin's theory of natural selection had a synchronic and a diachronic dimension, with species slowly evolving over centuries and struggling for existence at a particular point in time. Terminology from cell biology was used to metaphorically describe human communication, social fragmentation, and identity. It is through the use of the mode of speech, writing, or thought presentation that, on the one hand, the alleged superiority of human beings as well as their ability to communicate can be stressed, while, on the other hand, discourse presentation is also a means of meticulously describing social fragmentation and the complexities of human communication, as well as the relation between language and power.

5.2. *The Categories of Discourse Presentation*

5.2.1. Preliminaries

The rest of this chapter is devoted to an in-depth study of the different categories of the discourse presentation scales. I expand on the quantitative analysis presented in section 4.1 of Chapter 4 and contextualize further the significance of each category in relation to 19th-century discourse presentation in narrative fiction. I also look at each category on the discourse presentation scales in relation to one another, in relation to their counterparts with regard to speech, writing, and thought presentation and, at the same time, elaborate on their functional potential in context. Furthermore, an attempt is made in this study to retrieve lexico-grammatical features that are characteristic of the respective modes of speech, writing, and thought presentation.

To do so, all stretches of the different modes of discourse presentation are extracted. Then, following a corpus-stylistic approach (Busse 2010; Mahlberg 2013), repetitive formal linguistic features, keywords, and clusters are identified with the help of the programs *Wmatrix* (Rayson 2018) and *WordSmith Tools* (Scott 2004–2017) and statistical tests like the log-likelihood test. The individual stretches encoding the different modes of the speech, writing, and thought presentation from my 19th-century corpus of narrative fiction will further be compared with the more representative *A Corpus of Nineteenth-Century English* (CONCE) (Kytö et al. 2000). CONCE contains various genres; it is roughly made up of about one million words and is divided into periods of several decades. CONCE and its respective subparts will serve as a reference corpus in order to (a) retrieve, as mentioned, repetitive lexico-grammatical patterns that are characteristic of each mode on the speech, writing, and thought presentation scales, and (b) to find out whether these can be used for developing tools that help to further (semi)automatic annotation of discourse presentation in general (see Chapter 6). The stretches representing the different presentation modes in my 19th-century corpus will accordingly be compared not with identified and tagged stretches of discourse presentation in CONCE, but with the complete texts compiled in CONCE. Keywords will be measured by the statistical test of log-likelihood. Although, for ease of presentation, I deal with each discourse presentation scale separately, the conclusions I eventually draw should be seen as emerging from the cumulative effect created by the use of the various interrelating categories in the novels I analyze. Novice readers are advised to familiarize themselves with all the categories prior to reading the following sections (see Chapter 2).

5.2.2. Speech Presentation Categories

5.2.2.1. Narrator's Presentation of Voice (NV)

In 19th-century narrative fiction, a narrator's representation of voice captures minimal reports of speech, but it does not contain a speech act. It consists of some information about a speech event or indications concerning the fact that someone speaks, as in "while she spoke" (*A Beleaguered City* 2000 [1879]: 126). It may also point to a desired hypothetical speech event. As Table 4.6 (in Chapter 4) illustrates, NV occurs second-least frequently on the speech presentation scale. The number of tags identified as NV in the corpus amounts to only 160 (which constitutes 3.2% of all tags identified in the corpus). They are represented by 1,050 words and have a mean length of 6.56 words per tag.

NV is also on fifth position in the 20th-century fictional sub-corpus by Semino and Short (2004: 67). Their mean length is one word longer than in the 19th-century corpus.

Despite the scarcity of its occurrence, NV can be fruitfully characterized by a number of functions:

a) They contribute to narrative progression (Toolan 2009) by means of encapsulating or prospecting dialogue. NV establishes a parallelism between what has been said and what is done while speaking (through paralinguistic narration);
b) They function to create a playful, ambiguous, or ironic tone through the narrator;
c) They represent a stress on *how* something is said and an interplay with other categories on the discourse presentation scale; and
d) they foreshadow the social function of conversation.

As far as the first function is concerned, an example from Shelley's (2003 [1818]) *Frankenstein* can be used:

> I clasped my hands, and exclaimed aloud, "William, dear angel! this is thy funeral, this thy dirge!" *As I said these words,* I perceived in the gloom a figure which stole from behind a clump of trees near me; I stood fixed, gazing intently: I could not be mistaken. (*Frankenstein* 2003 [1818]: 77, my emphasis)

On his way to his brother's funeral through the Alps, Victor again laments the murder of his brother and is aware that the Creature must have killed him. His feelings are expressed in: "William, dear angel! this is thy funeral, this thy dirge!" The locutionary force of this utterance is then re-expressed by the first-person narrator (who is also the focalizer and the focalized) through "as I said these words." The stretch of NV establishes the parallel nature between the words uttered and what is actually done. As such, the narrative and discoursal framework become more complex and ask the reader to establish a multifaceted (if not realistic) scene of processing words and deeds synchronously.

This reference back to the previous speech event can be incorporated in what Sinclair (2004) sees as one way of "trusting the text" (see also section 2.4.2 in Chapter 2). The subordinate clause "as I said these words" represents what Sinclair (2004) calls encapsulation—a phenomenon in which a sentence encapsulates what has been said in the previous sentence by means of reference. The textual function of this subordinated temporal clause connects the narrative through the simultaneous verbal and sensory activities that take place; that is, to perceive the Creature following Victor, and describing the emotional turmoil. As such, it is also one means of describing Victor as the focalized and the focalizer, as well as the fictional mind in action, and therefore of furthering narrative progression.

Another example of NV's first function (that is, narrative progression through encapsulation of progression) is provided in the following exchange between the conjuror and a baker in Disraeli's (2004 [1826]) *Vivian Grey*:

"I have no doubt his wine would be as ready as your tobacco, Mr. Smith; or a wafila from your basket, my honest cake-seller"; *and so saying*, with a long thin wand the conjuror jerked up the basket of an itinerant and shouting pastry-cook, and immediately began to thrust the contents into his mouth with a rapidity ludicrously miraculous. (*Vivian Grey* 2004 [1826]: 183, my emphasis)

The stretch of "and so saying" summarizes the words of the conjuror, but at the same time foregrounds—almost like a stage direction—the simultaneity of the conjuror's paralinguistic activities accompanying his words.

Sinclair's (2004) emphasis on "trusting the text," as described in previous chapters, is not simply realized by encapsulation but also by means of prospection. Sinclair states that prospection functions by foreshadowing semantically, syntactically, and pragmatically what is about to be said. In Stevenson's (2003 [1886]) *Dr. Jekyll and Mr. Hyde*, the lawyer asks a reassuring question to Poole, after the lawyer has witnessed Jekyll's fear of being murdered. This question is prospected through a fixed expression as NV in "and had a word or two with Poole":

On his way out, the lawyer stopped *and had a word or two with Poole*. "By the bye," said he, "there was a letter handed in to-day: what was the messenger like?" (*Dr. Jekyll and Mr. Hyde* 2003 [1886]: 68, my emphasis)

Second, and frequently, NV summarizes the speech event. As in the examples mentioned earlier, it also often functions to simultaneously foreground a playful comment on the side of the narrator (function [b] in the preceding). A very illustrative example can be found in Austen's (1985 [1816]: 262) *Emma*:

To her voluntary communications Emma could get no more approving reply, than, "Very well. If the Westons think it worth while to be at all this trouble for a few hours of noisy entertainment, I have nothing to say against it, but that they shall not chuse pleasures for me.—Oh! yes, I must be there; I could not refuse; and I will keep as much awake as I can; but I would rather be at home, looking over William Larkins's week's account; much rather, I confess.—Pleasure in seeing dancing!—not I, indeed—I never look at it—I do not know who does.—Fine dancing, I believe, like virtue, must be its own reward. Those who are standing by are usually thinking of something very different." (*Emma* 1985 [1816]: 262, my emphasis)

The narrator summarizes Emma's excitement about the ball with a topicalized and foregrounded prepositional phrase "to her voluntary communications." The narrator misrepresents and downgrades her implied verbosity and ridicules the importance the ball has for Emma by implying that her exact words are not important. As such, the narrator aligns with Mr. Knightley because he becomes the focalized and his rejecting attitude is presented to the reader in a long stretch of DS and IS.

Information about the speech event is also enhanced by additional paralinguistic comments—that is, by including references to how something is said (that is, function [c] in the preceding). As such, NV further contributes to the description of the social nature of language (function [d]). NV provides comments on the attitude of the speaker and creates a particular atmosphere. At the same time, it informs the reader of whatever issues the narrator considers to be important and also of whether the narrator distances himself or herself from the focalized character. Examples from the corpus are "she fretted and sighed," "talked merrily," "said with much archness and he-he-ing," "quoting poetry," "speaking with great favour," or "the menacing manner."

Another example can be found in *North and South* (Gaskell 2003 [1854]: 96–97):

> She was ill at ease, and looked more than usually stern and forbidding, as she entered the Hales' little drawing-room. Margaret was busy embroidering a small piece of cambric for some little article of dress for Edith's expected baby. "Flimsy, useless work," as Mrs. Thornton observed to herself. She liked Mrs. Hale's double knitting far better; that was sensible of its kind. The room altogether was full of knick-knacks, which must take a long time to dust; and time to people of limited income was money. *She made all these reflections as she was talking in her stately way to Mrs. Hale,* and uttering all the stereotyped commonplaces that most people can find to say with their senses blindfolded. (*North and South* 2003 [1854]: 96–97, my emphasis)

The stretch of NV "as she was talking in her stately way to Mrs. Hale" links the discourse presentation mode of speaking with that of thinking in the previous stretch of a rare case of a summarizing NT "she made all these reflections." Mrs. Thornton is portrayed as a social eremite who is able to criticize the superficial establishment of phatic communication and politeness with strangers and severely loathes the atmosphere as well as the life of the Hales. But it is only revealed to the reader as a private reflection. In terms of the number of words used for these private reflections, more prominence is attributed to them than to the public conversational exchange with Mrs. Hale. The speech event is described as social, and additional paralinguistic information is given by means of the adjective "stately," which describes the pride and arrogance of her voice and also represents an intertextual connection with the description of the bodily movements of the Ghost in Shakespeare's *Hamlet.* The Ghost in *Hamlet* is described as "with solemn march / Goes slow and stately by them" (Act 1, Scene 2, Lines 201–202; Evans 1997: 1193).

As has been shown, 19th-century narrative fiction frequently contains repetitions of references to verbal activities. The patterned lexico-grammatical quality of these becomes visible when the encoded stretches of NV from my 19th-century corpus are compared with the 19th-century CONCE corpus, initially without the fictional subpart, by calculating keywords on the basis of the statistical test of log-likelihood.[1] The following lexemes suggest themselves as statistically foregrounded. At the same time, they reveal the clearly communicative and transactional nature of NV, because they are all verbal in nature or show a verbal process that has taken place, is summarized, or reported on. These lexemes that concretely realize NV will play a crucial role for devising tools for semi-automatic annotation of discourse presentation (see Chapter 6). Keyness figures are given by the statistical log-likelihood measurement. Anything with a log-likelihood figure which is > 6.0 is said to be marked (Rayson and Garside 2000). As can be seen in the following list, the keyness figures that result from the comparison by far surpass that threshold. These keywords are

- *words* (n.) (keyness 181.70)
- *voice* (n.) (keyness 142.73)
- *spoke* (keyness 64.87)
- *conversation* (keyness 35.72)
- *word* (n.) (keyness 29.08)
- *voices* (keyness 26.36).

A comparison with the fictional sub-corpus of CONCE shows similar results, because lexemes that semantically denote that speech has taken place are also key. These are

- *words* (n.) (keyness 138.17)
- *voice* (n.) (keyness 103.21)
- *spoke* (keyness 46.33).

To sum up, NV is functionally closer to discourse presentation than originally assumed because it fulfills a crucial function in stressing a complex parallelism between words spoken and actions performed. Further, it is possible to identify recurrent lexemes of NV in 19th-century instances of NV which construe functions of encapsulation and prospection and are realized by lexemes that refer to the semantic field of verbal processes and practices, such as *speak* or *voice*.

5.2.2.2. Narrator's Presentation of Speech Acts (NRSA)

NRSA represents the third largest category of discourse presentation in my corpus as a whole (8.1% of all tags, 408 tags in total), following DS and FDS, as is illustrated in Table 4.6 in Chapter 4. Their mean length is 7.3 words per tag. In Semino and Short (2004: 67), NRSA is on fourth position in the corpus overall.

As regards the speech presentation scale, NRSA is on the same position in the 20th-century corpus as it is in the 19th-century corpus, but the mean length of the respective stretches is 4.52 words per tag longer in the 19th-century data. In my corpus, NRSA shows a more extensive move to the speaker of the utterance than NV because it tells us the speech act value of what is said and may sometimes include a specification of the topic by means of a noun phrase. Although Waugh (1995) once called it "condensed forms of an indirect speech act" (Waugh 1995: 160–161), and even though it is often described as specifying nothing more than the illocutionary force of an utterance as well as only referring to a single person's utterance, NRSA takes on a specific function in 19th-century narrative fiction. It frequently contributes to narrative progression by means of prospecting or encapsulating utterances (as also described in relation to NV) which are either reported in the preceding or the following clause. Often these stretches are also introduced by (coordinating) conjunctions, such as *and, but,* or *after*. An example to illustrate this is "and inviting her to a secret conference" (*Northanger Abbey* 1985 [1818]: 151). In this scene, Catherine is reported to be in need of Isabella's conversation. Yet, the narrator ironically comments on this need by describing it as a "five-minutes longing of friendship" (*Northanger Abbey* 1985 [1818]: 151): When Isabella suddenly appears, she tries to arouse Catherine's attention by announcing a secret conversation with her. The stretch of "and inviting her to a secret conference" furthers the progression of the narrative by enticing the reader to find out what the conversation will be about. At the same time, this stretch serves to create tension and to satisfy readers' curiosity concerning revelations about romantic affairs between the characters (Isabella finally reveals to Catherine that John is in love with the latter). The prospecting function of this stretch is further reinforced by Catherine's direct reminder in: "But I thought, Isabella, you had something in particular to tell me?" (*Northanger Abbey* 1985 [1818]: 151), which follows Isabella's platitudes about her independence of mind.

In the following example from Dickens's (1993 [1837]: 123–124) *Oliver Twist*, the narrator's paralinguistic descriptions of Mr. Grimwig, Mr. Brownlow, and Mr. Bumble have to be seen in interaction with the reporting of speech in NRSA in the stretch following "commenced his story" because the speech act is summarized by a verb followed by a noun phrase:

> Mr. Brownlow looked apprehensively at Mr. Bumble's pursed-up countenance; and requested him to communicate what he knew regarding Oliver in as few words as possible. Mr. Bumble *put down his hat; unbuttoned his coat; folded his arms; inclined his head in a retrospective manner; and, after a few moments' reflection, commenced his story. It would be tedious if given in the beadle's words*: occupying, as it did, some twenty minutes in the telling; but the sum and substance of it was, that Oliver was a foundling, born of low and vicious parents. That he had, from his birth, displayed no better qualities than treachery, ingratitude, and malice. That he had terminated his brief career in the place of his birth, by making a sanguinary and cowardly attack on an unoffending lad, and running away in the night-time from his master's house. (*Oliver Twist* 1993 [1837]: 123–124, my emphasis)

Mr. Bumble is described as celebrating the fact that he is given word and that he is in the know about Oliver. The fact that his paralinguistic movements of unbuttoning his coat, and so on, are described is not only a particular Dickensian strategy accompanying the presentation of speech and thought, but also creates tension, and through the announcement of a story which is about to begin construes the reader's expectation to actually listen to the story about Oliver Twist and his whereabouts, which Mr. Brumble is expected to report. Note also how the conjunction "and" as well as the prepositional phrase "after a few moments' reflection" are used as means to progress the narrative, before finally "he commenced his story" is reported in NRSA. The narrator delays the telling of the story by means of emphasizing the physical and paralinguistic components of Mr. Brumble's peculiarities, and at the same time characterizes Mr. Brumble's own sense of importance and verbosity in "It would be tedious if given in the beadle's words." Coherence and prospection are created via recourse to the lexical items of *story* and *words*, which, as I argue, are also diagnostic to mark not only NRSA as a speech presentation mode, but to illustrate that a speech summary has taken place.

A similar narratological strategy of creating irony can be observed in Austen's (1985 [1818]: 150) *Northanger Abbey*:

> *But so active were her thoughts*, that when *these inquiries were answered*, she was hardly more assured than before, of Northanger Abbey having been a richly endowed convent at the time of the Reformation, of its having fallen into the hands of an ancestor of the Tilneys on its dissolution, of a large portion of the ancient building still making a part of the present dwelling although the rest was decayed, or of its standing low in a valley, sheltered from the north and east by rising woods of oak. (*Northanger Abbey* 1985 [1818]: 150, my emphasis)

Catherine's excitement at being able to stay with the Tilneys at Northanger Abbey is expressed not only by a stretch of NT—"but so active were her thoughts" (*Northanger Abbey* 1985 [1818]: 150)—but also by a rather reductive stretch of "these enquiries were answered," which does not reveal to the reader the exact words of her questions about *Northanger Abbey*. Instead, the sequence "these enquiries were answered" only highlights the speech act. Note the deictic demonstrative pronoun "these," which signals the summarizing function of "reports" as it refers to something that was said before.

NRSA is also used to inform the reader about the establishment of phatic communication, superficial compliance with social decorum, or of summarizing the social functions of conversation, such as welcoming somebody. In Thackeray's (1910 [1846–1847]: 119) *The Book of Snobs*, the first-person narrator seems to be rather ashamed at entertaining Mrs. Ponto by pretending to be at home within the circle of the genteel families of England. A stretch of NRSA in "I indulged Mrs. Major Ponto with a deal of information about the first families in England" summarizes what has been presented to the reader as IS or DS:

> I am ashamed to say *I indulged Mrs. Major Ponto with a deal of information about the first families in England*, such as would astonish those great personages if they knew it. (*The Book of Snobs* 1910 [1846–1847]: 119, my emphasis)

NRSA also introduces an utterance, which is then reported, for example, in DS in the following stretch from Shelley's *Frankenstein*:

> While I was thus engaged, Ernest entered: he had heard me arrive, *and hastened to welcome me*: *"Welcome, my dearest Victor,"* said he. "Ah! I wish you had come three months ago, and then you would have found us all joyous and delighted.

You come to us now to share a misery which nothing can alleviate; yet your presence will, I hope, revive our father [. . .]." (*Frankenstein* 2003 [1818]: 79, my emphasis)

The stretch "and hastened to welcome me" (*Frankenstein* 2003 [1818]: 79) prospects—here literally repeats—Ernest's actual DS stretch in "Welcome, my dearest Victor!" Victor, as a first-person narrator, heterodiegetically focalizes Ernest's expression of despair at their brother's murder that he tries to redress by complying with the rules of social decorum. Hence, we find the repetition of the expressive speech act of a welcome.

In the example from *Frankenstein* just quoted, the repetition of the level of the speech act (not the level of the word) seems to be important. This shows one of the functions of NRSA, which often foregrounds the speech act as such, rather than the exact words. Thus, for instance, Clerval's consolatory words after being informed about the murder of Victor's brother are reported as "Clerval endeavoured to say a few words of consolation" (*Frankenstein* 2003 [1818]: 75).

Table 4.6 in Chapter 4 shows that almost one-third of the stretches of NRSA are embedded.[2] This underlines Semino and Short's (2004) observation that these condensed forms of discourse presentation are easier to embed than, for instance, stretches of DS or FDS. There are only a few cases in the corpus in which the report of a promise is embedded and presented as NRSA, as in a passage from Gaskell's (2007 [1853]) *Cranford*, where Betty's utterance is embedded in a stretch of DS as NRSA: "only I had given missus my word" (Gaskell 2007 [1853]: 46). Another example is "she has been so kind as to promise it" from Austen's *Emma* (1985 [1816]: 266) in which Frank Churchill reports about Mrs. Weston's promise to write to him about news.

My identification of keywords in stretches of NRSA reveals the following lexical items when compared with the CONCE corpus (without the fictional subpart):

- *her* (38.88)
- *his* (37.75)
- *called* (34.05)
- *answer* (33.24)
- *welcome* (32.47)
- *question* (28.23).

What is striking in this list is the disproportionally high use of the possessive pronouns (both male and female) in relation to the rest of 19th-century English usage evident from CONCE. This seems to be vital and in need of more explanation; further, the use of speech-act verbs functioning as expressives and directives, for instance (Searle 1969, 1976, 1979). Although the actual use of a speech act is one of the prerequisites given in Semino and Short's (2004) definition of NRSA, the realization patterns of 19th-century NRSA are crucial especially with respect to developing automatic identification procedures of discourse presentation. In this regard, the keyness of the possessive pronouns draws attention to the fact that in NRSA reference is often made to somebody else's speech act.

When the stretches of NRSA are compared with the *fictional* sub-corpus of CONCE, only speech-act verbs emerge as key:

- *answer* (36.18)
- *question* (32.40)
- *called* (30.91)
- *say* (25.36).

Although the verb *say* has been identified as one of the most frequently occurring verbs in 19th-century discourse presentation, it is revealing to see that it is also disproportionally often used and key in NRSA.

To conclude, NRSA announces or summarizes a speech act, that is, it either precedes or follows more direct or character-oriented stretches of speech presentation. As such, it also has the function of structuring conversational turn-taking for the reader and, similar to NV, of adding a tone of, for instance, irony of the narratological voice to it. Diagnostic lexemes of NRSA are, accordingly, speech-act verbs.

5.2.2.3. Indirect Speech (IS)

In the 19th century—just as Semino and Short (2004: 67) conclude with regard to the 20th century—IS (indirect speech) is not the prototypical way of presenting speech. Although a well-known and much discussed category of speech presentation, IS is not even very frequent in the two corpora. It comes only on position four. With 175 tags, it amounts to 3.5% of all tags in my corpus. The average length of each tag is 10.71 words per tag. In Semino and Short (2004: 67), there are fewer tags for IS than in the 19th-century corpus, but the mean length of tags for IS, with 11.74 words per tag, is by one word slightly longer.

IS provides the propositional content of an utterance usually without reproducing the actual words, and, when seen as an individual category, it is important to note that it may not serve the purpose of dramatization. On the contrary, it almost fulfills the opposite function. IS is often described as having a summarizing function (Semino and Short 2004: 78) when the presentation of the propositional content rather than the lexico-grammatical form or the exact words are at stake. Because of its summarizing properties, IS is often used to represent a collective voice, where the name of the speaker(s) or origin of the source of what is being said are not important.

In the following example from *Wuthering Heights*, Nelly reports the servants' reply to her question as to whether they had seen Catherine in the following way: "The servants affirmed they had not seen her" (*Wuthering Heights* 2009 [1847]: 216). The fact that the servants are not given a voice of their own stresses their reluctance to engage in conversation, because they actually know where Catherine is. So, why is it that we, as readers, understand that the servants seem to know where Catherine is? In this example it is because, unlike prototypical IS, the exact words of the antecedent speech events are reported, which, in turn, creates a contrast between what is said and what is known.

Typical and clear instances in which IS focuses on the content of utterances rather than on the words are found, for instance, in the following stretch from Gaskell's (2007 [1853]) *Cranford*, in which the narrator reports Mr. Holbrook's passing away: "The next day Mrs. Pole brought us word that Mr. Holbrook was dead" (*Cranford* 2007 [1853]: 48). In order to understand the effect of this stretch of IS, it is important to bear in mind that the narrator has not chosen a stretch of narration to inform the reader about Mr. Holbrook's death, but has given controlled voice to Mrs. Pole, who informs Miss Matty in person about his death.

The following example from *Oliver Twist* (1993 [1837]) has already been used earlier but can equally be mentioned here in relation to IS:

> Mr. Brownlow looked apprehensively at Mr. Bumble's pursed-up countenance; and requested him to communicate what he knew regarding Oliver in as few words as possible. Mr. Bumble put down his hat; unbuttoned his coat; folded his arms; inclined his head in a retrospective manner; and, after a few moments' reflection, commenced his story. It would be tedious if given *in the beadle's words: occupying, as it did, some twenty minutes in the telling*; but *the sum and substance of it was, that Oliver was a foundling, born of low and vicious parents*. That he had, from his birth, displayed no better qualities than treachery, ingratitude, and malice. That he had terminated his brief career in the place of his birth, by making a sanguinary and cowardly attack on an unoffending lad, and running away in the night-time from his master's house. (*Oliver Twist* 1993 [1837]: 123–124, my emphasis)

In this example, Mr. Bumble depicts Oliver and his personal history to Mr. Grimwig. More importantly, the IS stretch "the sum and substance of it was that Oliver was a foundling, born of low and vicious parents" serves a crucial function. The narrator appears to characterize Mr. Bumble as a "flat character" incapable of producing substantial contributions and simply sticking to reporting clauses which prospect a summarizing function ("the sum and substance of it was"). So, in this case, IS is used to help characterization. Notice here the contrasting interplay between the speech presentation mode of hypothetical NV "in the beadle's words" with the stretch of NV in which the length of his story is summarized as in "twenty minutes in the telling." Besides aiding characterization, the functions of IS need to be seen in their interaction with other discourse presentation modes.

Genette's (1972: 172) distinction between "transposed speech" and "narratized speech" seems useful to aid to my analysis of IS. This distinction has only been indirectly referred to in Semino and Short's (2004) work although it crucially points out that IS does not usually present the exact words but only the illocutionary force or content of an utterance. Genette draws our attention to the fact that "transposed speech" seems to allow a more direct access to the lexicon and grammar used in the original discourse, while "narratized speech" reports the "substance of what was said, but not the actual verbal formula" (Barry 2002: 239; Genette 1980: 171–172). According to Barry (2002: 239), narratized speech turns "living speech into narrated event, and interposes the maximum distance between the reader and the direct impact and tone of the spoken words." Another feature conventionally associated with IS is the presence of the complementizer *that* at the beginning of the discourse presentation stretch. In 19th-century narrative fiction, in contrast, the stretch of IS is frequently introduced by a nonfinite infinitival clause beginning with the particle *to*. In fact, comparison of the stretches of IS and the CONCE corpus without the fictional subpart reveals the particle *to* as a keyword (with a keyness value of 69.01, when compared to the 19th-century non-fictional sub-corpus, and a keyness value of 59.81, when compared with the 19th-century fictional sub-corpus). The combination of these two parameters in 19th-century fiction appears to reveal interesting defining features about the 19th century. For instance, in Emily Brontë's (2009 [1847]) *Wuthering Heights*, Nelly, the first-person narrator, employs "narratized speech" introduced by a "to infinitive" clause. Nelly, requests Catherine to do something for her ("to read") and simply reports "I asked Catherine to read to me":

> At the close of three weeks I was able to quit my chamber and move about the house. And on the first occasion of my sitting up in the evening *I asked Catherine to read to me*, because my eyes were weak. We were in the library, the master having gone to bed: *she consented, rather unwillingly, I fancied*; and *imagining my sort of books did not suit her*, I bid her *please herself in the choice of what she perused.* (*Wuthering Heights* 2009 [1847]: 216, my emphasis)

The stretch of IS "to read to me," which is preceded by the reporting clause "I asked Catherine," summarizes her request. Narratized speech is followed by transposed speech in the next stretch a few lines further down, in which it seems that not only the propositional content is reported, but also the exact words "please herself in the choice of what she perused." Transposed speech, therefore, tends to be richer, not least because of the increase in the number of words used; Nelly is, in fact, attempting to minimize the face-threatening act imposed on Catherine by offering her to choose whatever she likes to read. It is worth mentioning, though, that these examples of IS appear alongside presentations of Nelly's thoughts concerning Catherine's possible reaction to her requests, as illustrated in "she consented, rather unwillingly, I fancied" and in "imagining my sort of books did not suit her." Catherine's thoughts of displeasure are inferred and she becomes the focalized. This effective interplay between what Nelly thinks and what she actually says suggests a contrast in attitude.

Another example of the effective contrast construed between the narrator-controlled IS and other speech presentation modes can be seen in Gaskell's *Cranford* (2007 [1853]):

> Mrs. Pole and I had the greatest difficulty in persuading her to go. *She thought it was improper*; and was even half annoyed when we utterly ignored the idea of any impropriety in her going with two other ladies to see her old lover. Then came a more serious difficulty. She did not think Deborah would have liked her to go. This took us half a day's good hard talking to get over; but, at the first sentence of relenting, I seized the opportunity, and wrote and despatched an acceptance in her name—fixing day and hour, that all might be decided and done with. *The next morning she asked me if I would go down to the shop with her; and there,* after much hesitation, we chose out three caps to be sent home and tried on, that the most becoming might be selected to take with us on Thursday. (*Cranford* 2007 [1853]: 38, my emphasis)

The stretch of "The next morning she asked me if I would go down to the shop with her" consists of the reporting clause "the next morning she asked me" and the reported clause realized as IS in "if I would go down to the shop with her." The stretch of IS, which is introduced through the adverbial of time stands in contrast to Mrs. Matty's initial hesitant attitude to accepting Mr. Holbrook's invitation, which in "She thought it was improper" is ambiguous, either presenting FIS or IS. Interestingly, the purpose of going to the shop is not mentioned, just the request of accompanying her. It is only in the coordinating clause with a spatial deictic adverb "and there," that the reader—with a slight tone of irony—is informed that she buys a new cap rather than a new dress.

Conventionally speaking, IS is introduced by the complementizers *that, if,* or *whether*. As mentioned, the comparison of stretches of IS with the fictional and nonfictional subparts of the 19th-century CONCE corpus reveals, however, that the *to*-particle is key (keyness 69.01, or 59.18, respectively) in my corpus. This illustrates that in 19th-century narrative fiction, infinitival stretches of the reported IS like "I asked Catherine to read to me" are the preferred constructions—a linguistic phenomenon that would be interesting to investigate further in other genres of the 19th century.

In IS, a third-person (rather than a first-person) possessive pronoun is also a diagnostic feature. Thus, when the stretches of IS are compared with the nonfictional sub-corpus of CONCE, the possessive pronoun *her* is key (28.88). The use of past tense forms is equally diagnostic if the stretch of IS is preceded by one of the complementizers mentioned before.

IS always involves a reporting clause through which the narrator controls the reporting of the speech act and modifies either the illocutionary force of the reported clause or how something is said. Typically, the reported stretch contains a verb indicating the speech activity. Semino and Short (2004: 79–80) point out that the variety of verbs used in the narrative fiction corpus is reduced when compared to the general set of reporting verbs for IS, which, they assume, results from the fact that IS is less frequent in fiction. In my corpus, verbs introducing the illocutionary force of the utterance are used most frequently, such as *declare, complain,* or *direct.* The manner in which something is said is rarely used to introduce stretches of IS. Other constructions from the corpus are the introduction via a noun phrase, as in "word spread that" or "the sum and substance of it was." But most frequently, in my corpus a finite reported clause is introduced by a finite reporting clause, such as "bring word," "return with a request," or "the final news arrived."

To conclude, IS shows the presence of the narrator through the reporting clause, and therefore moves toward the *telling* of discourse rather than the showing. This also coincides with the summary function identified in the 19th-century corpus. The effect is also that of "formal distancing between the reader and the depicted events" (Barry 2002: 238).

5.2.2.4. Free Indirect Speech (FIS)

FIS is the least frequent category tagged in my corpus as well as in the 20th-century fictional sub-corpus tagged by Semino and Short (2004). This is particularly striking considering the fact that (a) free indirect discourse (FID) in general has received great attention within the community (e.g., Palmer 2004), and (b) scholars like Toolan (2001) have claimed that FIS is particularly characteristic of the 19th-century novel. In my corpus, FIS is the category with both the fewest tags and the lowest number of words. FIS amounts to 41 tags, representing only 0.8% of all tags. These are represented by only 537 words, which makes up 0.9% of all the words in the corpus. With a mean length of 13.09 words per tag, FIS is longer than the summarizing categories (NV, NRSA, or IS), but much shorter than FIT, where we find a mean length of 22.39 words per tag.

Because of the low number of words for the stretches of FIS, a comparison with CONCE to retrieve keywords was not pursued. In Semino and Short (2004: 67), FIS tags are also rare (57 tags). Their mean length is 18.63 words per tag, which represents a longer mean length than for the 19th century. Although free indirect speech and thought (FIS and FIT) have already been discussed in previous chapters, it is worth revisiting them here together because—despite Toolan's (2001) claims—FIT is preferred to FIS in my corpus.

IS manages to reduce the distancing effect between the reader and the depicted events. FIS, nevertheless, is also reported speech, as is indicated by the switch from present to past tense, for instance. Barry (2002: 238) points out that FIS seems to suit narratives with internal focalization, since it seems natural to glide from FIS into recording the thoughts and feelings of the speaker. Barry goes on to point out that FIS is generally acknowledged to be a hybrid of direct and indirect features and, further, that it is said to move between mimesis and diegesis. Despite its lack of a reporting clause, FIS contains the narrator's intrusion through a switch from present to past, and by often reporting the exact words of a speaker. Importantly, this hybridity means that the reader has to infer from contextual clues *who* is speaking.

Despite the low number of FIS tags, some qualitative observations are necessary as they can help identify some seemingly repetitive features of FIS in 19th-century discourse. In the 19th-century corpus, the marker of freeness, that is the grammatical independence of the reported clause, is one reliable criterion. In the already quoted example from Gaskell's (2007 [1853]) *Cranford*, Miss Matty's reaction to Mr. Holbrook's invitation is reported in FIS in "She thought it was improper" and "She did not think Deborah would have liked her to go":

> Mrs. Pole and I had the greatest difficulty in persuading her to go. *She thought it was improper*; and was even half annoyed when we utterly ignored the idea of any impropriety in her going with two other ladies to see her old lover. *Then came a more serious difficulty. She did not think Deborah would have liked her to go.* This took us half a day's good hard talking to get over; but, at the first sentence of relenting, I seized the opportunity, and wrote and dispatched an acceptance in her name—fixing day and hour, that all might be decided and done with. The next morning she asked me if I would go down to the shop with her; and there, after much hesitation, we chose out three caps to be sent home and tried on, that the most becoming might be selected to take with us on Thursday. (*Cranford* (2007 [1853]: 38, my emphasis)

If "She thought it was improper" is defined as FIS, it can be identified as Miss Matty's words. The stretch of FIS in "She did not think Deborah would have liked her to go" is prospected in the narrative stretch of "Then came a more serious difficulty." Both of these stretches also contain openly uttered expressions of Miss Matty's thoughts and only superficial worries about 19th-century's social decorum. Miss Matty is really worried about her sister's reaction if she were to marry, as this would mean to leave her sister alone. The fact that these stretches are reported in FIS both represent a world-switch to Miss Matty, but, at the same time, also distances the reader from her because of the lack of the reporting clause.

Other features that show a move away from narratological control toward the evocation of the reported voice are syntactic in nature. For instance, main clauses and/or other syntactically equal sentence constituents are enumerated through the conjunction *and*. In Austen's (1985 [1816]: 262) *Emma*, three main clauses are listed to report—in a form of transposed speech—Emma's exact words in face of the postponement of the ball. In addition, modality in the choice of the auxiliaries *must* and *could* transfers a subjective tinge to the report. Furthermore, the enumeration of the present participles "planning, proceeding and hoping," which stresses the length of their waiting, also serve to almost iconically foreground the long period of indeterminacy during which it stands to question whether the ball will take place at all. At the same time, through this list of participle constructions, the narrator also ridicules the female characters' preoccupation with social entertainment:

> The preparations must take their time, nothing could be properly ready till the third week were entered on, and for a few days *they must be planning, proceeding and hoping* in uncertainty—*at the risk*, in her opinion, *the great risk of it being all in vain*. (*Emma* (1985 [1816]: 262, my emphasis)

Further revealing is the repetition of a stretch of Emma's words in "at the risk [. . .] the great risk," which serves to distance the narrator from Emma's words and at the same time to ironically exaggerate Emma's emotional turmoil (see also section 3.4.2 in Chapter 3 on the ambiguity in the interpretation of this example). Irony also seems to play a part in the way Mr. Woodhouse describes his being unable to attend the ball: "and as for the ball, it was shocking to have dear Emma disappointed; but they would all be safer at home" (*Emma* 1985 [1816]: 264).

Stretches of FIS are often prepared or projected by means of other speech presentation modes, as can be seen in the next two examples from Disraeli's (2004 [1826]) *Vivian Grey*. In the first, IS ("for his Excellency had persuaded our hero to accompany him") precedes two sentences of FIS, beginning with "On the morrow":

> *for his Excellency had persuaded our hero to accompany him for the summer to the Baths of Ems*, a celebrated German watering-place, situated in the duchy of Nassau, in the vicinity of the Rhine. *On the morrow* they were to commence their journey. The fair of Frankfort, which had now lasted nearly a month, was at its close. (*Vivian Grey* 2004 [1826]: 181, my emphasis)

In the second, NRSA anticipates the FIS stretches:

> the conjuror; who, with a light cap and feather in his hand, was now haranguing the spectators. *The object of his discourse was* a panegyric of himself and a satire on all other conjurors. *He was the only conjuror, the real one, a worthy descendant of the magicians of old.*
>
> "Were I to tell that broad-faced Herr," continued the conjuror, "who is now gaping opposite to me, that this rod is the rod of Aaron [. . .]." (*Vivian Grey* 2004 [1826]: 182, my emphasis)

NRSA in "The object of his discourse was" precedes the FIS stretch "He was the only conjuror, the real one, a worthy descendant of the magicians of old." In this FIS stretch, the cohesive repetition of the noun phrases "the only conjurer," "the real one," and "a worthy descendant" both encodes the orality of the speech event and highlights a clear rhetorical persuasive effect. (This example can, in fact, be interpreted differently.)

The following stretch of "He wouldn't" in the example of Brontë's (2009 [1847]) *Wuthering Heights* is embedded in Catherine's passage of DS. Although this stretch could also be labeled as IS if completed through the reporting clause in "he said," the position of the reported clause before the reporting clause makes it appear to be less controlled by the narrator and, hence, a stretch of FIS. As such, emphasis is made of the fact that Linton denied to play "blindman's-buff."

> After sitting still an hour, I looked at the great room with its smooth uncarpeted floor, and thought how nice it would be to play in, if we removed the table; and I asked Linton to call Zillah in to help us, and we'd have a game at blindman's-buff;

she should try to catch us: you used to, you know, Ellen. *He wouldn't*: there was no pleasure in it, *he said*; but he consented to play at ball with me [. . .]. (*Wuthering Heights* 2009 [1847]: 219, my emphasis)

To conclude, although FIS is not as frequent in the corpus as could have been expected, because of previous assessments by other scholarly work, it nevertheless seems to have a conspicuous function in being used to create irony, as well as in being a useful tool to summarize a stretch of antecedent speech.

5.2.2.5. Direct Speech (DS) and Free Direct Speech (FDS)

DS and FDS are those strategies of discourse presentation that are closest to the character in the narratological guidance of the narrative. In addition to presenting the speech act value and the propositional content of the utterance, DS and FDS provide the words and grammatical structures claimed to have been used in uttering the propositional content and associated speech act. DS and FDS bring with them the effect of vividness and dramatization. Toolan (2001: 120) stresses that to display ("show") the exact and idiosyncratic words of a character means to accept a scenic slowing of pace, and an enhanced focus on the specificity and detail of an interaction. There is a greater pressure on the narrator to make such texts interesting. If no contextual information or only a little introductory information is provided, for example, by means of reporting clauses, readers are challenged to follow the turn-taking between the interlocutors, as if they were reading a play-text. This allows readers to make complex inferences about power structures and relationships between interlocutors that lead to characterization, because the narrator chooses a more character-oriented strategy without much explanatory intervention.

These functional implications are supported by the quantitative findings in my corpus. Mention has been made of the fact that DS and FDS are the most prominent categories in the corpus, both in terms of the number of allocated tags and the number of words by which they are presented. In my 19th-century corpus DS tags are more frequent (663 tags, i.e., 13.2% of all tags) than FDS tags (413 tags, i.e., 8.2% of all tags). However, the overall number of words that represent those tags is higher for FDS (7,465 words, i.e., 12% of the total of words) than for DS (7,111 words, i.e., 11.4% of the total of words). Hence, stretches of FDS also show a longer average length than stretches of DS: for FDS the mean length of tags is 18.07 words per tag, while for DS it is 10.72 words per tag. It could therefore be argued that 19th- and 20th-century fictional narratives[3] make frequent use of DS and FDS both to aspire to some kind of higher degree of faithfulness and to represent the reported speech in a more vivid and dramatized manner. In Semino and Short (2004: 67), there are also more tags for DS than there are for FDS (i.e., 832 as against 737). The mean length for DS in the 20th-century corpus is with 12.45 words per tag, by almost two words longer than in the 19th-century corpus, while the average length of tags for FDS (18.07 words per tag) is by almost six words shorter in the 20th century.

To begin with the potential functions of DS and FDS in 19th-century narrative fiction, I quote the following excerpt from Dickens's (1999 [1860]) *Great Expectations* at length:

> "Well? Have you found it?"
>
> "Here it is," said Mr. Wopsle.
>
> "Now, follow that passage with your eye, and *tell me whether it distinctly states that the prisoner expressly said that he was instructed by his legal adviser* wholly to reserve his defence?"
>
> "Come! Do you make that of it?" Mr. Wopsle answered,
>
> *"Those are not the exact words."*
>
> *"Not the exact words!"* repeated the gentleman bitterly.
>
> *"Is that the exact substance?"*
>
> "Yes," said Mr. Wopsle.
>
> "Yes," repeated the stranger, looking round at the rest of the company with his right hand extended towards the witness, Wopsle.
>
> "And now I ask you what you say to the conscience of that man who, with that passage before his eyes, can lay his head upon his pillow after having pronounced a fellow-creature guilty, unheard?"
>
> We all began to suspect that Mr. Wopsle was not the man we had thought him, and that he was beginning to be found out.
>
> "And that same man, remember," pursued the gentleman, throwing his finger at Mr. Wopsle heavily, "—that same man might be summoned as a juryman upon this very trial, and, having thus deeply committed himself, might return to the bosom of his family and lay his head upon his pillow, after *deliberately swearing* that he would *well and truly* try the issue joined between Our Sovereign Lord the King and the prisoner at the bar, and would *a true verdict give according to the evidence*, so help him God!"
>
> We were all deeply persuaded that the unfortunate Wopsle had gone too far, and had better stop in his reckless career while there was yet time.
>
> The strange gentleman, with an air of authority not to be disputed, and with a manner expressive of knowing something secret about every one of us that would effectually do for each individual if he chose to disclose it, left the back of the settle, and came into the space between the two settles, in front of the fire, where he remained standing, his left hand in his pocket, and he biting the forefinger of his right. (*Great Expectations* 1999 [1860]: 107, my emphasis)

It is useful to resume the discussion of the "faithfulness debate" outlined in section 2.2 of Chapter 2 and to underscore my arguments against the proposals to subsume FDS under the general DS category. This exchange in *Great Expectations* is preceded by Mr. Wopsle's mock performance of a murder trial at court, which is based on a news report that Mr. Wopsle reads to Pip and a group of men in an inn. A stranger, who later turns out to be Mr. Jagger, a lawyer who is to tell Pip about his great expectations and who becomes his guardian, attacks the prejudiced condemnation of the alleged murderer and the men making fun of it by performing a mock-trial, although some witnesses have not been interrogated. Mr. Jagger stresses some legal issues and in a disdainful as well as sarcastic manner forces Mr. Wopsle to concede that he does not report correctly what the newspaper report actually says.

This exchange deals with issues of faithfulness and the difference between "the exact words" and "the exact substance," a concept that is complexly embedded in various writing and speech presentation categories. The preceding extract thus becomes a 19th-century statement not only about the different ways of reporting somebody's speech but also about the fact that the consequences of (mis)reporting can be severe. The noun *substance* is frequently used in 19th-century novels to announce a stretch of reported speech and to indicate that a focus is on the propositional content or the illocutionary force, rather than on the exact words. According to the OED, *substance* denotes the "essential nature" and "essence" of something and may also have a religious or moral connotation of truth (OED s.v. *substance*, n. 1). Interestingly, in my preceding example, *substance* collocates with "exact," which seems to both reinforce as well as contradict the idea of a substance itself, because a substance can only be exact in relation to the propositional content of the words. This collocation in the words of Mr. Jagger also illustrates his sarcasm.

Short (1988) as well as Semino and Short (2004) question whether FDS is a speech presentation category separate from DS, because it does not add a further faithfulness claim. Both FDS and DS contain—with or without the reporting clause—the exact words of the speaker. In addition, Semino and Short (2004: 89) add that novelists need not concern themselves with faithfulness because there has not been an anterior discourse. I refrain here from revisiting the faithfulness issue in relation to the categories established by Leech and Short (1981/2007a) and Semino and Short (2004) in general or with regard to Sternberg's (1982a, 1982b) and Fludernik's (1993) claims concerning the fact that in narrative discourse faithfulness is neither possible nor necessary. Nevertheless, I maintain that there is a distinction between the notion of a "verbatim report" and the notion of "faithfulness to an anterior discourse." For this distinction to be fully appreciated, a context-sensitive approach is indispensable. As we have seen, while the term *verbatim* indicates an exact reproduction, faithfulness in direct discourse "concentrates on those factors which are relevant in specifying as accurately as is feasible in context the precise communicative content of the discourse being reported" (Short et al. 2002: 328). Hence, the notion of faithfulness does not imply verbatim repetition of an original locution. Instead, it has to be understood as an approximation which is made vivid, for instance, in DS, and therefore is also perceived as such in narrative fiction.

Yet, there is another reason why the distinction between DS and FDS should be maintained when investigating 19th-century discourse presentation in narrative fiction.[4] This relates to the interplay between narration and discourse presentation (see also Chapter 7), on the one hand, and to a reinvigoration of Genette's (1972) understanding of the concepts of mimesis and diegesis and "tagged" and "untagged" speech, on the other. Mimesis—a classic concept amply discussed by narratologists, literary critics, and stylisticians—relates to the act of showing or dramatizing speech, which also implies that it is presented in a scenic way with a specified setting and making use of dialogue, which by definition "contains" speech. Mimesis is also a showing of what is done or said by the speaker; that is, it is staged so that we seem to see or hear things for ourselves. Diegesis, on the other hand, is telling or relating; narratives are presented in a more rapid and summarizing way and the narrator informs us of what happens.

Genette's distinction between "tagged" and "untagged" speech or thought draws directly on the notions of mimesis and diegesis. Genette's definition of "tagging" involves not only the label for the attached phrase in speech which indicates who the speaker is, but it also highlights the presence of the narrator and "tends to blunt the edge of the mimesis, edging the showing back towards the 'telling' " (Genette 1980: 162; Barry 2002: 237). Genette's emphasis on the presence of the narrator through the "tagging" of DS and IS or IT justifies why, on the level of narration and narrator control (rather than with regard to faithfulness), it is necessary to distinguish between DS and FDS.

In the example from *Great Expectations* quoted earlier (*Great Expectations* 1999 [1860]: 107), the necessity to differentiate between stretches of DS and FDS also becomes obvious because—although the passage is rich in sequences of vivid and immediate FDS—the narrator's control through the insertion of reporting clauses accompanying the stretches of DS is displayed at important points in the exchange. It would follow, therefore, that narratorial presence serves functions other than simply identifying the next speaker. As with many Dickensian reporting clauses, those occurring in this passage are also rich in the usage of paralinguistic information to provide the speech with an additional note of attitude. In the previously quoted passage, for instance, the lawyer's voice is described as "bitterly" and his hand and his finger play a prominent role: "with his right hand extended towards the witness" and "throwing his finger at Mr. Wopsle heavily" (see also Mahlberg 2007b, 2013).

Another example may be found in a passage from Brontë's (1985 [1847]) *Jane Eyre*, in which the first extensive conversational exchange between Mr. Rochester and Jane is shown (rather than told), in the presence of Mrs. Fairfax:

> "You have lived the life of a nun: no doubt you are well drilled in religious forms; —Brocklehurst, who I understand directs Lowood, is a parson, is he not?"
>
> "Yes, sir."
>
> "And you girls probably worshipped him, as a convent full of religieuses would worship their director."
>
> "Oh, no."
>
> "You are very cool! No! What! A novice not worship her priest! That sounds blasphemous."
>
> "I disliked Mr. Brocklehurst; and I was not alone in the feeling. He is a harsh man; at once pompous and meddling; he cut off our hair; and for

economy's sake bought us bad needles and thread, with which we could hardly sew."

"That was very false economy," remarked Mrs. Fairfax, who now again caught the drift of the dialogue. (*Jane Eyre* 1985 [1847]: 155, my emphasis)

The final line of this excerpt contains a stretch of DS, "That was very false economy," which is accompanied by a final reporting clause "remarked Mrs. Fairfax, who now again caught the drift of the dialogue." Because the final stretch of the passage is tagged DS, the narrator's mediation becomes foregrounded, especially after several interrogating turns of FDS between Mr. Rochester and Jane. The function of the reporting clause and the move from showing toward telling is not only to inform the reader that the speaker is not Mr. Rochester or Jane, but also to characterize Mrs. Fairfax. Mrs. Fairfax becomes the focalized character through an ironic comment about her finally taking up the speed of the conversation again, as is stressed by the meta-linguistic phrase "the drift of the dialogue." As such, Mrs. Fairfax's correct but somewhat misplaced expression of disapproval concerning Mr. Brocklehurst purchasing cheap needles to save money, together with the narrator's comment, foregrounds Jane's ability to stand up to Mr. Rochester's interrogation presented to us in FDS. It could be argued that the "untagged" FDS stretches provide the reader with instances of social criticism and distance the reporter from what the source says. If we look at the turn-taking mechanisms used by both speakers, Jane does not necessarily appear to be the least powerful of the two interlocutors. The interactional markers of length of turns, number of turns, topic switch and control, for example, are evenly distributed. Jane is cooperative in the literal sense of Grice's (1975) Cooperative Principle because she only answers what is necessary. Transactional markers in this passage, such as Mr. Rochester's questions, serve as prospective linguistic indicators for the reader, who would expect compliant answers from the addressee.

It is not only the frequency of categories but also the repetitive markers that linguistically materialize those categories which can shed light on the true nature of DS and FDS use. I therefore compare the FDS and DS instances found in my corpus with the whole of the nonfictional and fictional CONCE (Kytö at al. 2000) sub-corpora, respectively, in order to identify key words. The comparisons highlight certain over-representations of lexemes in my corpus that are worth investigating further.

First of all, I start by looking at FDS stretches in relation to the whole of the nonfictional sub-corpus of CONCE. Despite the fact that the corpus investigated in this study is fiction and that fictional dialogue cannot be equated on a one-to-one basis with natural conversation, it is still possible to use these results to draw some conclusions about 19th-century speech presentation. The following parts of speech appear as key: personal pronouns, personal names, and the auxiliary *do*. First-person personal pronouns (keyness value 85.89) and second-person personal pronouns (keyness value 129.67) are key, because self-reference is made in the stretches of DS and FDS, and the interlocutor is addressed by means of the second-person pronoun in DS and FDS. This underlines the turn-taking practices. Personal names are also significant because characters are either referred to or directly addressed by means of a vocative (e.g., *Dorian*, keyness value 58.72; *Harry*, keyness value 54.37; *Adèle*, keyness value 48.93). Finally, the use of the auxiliary *do* is also key (57.88), which seems to highlight both the use of questions and the use of negation in fictional dialogue. When the FDS stretches are compared with the entire fictional sub-corpus of CONCE, we can see that the second-person personal pronoun *you* is used even more prominently (keyness value 327.43), although the first-person pronoun is also over-represented (210.52). Furthermore, negation by means of the auxiliary *don't* (keyness value 59.20) is overused in my corpus, which stresses the spoken nature of FDS in 19th-century English fiction when viewed in relation to the CONCE fictional texts; in this respect, the stretches of DS as presented in my corpus would appear to stand closer to Present-Day English, as Biber et al. (1999) have pointed out.

For DS, similar results can be obtained when the stretches of DS are compared with the entire nonfictional sub-corpus of CONCE. Personal pronouns are key, such as *thou* (80.25), *you* (57.75), and *I* (55.96). Further, personal names, such as *Phillis* (keyness value 49.05) or *Ellen* (keyness value 41.02), are marked in the stretches of DS. The strategy of directly addressing characters by means of vocative forms can also be seen in the frequency of forms of address that seem—at least superficially—to be more directed at the social status of the addressee, such as *Missy* (keyness value 39.24), *Ma'am* (keyness value 38.27), or *Sir* (keyness value 29.58).

When compared to the fictional sub-corpus of CONCE, the key terms used in the stretches of DS become even more statistically and interpretatively relevant. The personal pronouns *you* (keyness value 211.65) and *I* (keyness value 164.49) are frequently used. The forms of address *Sir* (keyness value 57.99) and *Ma'am* (keyness value 35.16) are also key. The following list illustrates an additional number of key linguistic features that become key diagnostics in the projection of DS and FDS presentation in 19th-century fiction:

- present tense of *to be* = *is* (79.10)
- negation *don't* (46.47)
- *thou* (42.52) and *thee* forms (42.42)
- auxiliaries *will* (32.17), *shall* (31.98), and *can* (31.04)
- stance verb *know* (30.92)
- discourse marker *well* (30.98)
- deictic marker *here* 27.08.

It is illustrated that the direct forms of speech presentation contain the auxiliaries in direct forms, while the indirect forms of speech and thought presentation contain past tense forms such as *would* or *could*. The deictic marker *here* and the discourse marker *well* are clear linguistic markers of the spoken, which will also be presented for the first time as being diagnostic for an automatic identification of discourse presentation, outlined in Chapter 6.

It is highly significant that the comparison of the fictional sub-corpus of CONCE with stretches of DS reveals an under-representation of the verb *said* in the former, which, as we have seen, serves as the typical narrative marker to introduce reporting clauses. I discuss in detail the role and function of reporting verbs for DS presentation in section 7.1 of Chapter 7, where I use Caldas-Coulthard's (1994) reporting verbs typology to categorize the reporting strategies in my corpus and to compare them with the reporting stretches used in 20th-century narrative fiction.

The quantitative analysis of types, distribution, and lexico-grammatical patterns of DS and FDS would remain incomplete if these figures were not viewed in light of 19th-century attitudes toward speech in general, and to historical-political or literary critical conceptions of art, in particular. The orality of the presented material receives an additional dimension of immediacy, despite the fact that what is said cannot be proven to be true. In spite of this impossibility, my results seem to suggest that in 19th-century fiction, characters' social concerns are endowed with a voice that is allowed to be heard. Oscar Wilde also stresses the role of dialogue in *The Critic as Artist* (1997 [1881]), where he discusses the role of literature as *l'art pour l'art*:

> Dialogue, certainly that wonderful literary form, [. . .] can never lose for the thinker its attraction as a mode of expression. By its means he can both reveal and conceal himself, and give form to every fancy, and reality to every mood. By its means he can exhibit the object from each point of view and show it to us in the round, as a sculptor shows us things, gaining in this matter all the richness and reality of effect that comes from those side issues that are suddenly suggested by the central idea in its progress, and really illumine the idea more completely, or from those felicitous after-thoughts that give a fuller completeness to the central scheme, and yet convey something of the delicate charm of chance. (Wilde 1997 [1881]: 121)

Wilde stresses the fact that the writer/narrator/reporter can reveal his/her opinion, but also conceal it at the same time, because speech may be attributed to somebody else. Furthermore, the possibility of construing reality, that is, being mimetic in all its facets, is foregrounded in "give [. . .] reality to every mood" or in "the richness or reality of effect that comes from those side issues."

To conclude, the separation between DS and FDS seems to be in accord with Genette's "tagged" versus "untagged" speech distinction, because it takes account of the fact that the presence of the narrator in the DS reporting clause necessarily modifies the reader's perception of the DS stretch. Furthermore, the high proliferation of identified tags for DS and FDS can be correlated with contemporaneous 19th-century perceptions of the social and artistic functions of speech.

5.2.3. Writing Presentation Categories

5.2.3.1. Narrator's Presentation of Writing (NW)

The inclusion of the presentation of writing as a mode of discourse presentation has emerged from Semino and Short's (2004) analysis of 20th-century narrative fiction. One of their initial claims is that speech and writing presentation are closer to one another in terms of form and function than are speech and thought presentation. Table 4.7 in Chapter 4 has illustrated that the discourse presentation mode of writing presentation occurs least frequently. Despite its generally low frequencies of occurrence, this mode is, however, more frequent in the 19th than in the 20th century.

As could be seen from Table 4.7, 19th-century writers prefer to use writing categories that are situated at the narrator's end of the scale, that is NW, NRWA, and IW. DW, for instance, only amounts to 0.8% of all the tags identified in the corpus. This result stands in contrast to that for speech presentation categories, where DS was the most frequent form. Hence, despite the similarities in the formal attributes of DS and DW, the two categories should be discussed separately, as the difference in frequency seems to point to a difference in function. Furthermore, writing presentation in the 19th-century corpus does not exclusively include instances that are naturally written (such as the act of jotting down a note, or signing a petition, for instance), but also includes those instances that demand a polite and socially compliant reply in written form (e.g., thanking for, accepting or writing an invitation). Thus, although writing presentation and speech presentation share certain functions, one might argue that they differ in faithfulness claims, mainly due to the more permanent nature of the anterior discourse that is reported.

NW, like NV, captures minimal reports of writing, but it contains neither the writing act nor the actual words involved. It describes information about the writing event or the fact that someone has written something to somebody else and that some exchange of writing has taken place.

NW is the most frequent category of writing presentation in my corpus, represented by 39 tags, amounting to 0.8% of all tags, and with 277 words, making up 0.4% of all words in the corpus. In Semino and Short (2004: 100), NW is only on third position of the writing presentation scale, preceded by NRWA and DW. In my corpus, the mean length of NW stretches is 7.1 words per tag, which is almost two words more than in the 20th-century corpus. This is due to the fact that, in 19th-century narrative fiction, mention is habitually made of the fact that a note or a letter has been sent, while information about the circumstances is withheld.

Yet, the respective means by which texts are sent, for instance, by a letter-writer to an addressee, are usually indicated. Typical lexemes that refer to writing are especially nouns such as *note, letter, message,* and the verb *write.* This also corresponds to the keywords identified when stretches of NW are compared to the whole of the nonfictional sub-corpus of CONCE. These are

– *note* (keyness value 42.62)
– *letter* (keyness value 24.89)
– *message* (keyness value 24.04).

When the stretches of NW are compared with the fictional sub-corpus of CONCE, the nouns *note* (50.75) and *letter* (33.55) are also key. Examples are "a note came from Mr. Holbrook" and "The note was handed in" or "before reading the letter" and "I have just had a letter from John." In contrast to the 20th-century corpus, NW heads the writing presentation scale in the 19th-century corpus in terms of its frequency.

NW often places the emphasis on the fact that an interpersonal relationship between two characters is established, without paying attention to the actual words of writing or the writing acts exchanged. In the following example from Gaskell's (2007 [1853]: 45) *Cranford*, the NW stretch "Accordingly, I received a line or two from Martha every now and then" shows how Martha complies with the narrator's orders:

> *Accordingly I received a line or two from Martha every now and then*; and, about November I had a note to say her mistress was "very low and sadly off her food"; and the account made me so uneasy that, although Martha did not decidedly summon me, I packed up my things and went. (*Cranford* 2007 [1853]: 45, my emphasis)

NW also has a summarizing effect and therefore creates cohesion:

> *This wretched note was the finale of Emma's breakfast.* When once it had been read, there was no doing any thing, but lament and exclaim. The loss of the ball—the loss of the young man—and all that the young man might be feeling!—It was too wretched!—Such a delightful evening as it would have been!—Every body so happy! and she and her partner the happiest!—"I said it would be so," was the only consolation. (*Emma* 1985 [1816]: 263, my emphasis)

The NW stretch ("This wretched note was the finale of Emma's breakfast") is preceded by a report in FDW in which Mrs. Weston explains to Emma the facts of Frank's departure. As such, the noun phrase "This wretched note" summarizes or encapsulates the bad news. The demonstrative pronoun *this* anaphorically refers back to the preceding report.

An important message is also announced and introduced (and therefore prospected) by means of NW:

> A few days after, *a note came from Mr. Holbrook*, asking us—impartially asking both of us—in a formal, old-fashioned style, to spend a day at his house—a long June day—for it was June now. He named that he had also invited his cousin, Miss Pole; so that we might join in a fly, which could be put up at his house. (*Cranford* 2007 [1853]: 38, my emphasis)

Here Mr. Holbrook's invitation is initially prospected to the reader by a NW stretch "a note came from Mr. Holbrook." The importance of the invitation for Miss Matty is stressed by the choice of the discourse presentation mode that is used to convey the invitation. Given the fact that the relationship between Miss Matty and Mr. Holbrook is based on letters, the potential of written exchanges for establishing relationship receives a specific value.

To conclude, despite the scarcity of examples of this mode of writing, NW carries similar functions to NV as its corresponding mode on the speech presentation scale. It functions to prospect by pointing to a writing event that will be reported.

5.2.3.2. Narrator's Presentation of Writing Acts (NRWA)

The narrator's representation of writing acts (NRWA) reports acts of writing. In my corpus, NRWA occurs even less frequently than NW. 33 NRWA tags have been identified, which make up 0.7% of the overall number of tags. These are represented by 293 words, which are 0.5% of the words in the corpus. The mean length per tag is 8.87 words per tag, which is longer than that for NRSA (7.35 words per tag) and almost identical with NRTA (8.90 words per tag). The striking difference between the number of NRWA and NRSA tags has already been mentioned. While there are only very few instances of NRWA stretches, NRSA stretches come on third position of all identified tags (with 408 tags, i.e., 8.1% of all tags). NRTA tags are also much more frequent than NRWA, with 368 tags that amount to 7.3% of all tags. Hence, as regards the number of tags and the number of words (NRSA 2,999 words, i.e., 4.8% of all words; NRTA 3,753 words, i.e., 6.0% of all words), the thought and speech presentation modes are much closer to each other in terms of quantitative distribution than the writing mode of this category is to any of them.

NRWA is the most frequent category on the writing presentation scale in 20th-century narrative fiction (Semino and Short 2004: 100). Stretches of NRWA in the 20th-century corpus are with a mean length of 11.75 words per tag longer than those identified for the 19th century, which is only 8.87 words per tag.

Again, due to the scarcity of examples for NRWA, the lexico-grammatical patterns following keyword analysis were not identified with the help of CONCE for this category. Some qualitative observations can nevertheless be made. The examples of NRWA analyzed are not necessarily actions that are inherently written in nature (e.g., signing a petition), but rather instances which, according to social decorum, for instance, demanded a written response. Accordingly, NRWA is often used to describe expressive speech acts of thanking or accepting an invitation in the 19th-century corpus:

> This took us half a day's good hard talking to get over; but, at the first sentence of relenting, I seized the opportunity, *and wrote and despatched an acceptance in her name*—fixing day and hour, that all might be decided and done with. (*Cranford* 2007 [1853]: 38, my emphasis)

NRWA may also have summarizing functions, as can be seen in the following example from Shelley's (2003 [1818]: 75) *Frankenstein*:

> Clerval, who had watched my countenance as I read this letter, was surprised to observe the despair that succeeded the joy I at first expressed on *receiving news from my friends*. (*Frankenstein* 2003 [1818]: 75, my emphasis)

The NRWA stretch "receiving news from my friends" summarizes the content of the letter which Victor is reading.

To conclude, NRWA carries similar functions to that of NRSA, despite the fact that NRWA is much rarer in the 19th-century corpus than NRSA.

5.2.3.3. Indirect Writing (IW)

With 16 tags, IW amounts to only 0.3% of all the tags identified in the corpus. The identified 16 tags are represented by 232 words, which make up 0.4% of all the words in the corpus. IW is thus on fourth position of the categories on the writing presentation scale. It ranges behind NW, NRWA, and DW, but it is more frequent in the 19th-century corpus than in the 20th-century sub-corpus of narrative fiction, where only 5 occurrences are found (Semino and Short 2004: 100). As is the case with IS, IW does not necessarily mention the exact words of the speaker in full, but provides a summary of what is written. Similar to the 20th century, IW has the highest mean length of all words for writing presentation categories, although it is still shorter than in the 20th century: on average, there are 14.5 words per tag for the 19th century and 17 words per tag for the 20th-century stretches of IW. The mean length of 14.5 words per tag in the 19th century is, however, on fourth position of the overall mean length of all tags in my corpus, coming after FIT (22.39 words per tag), DW (21.54 words per tag), and FDS (18.07 words per tag). Again, due to the scarcity of examples of IW, lexico-grammatical patterns were not identified with the help of CONCE, but some qualitative observations can be made.

IW also has a summarizing function, because it usually involves a separate reporting clause and is used to focus on the content of the written message. As a brief example of how IW is used to summarize sequences of letters sent, consider the following from Hardy's *Jude the Obscure*: "Then Sue wrote to tell him the day fixed for the wedding" (*Jude the Obscure* 1975 [1891]: 164). Jude is informed about the date of Sue's marriage to Mr. Phillotson. Preceding this stretch of IW are examples of DW, which give an image of her exact words and therewith stand in contrast to the NRW and IW stretches. Therefore, IW is best to be seen in interaction with stretches of DW.

To conclude, examples of DW are rare, but if they occur, the degree of eloquence with which writing is presented is summarized in a rather elaborate way.

5.2.3.4. Free Indirect Writing (FIW)

FIW is the least frequent writing presentation category in both corpora. There are only 10 tags of FIW that could be identified in my corpus, amounting to 0.2% of all tags. These are represented by 102 words, amounting to 0.2% of all words. The mean length of words per tag is 10.02 words. In Semino and Short (2004: 100), there are only 4 tags of FIW. Again, due to the scarcity of examples of FIW, lexico-grammatical patterns were not identified with the help of CONCE, but some qualitative observations can be made.

FIW forms of writing presentation are linguistically more complex to identify because they display the linguistic mix of free indirect forms that is also visible in FIS. Just like FIS, FIW shifts linguistically and stylistically between mimesis and diegesis because the switch to the past shows the intrusion of the narrator. Often stretches of FIW are presented in a row of more than just one stretch of discourse presentation modes and categories. They may transfer to the reader the alleged urgency with which something is written, for example:

> The substance of this letter was forwarded to Emma, in a note from Mrs. Weston, instantly. *As to his going, it was inevitable. He must be gone within a few hours, though without feeling any real alarm for his aunt, to lessen his repugnance.* (*Emma* 1985 [1816]: 263, my emphasis)

The FIW stretch "As to his going [. . .] repugnance" conveys the fact that Frank is not able to stay any longer but, interestingly, it also seems to include his exact words. It provides more detail about what he said, which is now reported in the letter. By choosing the past tense form as a nonfactive marker, Mrs. Weston shows that she simply reports what has been said and that she is not making these statements herself. One might think that the use of FIW results from the avoidance of repeating the reporting clause. Yet, in the example given here, it adds to the vividness and, at the same time, reinforces the ironic narratological voice poking fun at Mrs. Weston's serious appraisal of Frank's need to leave.

To conclude, identifying both structural patterns of IW as well as their functional potential is difficult to assess systematically due to the scarcity of available material. As regards the functions of IW, they come close to that of IS: a summarizing function that is, however, elaborated on in an articulate way.

5.2.3.5. Direct Writing (DW) and Free Direct Writing (FDW)

DW is the third most frequent category of the writing presentation categories in the 19th-century corpus, while FIW does not occur at all. In other words, when writing presentation appears in a direct form, it is always accompanied by a signaling clause, making it DW presentation. DW is identified for 22 tags that represent 0.4% of all tags in the corpus. It is represented by 474 words, which makes up 0.8% of all words in the corpus. The mean length of words per DW tag is 21.54 words, which stands in contrast to the much shorter stretches for DT (average length of 7.57 words per tag) and DS (average length of 10.72 words per tag). In Semino and Short (2004: 100), DW is less frequent than in my 19th-century corpus. It occurs on second position of the 20th-century writing presentation categories. Yet, there are only 11 tags. The mean length of words representing these tags is 7.52 words, while in my corpus it is 21.54 words.

Despite the scarcity of examples in my corpus, which urges us to make generalized conclusions, it seems that in the 19th-century corpus DW is given more weight in terms of degree of lexical specificity and information encoded in this category. DW's heavier presence has immediate functional effects as well. First, in contrast to DS, DW does not (in fact, cannot) include immediate feedback or face-to-face communication. Second, DW also employs linguistic markers prototypically encoding more formal language than those found in DS examples. Therefore, the effects of vividness and dramatization normally associated with direct forms need to be related to the narrative viewpoints of the various reporters. DW includes not only direct stretches of letters that are quoted, but also advertisements in newspapers, such as, for instance, the reward for Oliver Twist.

As an illustration, we can consider the following stretch from Hardy's (1975 [1891]) *Jude the Obscure*. Sue's exact written words are given in the form of a letter in which she informs Jude about her marriage to Mr. Phillotson. The character is presented as reading the letter, but the reader also learns of Jude's feelings via a stretch of DT in "And yet, what could the poor girl do? He asked himself." The fact that the source that ultimately gives rise to Jude's thoughts is written creates a stronger claim toward faithfulness:

> MY DEAR JUDE,—I have something to tell you which perhaps you will not be surprised to hear, though certainly it may strike you as being accelerated (as the railway companies say of their trains). Mr. Phillotson and I are to be married quite soon—in three or four weeks. We had intended, as you know, to wait till I had gone through my course of training and obtained my certificate, so as to assist him, if necessary, in the teaching. But he generously says he does not see any object in waiting, now I am not at the training school. It is so good of him, because the awkwardness of my situation has really come about by my fault in getting expelled. Wish me joy. Remember I say you are to, and you mustn't refuse!—Your affectionate cousin,
>
> *SUSANNA FLORENCE MARY BRIDEHEAD.*
>
> Jude staggered under the news; could eat no breakfast; and kept on drinking tea because his mouth was so dry. Then presently he went back to his work and laughed the usual bitter laugh of a man so confronted. Everything seemed turning to satire. *And yet, what could the poor girl do? he asked himself*: and felt worse than shedding tears. (*Jude the Obscure* 1975 [1891]: 188, my emphasis)

Jude's thoughts create an interesting interplay between "writing" and "the truthfulness" of what has been written. Whereas the DT stretch seems to be used to accommodate his real feelings, Jude's answer realized in DW states otherwise:

> Jude screwed himself up to heroic key; and replied: MY DEAR SUE,—Of course I wish you joy! And also of course, I will give you away. What I suggest is that, as you have no house of your own, you do not marry from your school friend's, but from mine. It would be more proper, I think, since I am, as you say, the person nearest related to you in this part of the world. I don't see why you sign your letter in such a new and terribly formal way? Surely you care a bit about me still!—Ever your affectionate, JUDE. (*Jude the Obscure* 1975 [1891]: 189)

Thus, Sue's words presented as a written letter both illustrate the seriousness of her decision and the naïve attitude with which she goes about the marriage. Furthermore, the interplay of DW, on the one hand, and DT, on the other, is much more effective in foregrounding Jude's real feelings.

Finally, it is also worth discussing the keywords resulting from comparing the stretches of DW and the nonfictional sub-corpus of CONCE, especially because of the role played by personal names and place names, such as *Jude* (45.17), *Utterson* (30.11), *Bridehead* (30.11), or *Highbury* (26.29). This result not only is constructive of the forms of address and departing formula used to initiate and complete a letter, but also illustrates how deictic reference is made in order to inform the reader about locations of where to meet, or to index the place that is being referred to.

To conclude, despite the fact that there are only a few instances of writing presentation in the corpus of 19th-century narrative fiction, the length of information, as well as the degree of specificity given by stretches of DW, takes account of the fact that immediate feedback to what has been written in a letter or so cannot be expected.

5.2.4. Thought Presentation Categories

5.2.4.1. Direct Thought (DT) and Free Direct Thought (FDT)

I shall begin the presentation of the forms, distribution, and functions of the categories on the thought presentation scale by briefly recapitulating some of the quantitative figures. In my 19th-century data, NRTA is the most frequent category, representing 7.3% (368 tags) of all the identified tags and 34.2% of the thought presentation categories on the thought presentation scale. NI slides down to position number three (195 tags, i.e., 3.9%), preceded by IT (266 tags, i.e., 5.3%) in the 19th-century material, whereas it heads the thought presentation scale in the 20th century (Semino and Short 2004). FIT, which takes position number four of all the thought presentation categories, is proportionally more central to thought presentation than FIS is to speech presentation, although FIT is still more frequent in the 20th-century material than in the 19th century. In my corpus, FIT has 187 tags, which amounts to 3.7%. DT and FDT are not particularly frequent in my 19th-century data—in fact, they are the least frequent categories on the thought presentation scale. DT comes by 21 tags (i.e., 0.4% of all tags in the corpus). FDT only shows 3 tags, amounting to 0.1% of all tags of discourse presentation in the corpus. In the 20th-century corpus, FDT tags by far outnumber DT tags, while we find the reverse result in the 19th-century texts.

In contrast to the presentation of the different categories on the speech and writing presentation scales, let me begin the detailed description of the types, distribution, lexico-grammatical patterns, and functions of the categories on the thought presentation scale with the presentation of thoughts from the character's end of the scale, that is, with a closer inspection of DT and FTS. In contrast to the results computed for the direct forms of speech presentation, the direct forms of thought presentation, as mentioned, do not occur very frequently. Further, FDT and DT are only represented by a rather small number of words. DT tags are represented by 159 words, which amounts to 0.3% of all words and have a mean word length per tag of 7.57. FDT comes only with 29 words and a mean length of 9.66 words per tag, which has to be treated with caution because of the very few occurrences of FDT. Hence, I also refrain from computing keywords for the stretches of DT and FDT.

In the 20th-century corpus, there are 19 tags for DT and 58 tags for FDT (Semino and Short 2004: 121). The mean length of words for those tags is much longer than for my corpus: 14.03 words per tag for both DT and FDT.

Direct thought and free direct thought (DT and FDT) give access to a character's thoughts in a direct way, that is, both create the illusion that what is presented is what the character really thinks (Cohn 1978: 76). Both categories also seem to turn cognitive activities into words and foreground the impression that what is presented is a highly conscious affair. It is striking that both DT and FIT appear in such low numbers in both corpora. Perhaps one would have initially expected a different result because of the centrality of studies on thought presentation in general, or the fact that DS and FDS are the most frequent categories represented by most of the words in the corpus on the speech presentation scale. It seems that the style of thought presentation of 19th-century narrators in my corpus favors more complex and subtle summarizing modes of thought presentation, like NI or NRTA, or, as we have seen, lexically highly elaborate stretches of FIT.

According to Fludernik (1993: 77–78), DT and FDT categories occur at moments of high emotional intensity or sudden momentous realizations, which can be corroborated by the relatively short mean length of these stretches of 9.66 (FDT) and 7.57 (DT) words per tag. Further, the thoughts that are presented to us would count as exclamations (with incomplete sentences), which, in terms of Speech Act Theory (Austin 1962; Searle 1969, 1976), may count as expressive speech acts, always bearing in mind that thought presentation cannot be directly equated with speech presentation categories.

Despite their low number of tags, DT and FDT are multifunctional in 19th-century writing. For instance, a character might wish to present his/her opinion in speech but may not feel to be able to do so because of social constraints; if that is the case, DT or FDT still allow the reader to partake with the character's real attitudes, feelings, or opinions on whatever issue the character cannot openly verbalize.

DT and FDT are also used when the narrator explicitly creates a discrepancy between what is presented in speech and what is presented in thought, sometimes with the character reflecting on a sudden realization. To illustrate this, an incident from Stevenson's (2004 [1886]) *Dr. Jekyll and Mr. Hyde* can be quoted: " 'What!' he thought. 'Henry Jekyll forge for a murderer!' " (Stevenson 2004 [1886]: 21), where Utterson mentally expresses his surprise at the suspicion of Jekyll being a murderer.

Although both DT and FDT are dealt with here in one section, it should be stressed again that I consider DT and FDT as two distinct and different categories. As already discussed in relation to speech presentation, maintaining this distinction responds to functional (each mode projects different effects) and formal reasons (the presence of the reporting stretch in DT which necessarily entails narratorial intervention). FDT appears as more vivid, and the reader feels closer to the character's inner consciousness. The reporting verbs used to introduce DT are not restricted to the verb *think*; in fact, we find an ample variety of verb phrases, such as *observe to herself, the souls of each other cried out, his eyes added, cried his soul*, or *said to oneself*. All these verb phrases fall within the category of verbs of communication; however, they are often used reflexively to account for the fact that the activities presented are cognitive and take place in the focalizer's mind. Besides, only a clarifying reporting clause often illustrates the switch from speech to thought presentation. Consider, for instance, the following example from Thackeray's *Vanity Fair*:

> "The modern languages," says she modestly: "French, German, Spanish, and Italian, Latin and the rudiments of Greek if desired. English of course; the practice of Elocution, Geography, and Astronomy, and the Use of the Globes, Algebra (but only as far as quadratic equations); for a poor ignorant female, you know, Mr. Snob, cannot be expected to know everything. Ancient and Modern History no young woman can be without; and of these I make my beloved pupils PERFECT MISTRESSES. Botany, Geology, and Mineralogy, I consider as amusements. And with these I assure you we manage to pass the days at the Evergreens not unpleasantly." Only these, thought I—*what an education!* (*Book of Snobs* 1910 [1846-1847]: 123–124, my emphasis)

The stretch is preceded by a reporting clause (not quoted) which contains the perception verb *think*. Because of that, the whole stretch could be considered an example of DT. Yet, the expressive nature of the both admiring but also sarcastic "What an education" in response to the litany of subjects Mrs. Ponto pretends to be able to teach to her pupils may also serve as an example of FDT.

To conclude, compared to the attention that thought presentation (including DT and FDT) has received in the literature, there are surprisingly few examples of DT and FDT in my corpus. FDT and DT serve to highlight emotional reactions of a character or sudden realizations and revelations.

5.2.4.2. Free Indirect Thought (FIT)

The FIT category is situated in fourth position of the categories on the thought presentation scale in my 19th-century data; 187 tags (i.e., 3.7% of all tags) are stretches of FIT. (This amounts to 18.9% of all categories on the thought presentation scale.) This contrasts with 5% FIT tags in the 20th-century corpus of narrative fiction (Semino and Short 2004: 123). In Semino and Short (2004: 117), FIT comes on second position on the thought presentation scale (with 227 tags; following NI with 409 tags). Semino and Short (2004: 123) stress that FIT is mainly a fictional phenomenon because it hardly appears in the other corpora they have investigated.

As regards the number of words by which FIT is presented in my corpus (4,187 words, i.e., 6.7%), FIT strikingly appears on third position overall, only preceded by the number of words for DS (7,111 words, i.e., 11.4%) and FDS (7,465 words, i.e., 12.0%), although it should be stressed that some stretches vary in length. Even more striking is the fact that as regards the average length of tags according to the number of words, FIT is among the top discourse presentation categories with a mean length of 22.39 words per tag. The dominance of FIT and the presence of narrative progression in 19th-century narrative fiction thus appear to be mainly recognized by the reader due to the length of FIT stretches. In Semino and Short's (2004) sub-corpus of narrative fiction, both the number of FIT tags as well as their length seem to be responsible for this. In the 20th-century corpus, FIT stretches are also lexically dense, with a mean length of 25.83 words per tag.

As mentioned before, FIT has received considerable scholarly attention from a variety of perspectives. I would like to refer to the existent corpus-linguistic studies here. Toolan (2009: 137–138), for instance, implements a corpus-linguistic study of 20th-century short stories and identifies some formal linguistic means characterizing passages of FIT that also enhance narrative progression. He shows that "FIT is more rapidly detectable via surface signals than is sometimes supposed" (Toolan 2009: 135). This goes somewhat against Semino and Short (2004: 27–39), who draw our attention to the fact that discourse presentation in general and thought presentation in particular are too complex a discoursal phenomenon to be identified by repetitive linguistic features. Although Toolan (2009: 137) also stresses that contextual factors are needed to isolate FIT and that it is often difficult to distinguish between FIT and FIS, he identifies a set of patterns or "rules" whose occurrence can aid a possible automatic identification of FIT stretches. (He is, however, quick to ascertain that it is not possible to come up with a fully automated tagger or parser capable of isolating all instances of FIT.) Thus, the following markers would need to be included in any automated process of FIT identification:

a) narrative modal verbs which co-occur with a pronoun (excluding modals following *if*);
b) questions and exclamations;
c) flanking sentences containing subjective modals.

The following "rules" thus are made up of certain formal features which Toolan calls "diagnostic" (Toolan 2009: 138), that is, constitutive of FIT in 20th-century short stories.[5]

1) Toolan draws attention to the adjacent co-occurrence of a modal verb (*would, might, could,* and *must*) and a "pronominal Subject denoting a main character or phenomenon" (Toolan 2009: 138) but excludes negated modals.
2) Sometimes also the inverted modal as in "would she" appears, but also semi-modals, such as *need, used to,* or *ought to.*
3) A pronoun plus a modal followed by *have* (Toolan 2009: 143) is not a diagnostic.
4) A singular pronominal subject (in hetero-diegetic narrative, this is *he, she,* or *it*) also introduces FIT.

5) A further diagnostic is the fact that both pronoun and modal are in direct proximity. However, there may also be intervening material between pronoun and modal (as in, e.g., *he obviously must be*).
6) Toolan (2009: 143) excludes modals following *if* but includes interrogatives, exclamations, and clauses beginning with initial *wh*-word and a narrative tense verb.
7) Furthermore, all flanking sentences containing subjective modals are included.

Many of the features listed by Toolan (2009) are also "diagnostic" for FIT stretches in my 19th-century corpus. For example, when compared with the nonfictional sub-corpus of CONCE, the past tense singular form of the copula verb *be*, that is *was*, is the top keyword (76.14), followed by past tense *had* (67.44). Furthermore, modals, such as *could, should, might,* or *must,* co-occurring with a pronoun, are also among the formal elements which are "diagnostic" of FIT in 19th-century narrative fiction, just as they were in Toolan's short fiction corpus. *Might,* for instance, occurs in declaratives as in "What strength, or what constancy of affection he might be subject to, was another point" (*Emma* 1985 [1816]: 266) and the modal auxiliary *could* occurs in questions, as in "could he be the murderer of my brother?" Other features listed by Toolan (2009: 139) that can also be seen in the 19th-century corpus are, for instance, modals without the complementizers *if, whether,* or *that.* Because of the length of stretches of FIT, flanking sentences—that is, those stretches occurring immediately before and/or after a stretch of FIT—should be considered as well, as Toolan (2009: 140) suggests and as will also be illustrated in the following.

In addition, in my corpus the verb *seemed* (40.41), which is not mentioned to carry this function in Toolan (2009), is also key for FIT. The key status of the possessive pronouns *her* (35.34) and *his* (43.68) also illustrates that in FIT reference is made to characters by the use of pronouns rather than by personal names, which stresses the personal and character-oriented function of FIT. The key use of pronouns correlates with Toolan's (2009: 131) observations, although in the FIT stretches of my corpus, possessive pronouns seem to be more frequent (and statistically foregrounded). Interestingly, the personal pronouns *I* and *you* are under-represented in the stretches of FIT when compared with the nonfictional sub-corpus of CONCE (with a log-likelihood that is computed as –57.45 for *I* and –95.24 for *you*), and when compared with the fictional sub-corpus of CONCE (*you* with a log-likelihood of –24.93). In contrast to that, and as discussed earlier, in section 5.2.2.5, these two pronouns are particularly marked in direct stretches of DS and FDS. It appears that in speech presentation, these pronouns are used to emphasize the "origo" or deictic center, to underscore issues of immediacy, and it is also the case that characters speak about themselves or address the interlocutor. In FIT, a character's thoughts about others are more frequently presented.

Impersonal constructions such as *it was,* as in "It was too wretched," and existential *there* (Carter and McCarthy 2006: 287), as in "There was a great deal of friendly and of compassionate attachment on his side," represent additional diagnostic features to identify FIT and are not mentioned in Toolan (2009) or in any other study to have this function. Also, in my corpus, we find *it seemed*, as in "It seemed like the forerunner of something absolutely serious" (*Emma* 1985 [1816]: 265) or "Every thing seemed to cooperate for her advantage" (*Northanger Abbey* 1985 [1818]: 149). The use of the past tense verbs *was/were* and *had*, as in "These were thrilling words" (*Northanger Abbey* 1985 [1818]: 148) or "Certainly his being at Randalls had given great spirit to the last two weeks" (*Emma* 1985 [1816]: 266) is equally marked.

In addition, stance expressions (Biber et al. 1999: 899), such as the clausal "It was [. . .] a ticklish decision" and the stance adverbial *at least* in "It was, at least, a ticklish decision that he had to make" (*Strange Case of Dr. Jekyll and Mr. Hyde* 2003 [1886]: 68), further contribute to the reflective nature of FIT and mark functional items which can be additionally identified to have diagnostic value.

Other stance markers (Biber et al. 1999: 8) or "boosters" (Carter and McCarthy 2006: 283), such as *certainly, particularly, absolutely, mostly, evidently, indeed*, or clausal constructions like *it was excellent*, regularly appear in FIT stretches. They account for the fact that FIT is an "in-between" category, which also contains linguistic elements such as stance adverbials (Biber et al. 1999; Busse 2010) that are usually characteristic of spoken registers, even in historical discourse. Therefore, stance adverbials can be seen as an additional, formal feature that is "diagnostic" in stretches of FIT, although it also frequently appears in stretches of DS. In Simpson's (1993) terms, these add to the shading of the narrative and reinforce the point of view of the focalized. It can be seen that due to the occurrence of both deontic as well as epistemic expressions, the narrative may move between what Simpson (1993) has called "positive" and "negative" shading.

The same holds true for interjections or exclamations, lexically realized as *oh, god help me, yes, alas*, or *no*, which frequently occur in FIT and add to the emotional intensity that is transferred by FIT. For example, in Austen's (1985 [1816]) *Emma*, Emma reflects on Mr. Knightley's love for Mrs. Fairfax, but is then relieved that it is only friendship. The reader experiences her relief through the presentation of her thoughts in FIT: "There was a great deal of friendly and of compassionate attachment on his side—but no love. Alas! there was soon no leisure for quarrelling with Mr. Knightley" (*Emma* 1985 [1816]: 263).

Furthermore, nonfinite infinitival constructions of the exclamatory kind, as in "To receive so flattering an invitation" (*Northanger Abbey* 1985 [1818]: 148), or in the declarative "To sit there silent" (*A Beleaguered City* 2000 [1879]: 44), which are also often repeated, are characteristic of the FIT mode but have not been identified as such so far. Here is a correlation with the linguistic realization of stretches of IT, where we often find the same structure, but where that stretch is followed by a reporting clause.

Exclamations are often elliptic and consist just of a repetition of a noun phrase. But they may also be realized by complete sentences, and are also very characteristic of FIT in 19th-century narrative fiction. Here is an example from Austen's *Emma* (1985 [1816]) that abounds in the use of exclamatory utterances representing the agitation of Emma's mind:

> The loss of the ball—the loss of the young man—and all that the young man might be feeling!—It was too wretched!—Such a delightful evening as it would have been!—Every body so happy! and she and her partner the happiest! (*Emma* 1985 [1816]: 263)

Another feature that is characteristic of FIT in the 19th-century corpus is that of repetition. The repetition of noun phrases, for instance, appears not only in exclamatory expressions, as mentioned earlier, but also in examples of the following kind: "Her feelings, her preferences, had each known the happiness of a return" (*Emma* 1985 [1816]: 149). Both the topicalization of the noun phrases "her feelings" and "her preferences" and the repetition of the noun phrases intensify the importance of what is topicalized and also give a sense of the reflective nature of her thoughts.

A somewhat similar phenomenon can be observed in the following construction: "The Tilneys, they, by whom, above all, in the flattering measures by which their intimacy was to be continued" (*Northanger Abbey* 1985 [1818]: 149). This is called a header-tail construction (Carter and McCarthy 2006: 782) and refers to the redundant use of a pronoun that is anaphorically employed but that is too close to the antecedent noun to be grammatically necessary. The repetition of this pronoun, therefore, foregrounds its presence and underscores the noun phrase it refers to, "the Tilneys." This underlines Catherine's thinking process but also stresses the importance she places on the "Tilneys" and their role in making her stay at Northanger Abbey. These constructions are usually typical of spoken language, although in FIT instances they seem to reinforce the dynamic nature of the thinking process. So far, this strategy has not been identified to be diagnostic of FIT.

For clarity's sake, it may be useful at this stage to summarize the linguistic features mentioned so far, some of which being prototypically employed in 19th-century fiction, and others being shared by 20th-century fictional short stories as well. FIT's diagnostics seem to work on all linguistic levels: word, phrase, sentence, and discourse level:

a) past tense forms of the copula verb *to be* which stand in close proximity to personal (*he, she, it*) and possessive pronouns (*his, her, its*);
b) impersonal presentational constructions like *it was* and *there was*;
c) frequent usage of the construction *it seemed*;
d) the use of modals, such as *could, must, should, might*, which also stand in close proximity to a pronoun and occasionally to a stance adverb(ial), such as *certainly* or *indeed*; modals which are followed by a complementizer (*if, that*, or *whether*) can be excluded;
e) the use of the nonfinite infinitive construction in, for example, *to receive*;

f) the use of exclamations and questions (that is, inclusion of exclamation and question marks);
g) repetition of (frequently topicalized) noun phrases;
h) use of stance adverbials;
i) use of interjections.

The respective length of FIT stretches makes it necessary that preceding as well as following stretches be investigated. Further, there are prospecting or encapsulating stretches which announce thought presentation in general and FIT in particular; these are often characterized by constructions containing *all this* or *all these*.

In addition to a formal characterization of FIT diagnostics, these features also need to be considered with regard to their particular general functions. Pragmatically speaking, they often contribute to the creation of specific speech acts. Thus, for instance, the use of questions, which are as much characteristic of FIT in 19th-century texts as in Toolan's (2009) 20th-century corpus of short stories, stresses the emotional intensity of the thought act and reinforces the thinking process of leveling. Toolan (2009) describes the functionality of thought presentation in general as a means of narrative progression, because it is a form which distinguishes itself from orthodox narration and directly reported speech (Toolan 2009: 136). Further, FIT is a pointer to internal motives and crises of characters.

Due to the fact that FIT presents character-internal thoughts or a character's private reactions or hopes, which cannot be uttered in public because of the rules of social decorum, for instance, stretches of FIT can be seen as guides which aid readers' narrative expectations. Following Grice's (1975) concept of implicature, Toolan (2009: 137) emphasizes that "there must be a prospection-relevant point to the telling of those private thoughts" (Toolan 2009: 137) and sees FIT as sights of high narrativity representations of a character's thoughts. Due to the fact that FIT is probably the mode of discourse presentation that allows for the most intimate zooming into a character's thoughts, its prospecting function can be immediately seen. FIT is also an "in-between" category because it conventionally contains (linguistic) features of DT and IT.

The following examples illustrate some of the functions mentioned earlier. In the following example from Brontë's *Wuthering Heights* (2009 [1847]), Nelly attempts to distract Catherine from being tired and advises her to talk to her. Catherine's reply to that advice is not quoted in DS but commented on through Nelly's thoughts and her observation of Catherine's body movements:

> "Ellen, I'm tired." "Give over then and talk," I answered. That was worse: she fretted and sighed, and looked at her watch till eight, and finally went to her room, completely overdone with sleep. (*Wuthering Heights* 2009 [1847]): 216)

The stretch "That was worse" stresses Nelly's disparaging comment on Catherine's awkward behavior, when she reports this incident to Mr. Lockwood. Yet Nelly pretends to having kept up appearances when she tells this part of the story to Mr. Lockwood. We feel close to Nelly's thoughts through the deictic shift, which moves from Nelly's description of her own and Catherine's words to that of Nelly's inner thoughts in FIT. The linking element is the topicalized demonstrative pronoun *that*.

In the next example from Gaskell's *North and South* (2003 [1854]), Mrs. Thornton privately comments on Mrs. Hale's knitting. Her thoughts are presented in FIT (see also section 5.2.2.1 in Chapter 5):

> She liked Mrs. Hale's double knitting far better; that was sensible of its kind. The room altogether was full of knick-knacks, which must take a long time to dust; and time to people of limited income was money. (*North and South* 2003 [1854]: 96–97)

The narrator informs the reader that these are Mrs. Thornton's thoughts through a stretch of NT in "She made all these reflections." Interestingly, the narrator is able to present a common human practice of thinking and speaking simultaneously through subordinated temporal clause, which is preceded by a stretch of NT: "as she was talking in her stately way to Mrs. Hale, and uttering all the stereotyped commonplaces that most people can find to say with their senses blindfolded" (*North and South* 2003 [1854]: 96–97). This stretch is prospective, as through implicature, the reader is asked to understand (a) that there is a discrepancy between Mrs. Thornton's thoughts and what she says, and (b) that the presentation of Mrs. Thornton's thoughts at this point is highly relevant.

To conclude, stretches of FIT, which are represented by the highest number of words in the 19th-century corpus, can be identified by a variety of repetitive linguistic patterns, ranging from the repetition of modals to the repetition of syntactic constructions and lexical stance markers. In terms of function, in the 19th-century corpus it is also one of the most intimate ways of zooming into a character's mind. In terms of frequency of both identified stretches of FIT and the number of words by which it is represented, this strategy is more foregrounded in 19th-century narrative discourse than in that of the 20th century.

5.2.4.3. Indirect Thought (IT)

IT is the second-most frequent mode of thought presentation in my corpus. It occurs with 266 tags, making up 5.3% of all identified tags. These are represented by 2,368 words, which amounts to 3.8% of all the words in the corpus. The mean length is 8.9 words per tag. In Semino and Short (2004: 117), IT tags come on third position (85 tags) for the fictional sub-corpus. On average, with a mean length of 11.94 words per tag, these are represented by slightly more words than in the 19th-century corpus.

While Leech and Short (1981/2007a) claim that IT is the norm for thought presentation in 20th-century fictional narrative, Semino and Short's (2004) study shows that, in fact, it is not, because NI occurs more frequently. In the 19th-century corpus, the norm for thought presentation is NRTA (see Table 4.8, section 4.2, in Chapter 4). Leech and Short (1981/2007a) further claim that the thought presentation scale is more complex than the speech presentation scale, because, for instance, IT does not carry the same summarizing function as does IS, but instead it seems that we are mostly given the entire propositional content (Semino and Short 2004: 128). IT could thus be seen as the antipole to speech which, through the reporting clause, is interspersed with the narrator's voice.

Often, IT is an unspoken reaction to the speech of another character. Toolan (2009) does not see IT to be directly relevant to narrative progression because it shows direct narrator intervention through a reporting clause. It is less dramatic than FIT and allows for a more "mundane character deliberation" (Toolan 2009: 136). On a scale of character involvement, IT appears to be downgraded insofar as it only reports a character's thoughts through the voice of a narrator, without presentation of the actual cognitive activity. In my 19th-century corpus, the narrator's presence in IT and DT is most obvious through the reporting clauses. These appear to be highly varied and not restricted to a prototypical "he thought," or similar phrases. On the contrary, often the reporting clauses are highly creative and the type-token ratio, which measures lexical variability, is extensive. Consequently, IT brings in further lexical diversity, encoded mainly in the wealth of reporting verbs: *think* occurs most frequent (33 occ.), followed by *know* (10 occ.), *feel* (9 occ.), *see* (9 occ.), *remember* (5 occ.), *find* (4 occ.), *wish* (4 occ.), *hope* (3 occ.), *wonder* (3 occ.), *convince* (3 occ.), *determine* (3 occ.), *resolve* (3 occ.), and *suppose* (3 occ.). Other *verba sentiendi*, verbal, nominal, or adverbial expressions referring to thinking or believing, are (in alphabetical order as occurring in the 19th-century corpus of narrative fiction):

a dread came over me
a mutual thought
add
apprehension
ask oneself
beginning to hope
believe
completed her conviction
conjecture (vb.)
convince
dare in my own mind
decide
desire (vb.)
determine
discover
does/did not doubt
dream (vb.)
endeavour (vb.)
expect
fancy (vb.)
fear (vb.)
feel
feel instinctively
find
foresee
forget
get so far
hold
hope (vb.)
imagine
in (the) hope
intend
inwardly deplore
it appeared
it appears
know
like (vb.)
long (vb.)
my mind
natural for him
no doubt (adv.)
no objection
observe
perceive
persuade
prepare
prophesy
recollect
remark
remember
resolve
say to oneself
secretly
see
seem
seem impossible
small part of

stand uncertain	*to be certain*	*to suspect*
strive	*to be probable*	*understand*
suppose	*to be startled*	*urge* (vb.)
suspect (vb.)	*to be sure*	*was delighted*
the souls of each	*to be surprised*	*wish* (vb.)
think	*to be tempted*	*with a sudden*
to be afraid	*to be the thought*	*consciousness*
to be aware	*to have no doubt*	*wonder*

This list of verb, noun, and adverbial phrases shows acts of believing, desiring, intending, motivating, and planning. Apart from their obvious role as encoders of narratorial intervention in reporting clauses, these items also work as linguistic markers for IS speech annotation. Some rare examples are even used metaphorically, as can be seen in "It darted through her with the speed of an arrow" (*Emma* 1985 [1816]: 398). Here the thinking process is conceptualized in terms of movement (see Lakoff and Johnson 2003). This kind of conceptualization is also a stable and recurrent feature in 19th- and 20th-century discourse presentation, as discussed by Semino and Short (2004).

The differentiation between IT and DT can rely on quotation marks, as well as on the identification of whether a complementizer *that*, *if*, or *whether* follows the reporting clause. For my 19th-century corpus, the complementizer *that* is key for IT, both when compared to the fictional sub-corpus of CONCE (81.10) and to the nonfictional one (62.79). One example to illustrate this is: "This persuasion, joined to all the rest made her think that she must be a little in love with him" (*Emma* 1985 [1816]: 266).

Sometimes, the complementizer is left out, but the sentence following the reporting clause is still IT, such as in the following: "The entrance of her father put a stop to the civility, which Catherine was beginning to hope might introduce a desire of their corresponding" (*Northanger Abbey* 1985 [1818]: 148). In addition, a framing verb may also be part of a stretch of FIT. The framing verb then often follows the reported stretch, so that it may be difficult to decide whether the stretch is IT, FIT, or ambiguous, such as in "This, Emma felt, was aimed at her" (*Emma* 1985 [1816]: 262). Here the reporting stretch "Emma felt" does not take initial position, but rather foregrounds the demonstrative pronoun *this* and may be taken to function as a reporting clause for *this*, while "was aimed at her" is free and could therefore be labeled as FIT.

The function of IT becomes more complex when the reporting clause is moved to medial or final position, because there may be a move from IT to FIT:

> [. . .] his full nostrils, denoting, *I thought*, choler; *his grim mouth, chin, and jaw—yes, all three were very grim*, and no mistake. His shape, now divested of cloak, I perceived harmonized in squareness with his physiognomy: *I suppose* it was a good figure in the athletic sense of the term—broad chested and thin flanked, though neither tall nor graceful. (*Jane Eyre* 1985 [1847]: 151–152, my emphasis)

The reader is presented with a stream of Jane's thoughts in which she herself describes Mr. Rochester's outward appearance. The fact that the reporting clause "I thought" does not initiate the sentence makes it more difficult to decide whether we are presented with IT or FIT, to which the subsequent lines ("his grim mouth, chin, and jaw—yes, all three were very grim [. . .]") then move. It seems that the narrator provides the reader with one linguistic clue as to the fact that Jane's thoughts are presented here, and then moves on to the more vivid and dramatic presentation of her thoughts through FIT.

The reporting clause may also be an impersonal construction, but still expresses the character's stance: "but it appeared he was not in the mood to notice us" (*Jane Eyre* 1985 [1847]: 152). Although these are Jane's thoughts, which are not uttered in public, and "it appeared" is a clausal marker of stance, the reader gets the impression that she almost wishes to follow rules of social decorum and politeness in order to hide her irritation at Mr. Rochester's ignorance. Another feature which this example illustrates is the use of the pronoun *he* in the reporting clause, which is a statistically prominent linguistic feature in my corpus.

A stretch of IT also frequently contains the infinitive particle *to*, which realizes a stretch of IT if it is followed by a reporting clause, such as in "To see and explore either the ramparts and keep of the one, or the cloisters of the other, had been for many weeks a darling wish" (*Jane Eyre* 1985 [1817]: 149–150). In final position, the stretch "had been for many weeks a darling wish" functions as a reporting clause, and the construction beginning with "To see and explore" represents the reported clause. As mentioned, this infinitival construction may also be diagnostic of FIT. The difference between FIT and IT is that in FIT the reporting clause does not follow the infinitive construction. Admittedly, this complicates the automatic identification of such stretches including infinitival *to*, as they can be both IT and FIT.

Unlike IS, the classic examples of IT do not simply fulfill a summarizing function of a character's thoughts. We rather seem to be provided with the character's real thoughts and the apparent words that verbalize them by giving the illusion of verbatim repetition of processed words. IT is, however, less dramatic and less vivid than FIT because of the narrator's direct intervention through the reporting clause:

> "A porochial life, ma'am," continued Mr. Bumble, striking the table with his cane, "is a life of worrit, and vexation, and hardihood; but all public characters, as I may say, must suffer prosecution." Mrs. Mann, *not very well knowing what the beadle meant*, raised her hands with a look of sympathy, and sighed. (*Oliver Twist* 1993 [1837]: 119, my emphasis)

Mr. Bumble's comment is extensively stylized so that Mrs. Mann has difficulties in understanding him. Yet due to her subservience she does not ask the beadle about the content of his utterance. Instead, the narrator informs the reader about her lack of understanding through a stretch of IT "what the beadle meant," which is introduced by the reporting clause "not very well knowing." This deictic shift from speech to thought presentation affords another "deictic projection" (Stockwell 2002: 46) which the reader needs to perform to enter Mrs. Mann's reflections.

To conclude, IT usually presents a character's thoughts and does not just represent a summary of them. There are linguistic features particularly characteristic of IT which are foregrounded in IT constructions. Among them are the complementizer *that* and constructions beginning with infinitival *to*.

5.2.4.4. Narrator's Presentation of Thought Acts (NRTA)

Moving on to the more summarizing categories of thought presentation, I shall continue with a description of the types, distribution, and lexico-grammatical features as well as functions of NRTA. The category of NRTA consists of a transitive mental verb or a nominal construction, which is then followed by either a noun phrase or a prepositional phrase containing a noun phrase. Note the example from Brontë's (2009 [1847]) *Wuthering Heights*, quoted more fully later in this section, where Nelly reflects on Catherine's strange behavior: "I thought her conduct odd" (*Wuthering Heights* 2009 [1847]: 178).

NRTA is the most frequent category of thought presentation in my corpus—a result which stands in contrast to Semino and Short (2004), where NI dominates the rank scale. In my 19th-century corpus, NRTA receives 368 tags, which amounts to 7.3% of all tags. These are represented by 3,753 words, which is 6% of all words. The mean length of tags is 8.90 words per tag, so that it is on average the longest category on the thought presentation scale. In Semino and Short (2004: 117), NRTA comes on fourth position on the thought presentation scale (60 tags). With 9.41 words per tag, the mean length for each tag is slightly longer than in the 19th-century corpus.

A comparison of the stretches of NRTA with the nonfictional sub-corpus of CONCE reveals that the type *thought* (42.82), which can represent the noun *thought* or the verb in the past tense, is key. The same holds for the preposition *of* (42.32), which frequently follows the noun *thought*. Hence, it can be said that the construction *thought of* is, in addition to the other constructions identified in my corpus, a diagnostic marker of NRTA, such as in, for instance, "every thought of Mr. Thorpe's being in love with her" (*Emma* 1985 [1816]: 152) or "I thought of pursuing the devil" (*Frankenstein* 2003 [1818]: 78).

Although the notion of illocutionary force strictly speaking does not apply for NRTA, because it represents a thought act that is not communicative in the conventional, oral sense of the word, we can still see why NRTA is sometimes seen as a speech act or as a cognitive activity that is also presented as if it were spoken. NRTA does not contain an indication of the propositional content, but rather, someone performs mentally what would usually count as a speech act. NRTA is, however, less dramatic and less immediate than IT. When NRTA is used, there is also often a contrast between verbal behavior and private reflection (Semino and Short 2004: 130). It frequently occurs in the middle of the conversation and gives readers a brief insight into the thoughts that motivate the speech of one of the characters, as we have already seen:

> The following night she seemed more impatient still; and on the third from recovering my company she complained of a headache, and left me. *I thought her conduct odd*; and having remained alone a long while, I resolved on going and inquiring whether she were better, and asking her to come and lie on the sofa, instead of up-stairs in the dark. (*Wuthering Heights* 2009 [1847]: 216, my emphasis)

Nelly, as a homodiegetic narrator, considers Catherine's behavior abnormal, but she does not utter her strange feeling in public. Often, we also find mental acts addressed to somebody. NRTA can thus be seen as communicative in that it indicates to the reader what follows next. As such, it also has a prospective function because there is often more than one form of thought presentation in close proximity. NRTA may, for instance, introduce FIT.

To conclude, NRTA presents a summary of an assumed thought act that is realized by a variety of diagnostic lexico-grammatical features in the 19th-century corpus. It often occurs in immediate co-textual neighborhood to speech presentation scales to illustrate the contrast between speech and personal thought and opinion.

5.2.4.5. Narrator's Presentation of Thought (NT)

Narrator's presentation of/reference to thought (NT) is a category on the thought presentation scale which is newly introduced by Short (2007: 236). It constitutes straightforward thought presentation equivalences of NV and NW and should take their position on the thought presentation scale accordingly (Short 2007: 237). NT does not mention propositional content and does not stress illocutionary force. NT merely highlights the fact that a process of thinking takes place without specifying the contents of this thinking process, such as in stretches like "he began to think" in: "As he left the room, Lord Henry's heavy eyelids drooped, and he began to think" (*Picture of Dorian Gray* 1994 [1891]: 68).

NT is not very frequent in the 19th-century corpus, but it nevertheless occurs: only 36 tags (i.e., 0.7% of all the identified tags in the corpus) are stretches of NT. These are represented by 354 words, amounting to 0.6% of all the words in the corpus. The mean length is 9.8 words per tag. As Short newly introduced this category in 2007, there are no figures in the Semino and Short corpus of 2004, with which I compared my data.

In contrast to other thought or speech presentation modes, NT sets up a framework that may be contradicted by what follows it by means of speech. For instance, in the following example from Austen's *Emma* (1985 [1816]), the narrator's ironic comment on the alleged gravity of the situation is created through the exaggerated presentation of Frank's thoughts, on the one hand, and the fact that he is superficially presented as an accommodating and caring man, on the other. The stretch of NT in "He sat really lost in thought for the first few minutes" is to underline the extent to which Frank is overwhelmed by the decision he is forced to make. It also creates an atmosphere of silence and somewhat pompously prepares for his spoken utterance about leave-taking:

> He felt the going away almost too much to speak of it. His dejection was most evident. *He sat really lost in thought* for the first few minutes; and when rousing himself, it was only to say, "Of all horrid things, leave-taking is the worst." (*Emma* 1985 [1816]: 264, my emphasis)

The process of thinking without really informing the reader about the content of the thoughts is also exemplified in the following example:

> *But so active were her thoughts,* that when these inquiries were answered, she was hardly more assured than before, of Northanger Abbey having been a richly endowed convent at the time of the Reformation, of its having fallen into the hands of an ancestor of the Tilneys on its dissolution, of a large portion of the ancient building still making a part of the present dwelling although the rest was decayed, or of its standing low in a valley, sheltered from the north and east by rising woods of oak. (*Northanger Abbey* 1985 [1818]: 150, my emphasis)

The stretch of NT in "But so active were her thoughts" does not initially inform the reader about the exact content of Catherine's mental activity as it would have materialized in words. Instead, the stretch mainly underlines Catherine's agitation about going to Northanger Abbey. Also this stretch serves as a signpost that a thinking process is soon to take place through nouns like *thoughts, meditation, reflections* and verbs like *think.*

At the same time, NT functions to encapsulate (Sinclair 2004) a thinking process that has previously been presented in FIT. We have already encountered the following example in which thought presentation happens simultaneously to speech presentation, here in NV:

> She liked Mrs. Hale's double knitting far better; that was sensible of its kind. The room altogether was full of knick-knacks, which must take a long time to dust; and time to people of limited income was money. *She made all these reflections* as she was talking in her stately way to Mrs. Hale, and uttering all the stereotyped commonplaces that most people can find to say with their senses blindfolded. (*North and South* 2003 [1854]: 96–97)

That a stretch of NT also functions as a means of prospecting a longer stretch of thought presentation can also be seen in the example quoted at the beginning of this section: "As he left the room, Lord Henry's heavy eyelids drooped, and he began to think" (*Picture of Dorian Gray* 1994 [1891]: 68). This instance of NT is followed by a long stretch of FIT, in which Lord Henry muses about Dorian.

The following example of NT subtly creates a contrast between saying and thinking. Phillis does not dare to express his opinion on reading psalms, and even the reader is not informed about what he is actually thinking, because we only find "though I was thinking a great deal":

> "I dare say you railway gentlemen don't wind up the day with singing a psalm together," said he; "but it is not a bad practice—not a bad practice. We have had it a bit earlier to-day for hospitality's sake—that's all." I had nothing particular

to say to this, *though I was thinking a great deal.* (*Cousin Phillis* 1972 [1863]: 15–16, my emphasis)

Other manifestations of NT rely heavily on the metaphorical realization of this particular category, in which thinking is conceptualized as physical movement, as can be seen in the following examples: "So active were her thoughts" (*Northanger Abbey* 1985 [1818]: 150), "The multitude of feelings that crowded into my mind" (*Frankenstein* 2003 [1818]: 76), and "At those words, the truth rushed at last into my stupid old head" (*The Moonstone* 1998 [1868]: 142). That this is a very deeply ingrained conceptual metaphor can be seen from the fact that verbs of motion which metaphorically present cognition can already be found in Old English (Möhlig-Falke 2012: 183). The stretch of NT becomes personified, and the mind is described not only as being active and in movement, but also as being constantly in attention (OED s.v. *active* adj., 1.a.):

> But I did not feel the inconvenience of the weather; *my imagination was busy in scenes of evil and despair.* I considered the being whom I had cast among mankind, and endowed with the will and power to effect purposes of horror, such as the deed which he had now done, nearly in the light of my own vampire, my own spirit let loose from the grave, and forced to destroy all that was dear to me. (*Frankenstein* 2003 [1818]: 78, my emphasis)

To conclude, NT is a useful and revealing thought presentation category to illustrate a characters' mental and cognitive activities. It enables the narrator to realize the linguistic presentation of the simultaneous, complex, and non-linear interplay between what a character thinks and says at the same time. The fact that NT occurs in fictional samples of 19th-century narrative fiction illustrates the degree of sophistication with which 19th-century novelists were able to elaborate on that interplay.

5.2.4.6. Internal Narration (NI)

NI is on third place on the scale of thought presentation categories, following NRTA and IT. NI has been tagged 195 times in my corpus, which amounts to 3.9% of all identified tags. These are represented by 1,491 words, which is 2.4% of all words. Stretches of NI are rather short with a mean length of 7.64 words per tag, even though this is longer than the mean length of tags for the corresponding category on the speech presentation scale, NV, with on average 6.56 words per tag. NI further occurs more frequently and is represented by more words than NV, which occurs with 160 tags (i.e., 3.2% of all tags in the corpus) and 1,050 words (i.e., 1.7% of all words in the corpus).

In Semino and Short (2004), NI is the most frequent category (with 409 tags). NI is a summary of a character's mental state, and it remains to be discussed whether its high number corresponds to the high number of FIT tags in Semino and Short's (2004) corpus (see section 2.1.6 in Chapter 2). On average, the tag length for NI is much longer in the 20th-century corpus, amounting to 13.40 words per tag, as against 6.56 words per tag in the 19th-century data.

NI includes the presentation of mental states or a mind state and their changes. These involve cognitive and affective phenomena which do not amount to specific thoughts. Semino and Short (2004: 226) and Toolan (2001: 148) suggest that NI should be seen outside the thought presentation scale, because they present statements that the narrator makes about the inner world of the character. Further, they may be more straightforward minimal presentations of a character's thoughts leading to NT, or they may describe emotional processes or states that endure over a long period.

Short (2007: 236), however, stresses that NI describes an emotion which is related to the speaker's current context in the relevant fictional or nonfictional world. It can also be an emotional reaction triggered by cognitive processing. We often draw on our experience of our body and the physical world to talk about the less palpable domain of our mental and affective experiences.

Verbs and adjectives that normally project NI are, for instance, the nouns *fear* or *shock*, the verbs *petrify* or *unhappy*, or the adjectives *sad* or *grave*. In order to find more reliable semantic clues that would help identify stretches of NI, I ran my corpus of labeled sequences of NI through the semantic tagger of *Wmatrix* (Rayson 2018). By doing so, I attempted to classify NI diagnostics in a semantically more systematic way. Needless to say, I paid special attention to the historical meanings of the respective verbs, so contextualization is also of particular importance here. The software *Wmatrix* categorizes my NI diagnostics into the following semantic domains:

- fear/shock and bravery (*fear, terror, dread, petrify, startled*);
- state of being sad (*unhappy, sad, grave, remorseful, melancholy*);
- state of being content and happy (*glad, satisfied, proud, pleasure*);
- states of being interested, excited, energetic, and the opposite (*passion, excited, impress, passive*);
- something that is unexpected (*astonishment, amazed*);
- violence, anger (*angry, anger, vexation*);
- emotional experiences (*emotion, shudder, temper, feel*).

As discussed throughout this book, I attempt to perform a systematic and methodical analysis of discourse presentation categories by taking advantage of various software packages. More importantly, this classification appears to support certain claims that discourse presentation scholars have made with regard to thought presentation techniques in general. For instance, the preceding semantic classification confirms Palmer's (2004) claims in relation to the ample diversity of mental states capable of presenting thought in narrative fiction. These descriptions also often go hand in hand with some physical action, as shall be seen in the following. Again, as is the case for the rest of the thought presentation categories which are closer to the narrator end of the scale, the report of mental states is frequent and may have intermental and intramental (Palmer 2004: 224) effects on the presentation of the social mind of the reader.

Often, NI is used in contexts of narrative progression. This is irrespective of characters who are presented to be consciously aware of their feelings or to whom some mental state is attributed through observation. Emotional processes are also often expressed in line with body movements, reactions, or references to the senses:

> and when *I could hardly see the dark mountains; I felt still more gloomily*. The picture appeared a vast and dim scene of evil [. . .]. (*Frankenstein* 2003 [1818]: 76, my emphasis)

Here the stretch of NI "I felt still more gloomily" is accompanied by descriptions of how Frankenstein's eyes cannot see the mountains because the night is so dark. The Gothic description of the setting stirs up a deep-seated fear of the Creature and his brother's murder because this intramental state of mind is accompanied by a description of the setting that evokes certain scripts of the endangering, majestic, and overpowering Alps.

In Gaskell's (2007 [1853]) *Cranford*, physical action and body movements are used to describe Miss Matty's state of mind after she is informed about Mr. Holbrook's death:

> I saw *Miss Matty could not speak, she was trembling so nervously*; so I said what I really felt; [. . .] But the effort at self-control Miss Matty had made to conceal her feelings—concealment she practised even with me, for she has never alluded to Mr. Holbrook again, although the book he gave her lies with her Bible on the little table by her bedside; she did not think I heard her when she asked the little milliner of Cranford to make her caps something like the Honourable Mrs Jamieson's, or that I notices the reply—
>
> "But she wears widows' caps, ma'am?"
>
> "Oh! I only meant something in that style; not widows', of course, but rather like Mrs Jamieson's."
>
> The effort at concealment was the beginning of *the tremulous motion of head and hands* which I have seen ever since in Miss Matty. (*Cranford* 2007 [1853]: 48, my emphasis)

This passage abounds in complex presentations of discourse modes, which move between the description of thought to that of speech and back to that of thought. They construe Miss Matty's state of mind, both from an intramental and intermental (Palmer 2004: 226) perspective. What construes her feeling is not a description of "inner speech," but a description of her body movement as in "she was trembling so nervously" and the narrator's observations that she "could not speak," which allow the reader to infer how much she must be in shock. A description of a shivering woman activates a schema of either fear or devastation which the reader can draw on. This narrative description therefore also contains a description of her state of mind. Within the narrative, there is some group dynamics as well because the narrator Mary is also affected. She feels so sorry for Miss Matty that she—almost on Miss Matty's behalf—expresses "what I really felt." Here we can see the synergetic effect of a presentation of an intermental state of mind and how it affects Miss Matty's outward appearance and her behavior (reported about in anecdotal DS in the incident about the caps) as well as that of the others surrounding her. Hence, presentations of states of mind can never be seen in isolation as they are social and dialogic (Palmer 2010). Notice also the cohesive lexical ties that are created through the repetition of verbs and nouns referring to states of mind in "feeling" or "concealment," which is taken up again in "the effort of concealment." Palmer (2004: 224) is therefore right to stress that mental states are often accompanied by physical action (see also Chapter 7), which can be caused by and emerge from emotions and feelings.

To conclude, this section has illustrated that it is possible to further categorize passages of NI according to whether they refer to expectations, psychological actions, or positive and negative emotions. It has also illustrated that this report of a state of mind is dialogic and contextual and can serve as both prospecting and encapsulating both physical and mental action.

5.3. Subcategories of Speech, Writing, and Thought Presentation

The following section outlines the interpretative complexities of ambiguous speech, writing, and thought presentation, addressing those stretches of discourse presentation which cannot be unambiguously assigned to a specific category, but which seem to belong to more than one. These ambiguous cases may either be categorized as two categories on the same discourse presentation scale, but they may also move between two categories on two different scales of discourse presentation or even narration. The following chapter will furthermore analyze how hypothetical speech, writing, and thought presentation is realized in the 19th-century corpus of narrative fiction. Embedded speech presentation, which would be another topic worth pursuing, is treated in Busse (2010) to which the reader is kindly referred. This study uses the same corpus to quantitatively and qualitatively outline the types, distributions, and functions of embedded discourse presentation, drawing on a cognitive stylistic framework.

5.3.1. Ambiguous Tags

Stretches of discourse presentation which are ambiguous between different categories are relevant to discuss in order to fully understand the workings of discourse presentation in 19th-century narrative fiction. This chapter will show that, contrary to what Fludernik (1993) claims, it is not only possible but also profitable to take account of ambiguous cases in a corpus-based approach, and all but "useless for interpretation" (Fludernik 1993: 9).

Four percent of all identified tags in the 19th-century corpus must be classified as ambiguous, which is a lower percentage than the 9.3% of ambiguous cases found by Semino and Short (2004: 183) in their 20th-century data. All in all, I have identified 88 different ambiguous categories. These fluctuate between different categories. Among the more frequent ones are instances fluctuating between FIS-FIT (4), N-FIS (5), N-NI (14), N-NRSA (5), N-NV (6), and NI-NT (5). Fluctuation between N-FIT, with 45 instances, occurs most frequently.

In evaluating these cases, it is useful to differentiate between those that involve two adjacent categories on the same scale and those that involve non-adjacent categories on the same and from different scales of speech, writing, and thought presentation.

Most of the ambiguous cases seem to fall between the narration (N) and free indirect categories, be they free indirect speech, thought, or writing. An example from Austen's *Emma* (1985 [1816]: 265) may illustrate this: "A few awkward moments passed, and he sat down again." The second part of this sentence is paralinguistic narration ("and he sat down"). The first part may, however, function as both narration and FIT, due to the adjective "awkward," which could be either attributed to Emma's thinking processes or to the narrator's comment on the situation. Such ambiguity between the free indirect forms of discourse presentation and narration has often been noted, especially in discussions of thought presentation in fictional narratives (Fludernik 1993: 149–151; Leech and Short 1981: 339–340; Toolan 2001: 131).

Another borderline case between N-FIS may be seen in the following example: "On the morrow they were to commence their journey. The fair of Frankfort, which had now lasted nearly a month, was at its close" (*Vivian Grey* 2004 [1826]: 181). These words could be understood as being words uttered by the Baron, but they might also be understood as a comment by the third-person narrator.

Tags fluctuating between N and free direct forms are less frequent. Rather more frequent is ambiguity between adjacent categories on the same scales, such as N-NRSA. Consider, for instance, "and showed him, with great attention and respect, to the house" (*Oliver Twist* 1993 [1837]: 119). In this example, it is not fully apparent whether speech is involved at all.

Ambiguity between non-adjacent categories presents more challenges for the analyst, as one has to decide whether the stretch in question is speech, thought, or writing presentation. We find, for example, stretches containing possible IS-IT or NRTA-NRSA or NRSA-NRWA cases. The implications as to how the reader processes these may be deeply significant for the interpretation of the text. For instance, in "for the death of Sir Danvers was resented as a public injury" (*Dr. Jekyll and Mr. Hyde* 2003 [1886]: 71), the question is whether this is a report of a speech act or a general report of a writing act.

We also find examples in the corpus where an ambiguity exists between a stretch of FIS-FIT. Thus, in "I expected Miss Matty to jump at this invitation; but, no! Miss Pole and I had the greatest difficulties in persuading her to go" (*Cranford* 2007 [1853]: 48), the first stretch consists of NRT and IT. The stretch "but no!" can be either attributed to the narrator or to an emotional outburst on Miss Matty's part, which is reported about by the narrator.

As regards adjacent categories, they may occur on all levels of discourse presentation. For example, in "But the effort at self-control Miss Matty had made to conceal her feelings" (*Cranford* 2007 [1853]: 48), the stretch "the effort at self-control Miss Matty had made" may be a stretch of NRTA or a stretch of NRT introducing IT. The last part of that example, "to conceal her feeling," could be understood as the narrator's description of Miss Matty's feelings, which would turn that stretch into either NI or N; additionally, it could also be a stretch of embedded NT, in which it is indicated that a thinking process is taking place. As can be seen, the characterization of these cases gives rise to a lot of interpretative work which also attests to the richness of the narrative itself.

Other ambiguous cases shift between the adjacent categories of NV and NRSA. Thus, in "Upon this we all took courage to unite a confirmatory murmur" (*Great Expectations* 1999 [1860]: 177), the question is whether "we all took courage to unite a confirmatory murmur" is just the utterance of a voice, which would, however, include a confirmatory speech act indicated by the adjective "confirmatory."

When NI-NRTA occur in an ambiguous tag, it is often difficult to distinguish whether a real act of thinking has taken place, or whether just a mental process is being reported. Thus, in "his wish of staying longer, evidently did not please" (*Emma* 1985 [1816]: 262), the stretch "evidently did not please" can be described as just a state of mind, but it may also imply a thinking process with a thought act.

The fact that these ambiguous cases exist also illustrates the narratological move in presenting the complexity of discourse presentation, which is reinforced through the frequent ambiguity between the N and FIT categories. The distinction between free indirect and free direct forms is more pronounced in the 19th-century corpus than in Semino and Short's (2004: 197) corpus of 20th-century narrative fiction, but fuzziness may also exist between adjacent categories in the latter, for example N-NV, or NV-NRSA categories.

5.3.2. Hypothetical Speech, Writing, and Thought Presentation

Presentation of hypothetical speech, writing, and thought refers to instances of discourse presentation which refer to the future, are counterfactual, or imaginary. Few studies have focused on this phenomenon so far (see Fludernik 1993; Semino and Short 2004: 153–200; Sternberg 1982a, 1982b; Tannen 1989), and often their focus lies on hypothetical discourse presentation with IS or IT presentation as hosts, that is, the originating discourse presentation mode.[6] Furthermore, it appears that instances of hypothetical writing presentation are rarely included. Tannen (1989: 14–16), for instance, provides real-life examples involving the verbalization of other people's thoughts or reactions, whereas Fludernik (1993) discusses fictional extracts where thoughts, reactions, and attitudes are imputed to others in the form of direct discourse and FID.

Although hypothetical discourse presentation covers a wide range of phenomena, what unites the variety of incidences is their common ontological status, that is, they are explicitly presented as occurring not in what counts as the actual world of the text, but in non-actual scenarios of various kinds.

Semino and Short (2004: 160) present a "typology" of hypothetical discourse presentation, distinguishing between the typical scenarios of presenting potential speech, thought, or writing. The presentation of wishes, obligations (rules), intentions, predictions, and interpretations of the verbal and nonverbal behavior of others, where statements may also count as predictions, is strongly related to this. In addition, Semino and Short (2004: 163) also find cases in their corpus in which future utterances (i.e., somebody being surprised about something in the future) are reported. These are less obvious cases because the narrator or reporter guesses what could be thought, but the function is also to present somebody's thoughts in a dramatic and lively way. Negative meaning and expressions may also entail hypothetical discourse presentation, because negation is not actual and therefore tagged as hypothetical.[7]

The analysis of 19th-century narrative fiction reveals instances of hypothetical speech presentation. To begin with a typical case of speech speculation, consider the following excerpt from Hardy's *Jude the Obscure* (1975 [1891]: 190):

> "What's the matter, Jude?" she said suddenly. He was leaning with his elbows on the table and his chin on his hands, looking into a futurity which seemed to be sketched out on the tablecloth. "Oh—nothing!" "You are 'father,' you know. That's what they call the man who gives you away." *Jude could have said "Phillotson's age entitles him to be called that!"* But he would not annoy her by such a cheap retort. (*Jude the Obscure* 1975 [1891]: 190, my emphasis)

So far, I have discussed a variety of examples from this novel where Jude's thoughts are clearly presented in contrast to what he subsequently verbalizes for reasons often related to politeness constraints and 19th-century social decorum. This discrepancy between what is said and what is thought is constructed in an even more vivid and lively manner. To use concepts from Text World Theory (Werth 1999; Gavins 2007), one could argue that the world-switch from DS to a hypothetical stretch of DS, which is introduced by the reporting conditional clause "Jude could have said," creates a sense of immediacy, which the reader has to process through the switch to the epistemic modal *could have said*. The focus of attention is now in the enactor's deictic center and a situation remote from their originating world is being described. Jude's potential reply is expressed in hypothetical form, as one of the few incidences of hypothetical DS: "Phillotson's age entitles him to be called that!" The narration then shifts back to that of the narrator, who comments on Jude's thoughts and creates another negated epistemic modal-world through "But he would not annoy her by such a cheap retort." The narrator is in the know about Jude's real feelings about Sue's marriage and therefore illustrates the complexities of communication between two potential lovers who are not allowed to admit their real feelings. As an interpretation of someone's nonverbal behavior, this is also an incident of "intersemiotic transfer" (Sternberg 1982a: 134), which involves the verbalization of mute reality and gives a sense of immediacy and drama (Sternberg 1982a: 135).

Hypothetical discourse presentation is also frequently introduced as counterfactual with the help of *as if* clusters (see Mahlberg 2007a, 2007b, 2013). In the following example, the stretches in italics are NRSAh: "and her lips suddenly parted *as if she were going to avow something.* But she went on; and whatever she had meant to say remained unspoken" (*Jude the Obscure* 1975 [1891]: 193, my emphasis). This shows that Sue is almost about to admit her real feelings for Jude, but in the end, remains silent. The stretch "whatever she had meant to say," which oscillates between hypothetical NRSA and IS, is equally hypothetical (despite not being introduced by *as if*) because a potential speech act is immediately denied through the morphological negation in "unspoken." Both sentences shift again from the thoughts of the character to the narrator's.

In the following example from Austen's (1985 [1818]) *Northanger Abbey*, a hypothetical NRSA in "many were the inquiries" is partly topicalized through moving the adjective *many* to the front of the sentence in order to somehow stress Catherine's urge in wanting to know everything about Northanger Abbey: "Many were the inquiries she was eager to make of Miss Tilney; But so active were her thoughts, that when these inquiries were answered" (*Northanger Abbey* 1985 [1818]: 150). The noun "inquiries" specifies only the speech act, but the exact content is not given. Catherine's alleged eagerness, however, is immediately refuted by means of the conjunction *but*, which as a coordinating conjunction construes contrast, while from a textual point of view, it creates coherence (Biber et al. 1999: 81). It could be argued that both topicalization and the past-tense attitudinal marker "was eager" lead the reader to assume that Catherine does not really ask all those questions and that she is not really listening to Mrs. Tilney's replies, because her imagination has gone wild. This is subtly but effectively indicated through the use of *but*, marking a move to her thoughts through the metaphorical NT instance "but so active were her thoughts," in which thought is conceptualized as movement. In "'But I thought, Isabella, you had something in particular to tell me?' 'Oh! Yes, and so I have. But here is a proof of what I was saying'" (*Northanger Abbey* (1985 [1818]: 151–152), Catherine reminds Isabella of a particular incident she had meant to talk about to Catherine. At this point in time, it is still hypothetical and therefore not part of the actual world because Isabella has not yet told Catherine about John's letter and his love for Catherine.

Due to the fact that hypothetical discourse presentation is not part of the actual world that is reported or described, it can be assumed that there are linguistic expressions marking counterfactuality, such as *as if*, or conditional auxiliary verbs, which point to the introduction of hypothetical speech, that is, to the world-switch to an epistemic modal world. They are therefore also relevant to what Toolan has defined as narrative progression (Toolan 2009). To identify their diagnostic features, I extracted all stretches of hypothetical discourse presentation. Again, I compared these with the fictional sub-corpus of CONCE, and the results confirm the keyness of the conjunction *if* with a value of 24.04.

Table 5.1 provides the raw numbers and percentages of tags of hypothetical discourse presentation in relation to the overall number of discourse

TABLE 5.1 Figures for Hypothetical Discourse Presentation in the 19th-Century Corpus

DISCOURSE PRESENTATION MODE	HYPOTHETICAL	HYPOTHETICAL / INFERRED	EMBEDDED / HYPOTHETICAL	RAW NUMBERS	PERCENTAGES COMPARED TO OVERALL DISCOURSE PRESENTATION
NV	4	0	9	13	0%
NRSA	11	1	52	64	0.3%
IS	3	0	13	16	1.3%
FIS	0	0	0	0	0.3%
DS	3	0	2	5	0%
FDS	0	0	0	0	0.1%
NI	5	0	3	8	0.2%
NT	1	1	1	3	0.1%
NRTA	10	2	19	31	0.6%
IT	7	1	9	17	0.3%
FIT	0	0	0	0	0%
DT	0	1	0	1	0%
FDT	0	0	0	0	0%
NW	0	0	2	2	0%
NRWA	0	0	6	6	0%
IW	0	0	2	2	0%
FIW	0	0	0	0	0%
DW	0	0	0	0	0%
FDW	0	0	0	0	0%
Total	44	6	118	168	3.3%
Percentages of Hypothetical Discourse Presentation	26.2%	3.6%	70.2%		

presentation tags in the respective categories of speech, writing, and thought presentation.

As Table 5.1 reveals, hypothetical discourse presentation is not frequent in the corpus. Only 3.3% of all identified tags mark a presentation of hypothetical speech, writing, or thought presentation. Yet, hypothetical discourse presentation is more frequent than in the 20th-century corpus, where 2% of all tags in the entire corpus are hypothetical (393 tags, with only 110 of them occurring in the fictional sub-corpus; see Semino and Short 2004: 169). Hence, it can be said that 19th-century narrative fiction contains more speculation of what somebody else may or might have said, thought, or written, or will say, think, or write. Also, it seems that there is relatively more hypothetical *thought* presentation in the 19th-century corpus than there is in Semino and Short's corpus (Semino and Short 2004: 159–163). In my corpus, of the overall occurrence of hypothetical discourse presentation, 45.2% belong to hypothetical speech presentation, 35.7% belong to hypothetical thought presentation, and only 6%

belong to hypothetical writing presentation, although it should be borne in mind that the raw figures for the respective tags are very low.

Further, hypothetical discourse presentation is also more frequently embedded in my 19th-century corpus than in the 20th-century corpus. In Semino and Short (2004), about 63% of hypothetical cases are embedded, with about 67% of all cases of embedded hypothetical discourse presentation occurring in speech presentation. In my 19th-century corpus, a similar tendency can be observed: embedding is most frequent in hypothetical speech presentation, with 70.2% of all hypothetical tags being embedded, that is, a higher percentage than in 20th-century writing.

All the subcategories of hypothetical discourse presentation that occur in the 20th-century corpus of narrative fiction also appear in the 19th-century corpus. Generally speaking, hypothetical discourse presentation renders the presentation of other-people's speech, thought, or writing more fine-grained and complex. As far as this study is concerned, the identification of these subcategories further reinforces 19th-century idiosyncrasies, as they become the linguistic materialization of external concerns, such as attempts at presenting the human psyche and the complexities of human communication.

Semino and Short (2004: 167) claim that all categories of speech presentation in their corpus can be turned into hypotheticals. It appears that hypothetical speech presentation in the 20th-century corpus tends to occur mainly as NRSAh, with FISh having the fewest instances. DS and FDS together make up half of all the hypothetical forms in the 20th-century corpus. In my own analysis of 19th-century narrative fiction, I find that almost all categories of speech presentation occur as hypotheticals with the exception of FIS and FDS, because the free indirect forms of speech presentation are more difficult to present as hypothetical than those categories that have a discourse-summarizing function. NRSAh is by far the most frequent category of hypothetical speech presentation, and the same holds true for NRTAh. The hypothetical categories which are at the left-hand side of the discourse presentation model, that is, those categories which are closer to the narrator, are easier to embed because they consist of compressed forms which do not, for instance, include the exact words a character might have used.

The fact that there is more hypothetical thought presentation in the 19th-century corpus than in the 20th-century corpus seems to highlight the role of omniscient narrators having access to the thoughts of characters. Equally, as mentioned before, these results also support 19th-century concerns with the psyche, as authors were eager to illustrate linguistically impossible ontological leaps in which narrators do not simply verbalize what people think, but also hypothetically speculate with regard to what they may have thought.

From a theoretical point of view, instances of hypothetical discourse reporting have been used to refute the notion of faithfulness. Because they are explicitly expressed as something that is not part of the actual world, faithfulness and its relevance for determining the ontological status of a discourse report have been questioned. However, I comply with Semino and Short (2004: 167) in stressing that the occurrence of hypothetical discourse presentation is not frequent enough to be used as a line of argument against the concept of faithfulness.

5.4. Summary and Further Reflections

This chapter has so far discussed the modes of speech, writing, and thought presentation in quantitative and qualitative contexts. It has established the quantitative distribution of the scales of discourse presentation and their respective modes. Generally speaking, in the 19th-century data the distribution is similar to that of 20th-century narrative fiction, as outlined by Semino and Short (2004), but there are fewer tags identifying discourse presentation, which means that there is more narration. And yet the average length of sentences realizing discourse presentation is longer than in the 20th-century corpus. The distribution of the different modes of discourse presentation has been placed within the 19th-century context, showing, for instance, a preponderance with the psyche and consciousness, illustrations of fictional minds, and narrating as a response to coeval 19th-century theories of vision and the psyche.

All modes on the different scales have been analyzed in detail and their quantitative occurrences have been compared with those in 20th-century narrative fiction. The categories have proven to be of sufficient robustness to analyze the discourse presentation modes in the 19th-century narrative corpus. Identifying repetitive patterns on the lexico-grammatical and pragmatic levels, following Hoey's (2005) approach of lexical priming, is a novice way of measuring and describing the interplay between function and form in this complex discoursal framework. This procedure enhances a reader-oriented approach to explaining narrative progression (Toolan 2009) and the role of discourse presentation in it.

Some of the findings obtained correlate with those in Semino and Short (2004). Thus, for instance, in both corpora DS is the norm for speech presentation. In other cases, it was necessary to elaborate on the Semino and Short (2004) framework, such as for NI, where subcategories that embrace different kinds of internal narration are suggested.

As an afterthought to the quantitative investigation of discourse presentation categories identified in the 19th-century corpus of narrative fiction, a few comments on the interplay between discourse presentation scales, on the one hand, and the—more functionally situated—notion of speech, writing, and thought summary, on the other, is in order. The following stretch of discourse presentation from Dickens's (1993 [1837]: 123–124) *Oliver Twist* may serve as an example of how stretches of discourse presentation can be identified as representing a particular mode of discourse presentation and, at the same time, function as a summary of antecedent speech, thought or writing:

</sptag>
<sptag cat=N w=4>
It would be tedious
</sptag>
<sptag cat=NVh who=A next=NRTA w=6>
if given in the beadle's words:
</sptag>
<sptag cat=N w=1>
occupying,
</sptag>
<sptag cat=NRSA who=A w=3>
as it did,
</sptag>
<sptag cat=N w=3>
some twenty minutes
</sptag>
<sptag cat=NV-NRSA who=A w=3>
in the telling;
</sptag>
<sptag cat=NRSA-NRS who=A A w=8>
but the sum and substance of it was,
</sptag>
<sptag cat=IS who=A next=N w=60>
that Oliver was a foundling, born of low and vicious parents. That he had, from his birth, displayed no better qualities than treachery, ingratitude, and malice. That he had terminated his brief career in the place of his birth, by making a sanguinary and cowardly attack on an unoffending lad, and running away in the night-time from his master's house.
(*Oliver Twist* 1993 [1837]: 123-124)

Structurally speaking, the stretches "if given in the beadle's words" and "in the telling" are examples of hypothetical NV for the former and a mixture of NV and NRSA for the latter. These stretches, however, also clearly mention that speech takes place or that a story is told. In fact, the content is summarized, or an announcement of a summary of the content is given, which is then followed by "that Oliver was a foundling, born of low and vicious parents [. . .]," etc. The narrator comments on the beadle's verbosity by saying that "it would be tedious if given in the beadle's words, occupying as it did, some twenty minutes." In other words, the narrator only provides some of the obviously more relevant bits of information in IS.

Short (2012) suggests a distinction between speech and writing summary scales, which go hand in hand with the speech and writing presentation scales, to account for the fact that much of speech and writing presentation is a summary of an antecedent discourse and not always faithful to the exact words used by the speaker. The speech summary scale (and the writing summary scale, accordingly) is parallel to the speech presentation scale in terms of categories, but with different effects. For the summary scales, the faithfulness categories apply only in terms of content that is reported about. As such, the categories can be ambiguous between speech presentation and speech summary.

Short's argument relies on the fact that for speech presentation, especially in NRSA, the notion of a summary is most obviously apparent. In addition, there is always a domain above the proposition, which may be an entire conversation, or a whole text or part of one, as illustrated in the examples mentioned earlier. For the speech presentation scale, it has conventionally been assumed that a single proposition is its domain. This is why whatever is presented in a particular mode of speech presentation is a translation from an antecedent discourse. Further, the concept of faithfulness is most prevalent here.

Although the present study has applied the faithfulness claim on a structural level, as it serves as a useful aid for the annotation process, the notion of faithfulness has also been criticized with respect to narrative fiction because it cannot be assumed that there is any antecedent discourse. What is crucial in discourse presentation is how the report of others' speech, thought, or writing is presented, that is, which mode is chosen. One could say that there are different ways as to how a speech event is translated into one of the speech presentation modes and that these different ways may also contain summaries of antecedent texts or discourses, which are then translated into IS, DS, or FDS, and so on. At the same time, there are different ways—that is, styles—of how speech can be summarized.

The question here is whether it can be justified to say that all discourse modes contain an aspect of summary. Perhaps both discourse presentation and discourse summary interact, because embedding takes place, too—to the extent that a narrator chooses to summarize an allegedly antecedent speech event and may also summarize parts of the antecedent discourse. Pragmatic inference is necessary to identify the discourse presentation category and to determine the effects of the discourse presentation mode chosen, as well as what is presented within. Often this is ambiguous. Again, one should ask whether the notion of faithfulness is not simply too strong and dominating, as it blurs the strategies and styles of conventional "polishing up" or bowdlerism of what has been said before.

Another general question that forces itself on the analyzer is what exactly we need to code in the annotations: is it the structure itself or its effects? This dilemma is most prevalent in discourse presentation, where we may get several levels of embedded discourse presentation, as in, for instance, Brontë's (2009 [1847]) *Wuthering Heights*. Here, one level of discourse presentation is

Nelly telling Heathcliffe and Catherine's story to Mr. Lockwood. Other levels are those that report on their discoursal interactions, for example.

The discussion of embedded discourse presentation is closely followed by whether thought can be summarized at all. In classical narratological theory, the assumption has prevailed for a long time that the categories that are applied to fictional speech can easily be transferred to the presentation of fictional thought. As mentioned, Fludernik (1993: 281) calls this the "direct discourse fallacy," that is, the constant equation of thought with speech or "inner speech," and the overestimation of the verbal component in thought (Palmer 2004: 71). Chatman (1978: 182) points out that the "most obvious and direct means of handling the thoughts of a character is to treat them as 'unspoken speech.'" As discussed before (see section 5.2.4), in the 19th-century corpus the modes of thought presentation that occur most frequently are those that—structurally speaking—are situated on the narrator end of the scale, already containing an element of summary. It can thus be argued that the direct discourse fallacy does not hold and that, following Palmer (2004), this approach does not do justice to the complex workings of the fictional mind and consciousness because it ignores the presentation of beliefs, intentions, purposes, and dispositions (see also Cohn 1978: 61). As Palmer (2004, 2010) stresses, the mind is active and social; presentations of consciousness through the variety of discourse presentation modes that characters are attributed with have to be seen in interaction with those of other, preceding discourses, and so on. As such, the more diegetic forms of thought as well as speech report are not necessarily privileged over the more mimetic—and at times more "glamorous" (Palmer 2004: 57)—forms of FIT. Speech, thought, and writing reports—that is, for instance, NV, NI, and NW, or NRSA, NRTA, and NRWA—are equally important.

Especially for thought reports, it is necessary to notice that states of mind are being portrayed—rather than summarized. These strategies contribute equally well, if not more effectively than a description of a flow of consciousness, to characterization.

In addition, what is often labeled as "inner speech"—that is, DT or FIT—often receives most attention because of its seeming similarity with speech, but may nevertheless be too one-dimensional. As Palmer (2004: 183–184) notes, all discourse presentation modes have to be treated equally within a framework of characters' minds in action, which may consist of the following components: "the total perceptual cognitive viewpoint; ideological worldview; memories of the past; and the set of beliefs, desires, intentions, motives, and plans for the future of each character in the story as presented in the discourse" (Palmer 2004: 183–184).

CHAPTER 6 | Toward Developing a Procedure for Automatically Identifying Speech, Writing, and Thought Presentation

SEMINO AND SHORT (2004: 27–39) explain that due to the discourse complexity of presenting other persons' speech, thought, or writing, it is difficult to find automatic procedures for this kind of identification, especially when it comes to categories that are structurally "in-between," such as FIT and FIS, and because of the fact that both structural and functional criteria are needed to identify different modes of discourse presentation. They also stress, however, that their definitions for the respective categories can serve as starting points for an automatic annotation of discourse presentation (Semino and Short 2004: 224).

6.1. *Preliminaries*

This section will illustrate that although discourse presentation in 19th-century narrative fiction is a highly complex discoursal phenomenon in need of contextual qualitative analysis, it is possible to identify repetitive lexico-grammatical features and to set up some rules for the automatic annotation of discourse presentation, based on the manual annotation of this corpus. The detecting procedures take account of the variety of modes of speech, writing, and thought presentation. The purpose of this analysis is to facilitate to a considerable degree the laborious and time-consuming manual annotation procedure.

Preliminary work on the automatic identification of discourse presentation has been done by Ostdijk (1990) as well as Dodgson (1995). De Haan (1996, 1997) elaborates on the typical features of dialogue: lexical density, sentence structure, word order, and length of utterance. Axelsson (2009) focuses on the challenges of automatically tagging DS and calls for corpora that include information about and annotations for DS. Mamede and Chaleira (2004) use rule-based systems for segmentation and classification in their attempt to automatically tag direct and indirect discourse in Portuguese children stories.

Speech, Writing, and Thought Presentation in 19th-Century Narrative Fiction. Beatrix Busse,
Oxford University Press (2020). © Oxford University Press.
DOI: 10.1093/oso/9780190212360.001.0001

Elson and McKeown (2010) apply a machine-learning approach for quoted speech attribution to speakers in news reports and literature. McCarthy and O'Keefe (2012) show how quotes can be extracted and attributed. They use rule-based systems for segmentation and classify them for machine-learning algorithms.

Brunner (2013, 2015) applies Semino and Short's (2004) model of discourse presentation for the tagging of contemporary German narrative fiction. Using both a rule-based system and a machine-learning approach, she stresses that a rule-based approach is more useful for automatic tagging for so-called clear surface structures like DS, while so-called recognizers based on machine-learning are more useful for the free indirect forms (Brunner 2013: 572). On the basis of the complete Charles Dickens's corpus of narrative fiction, Mahlberg and Smith (2010) have developed some procedures to automatically identify sequences of discourse presentation in quotation marks, but, it should be noted that these can be direct speech, writing, or thought presentation; the script also annotates "suspensions," that is, annotations of a character's speech through the narrator.

In Chapter 3, I suggested a five-step qualitative procedure for the manual annotation of speech, writing, and thought presentation, which as an analytical tool is recommended to be carried out during the manual annotation of discourse presentation. Thus, I suggest that it should at first be decided whether a stretch of texts is speech, writing, or thought presentation, or narration. If it is a form of discourse presentation, then the annotator can decide which category of the scale is used and how many words the stretch comprises. Such a procedure would not work for the automatic annotation of discourse presentation because the system, that is, the respective algorithms, first need to be fed by specific knowledge of the respective categories on each scale. Hence, an initial identification of whether a stretch of discourse is speech, writing, or thought presentation, or narration, would include too high a rate of error. Manual annotation must therefore be differentiated from the procedures, which should help to develop an algorithm for automatically annotating stretches of discourse presentation and which I am going to suggest in this chapter. These procedures are based on the quantitative and qualitative results of the investigation that have suggested a number of structural and functional parameters, such as the average length of the different categories on each scale, the keywords detected, the use of modality and negation, lexico-grammatical and even pragmatic observations.

In addition to the implementation of an algorithm for the automatic annotation of discourse presentation, one would also have to consider how an automatic annotation system needs to be modeled, a question that is also addressed by some of the studies mentioned earlier. From the perspectives of natural language and machine-learning approaches, this includes considerations about how to segment individual stretches of discourse presentation and how to classify them. These are probably two processes that run synchronously during cognitive processing and of which an automatic procedure must take account.

It is not my intention to test the advantages and disadvantages of rule-based systems, machine-learning approaches, or a combination of both. Rather, this chapter will suggest procedures that help to classify and annotate the specific categories, which in turn will then serve as the basis for specific feature extraction processes that may support the development of algorithms for the automatic annotation of discourse presentation.

6.2. *The Procedure*

To begin, I suggest that the annotation of the corpus is initially enhanced by running the corpus through a POS (Parts of Speech) tagger using CLAWS (Garside et al. 1987) and a semantic tagger such as that built into *Wmatrix* (Rayson 2018), because particular word forms mark particular stretches of discourse presentation. For historical data, this tagging needs to be proofread to confirm their historical accuracy. It is most likely that this process is also enhanced by a segmentation of the respective text into units like sentence, clause, or utterance, the usefulness of which probably requires further testing.

Despite the fact that speech presentation is the most frequent of all discourse presentation scales in the 19th- and 20th-century data, it still makes sense to begin the automatic annotation procedure with the identification of the direct and free direct forms of speech, writing, and thought presentation, that is, (F)DS, (F)DW, and (F)DT. These are easiest to detect because of the typographical marking by quotation marks, which can be looked for at the beginning and end of a stretch (cf. Mahlberg and Smith 2010). For the direct stretches (DS, DW, and DT) an additional marker is the reporting clause accompanying them.

In order to differentiate (free) direct speech from (free) direct thought or writing presentation, it is necessary to include in the automatic annotation process the repetitive lexico-grammatical features that have been identified and have turned out to be diagnostic of (F)DS, (F)DT, or (F)DW, respectively. For DT, for instance, such keywords are first- and second-person pronouns as well as personal names, which can either be used as third-person references or as vocatives to address the interlocutor in the exchange that is reported. In a corpus, these can be tagged through POS tagging. If used as vocative forms, personal names fulfill a transactional function—and in Toolan's (2009: 144) terms a prospective function, because the reader expects a reciprocity in address term usage. In addition, an address term is interpersonally related to the speaker whose words are presented (Busse 2006).

Other address forms that have been identified as key in the 19th-century corpus are *sir* and variants of *madam*. Hence, they mark spoken conversation or adjacency pairs, often characterized by reciprocity. If these forms are automatically annotated in a corpus, they serve as signifiers or boundary markers for DS and FDS, because they often—however, not exclusively—begin or terminate a stretch of direct speech.

Further interactional features that have been identified as key in (F)DS and can be used for automatic annotation are the discourse marker *well* and the deictic marker *here*, which can also be automatically searched. Other constructions are the use of the copula verb *be* followed by an adjective and sometimes a clause.

Pauses are indicated by dashes, as seen, for instance, in the 19th-century grammar by Brown (1860; see section 5.1 in Chapter 5 of this volume). Another characteristic feature, which is also typical of present-day spoken English (Biber et al. 1999: 159), is the use of negation (and here a distinction has to be made between whether negation occurs in FIT or in stretches of reported DS or FDS, where it is a frequent phenomenon). The search thus needs to detect forms of negated *n't* and *not*. Further, the modals *will, shall*, and *can* are key in stretches of DS and can be identified automatically.

Stance and other modal forms by which speakers express their attitude are equally crucial. Among the key terms identified is the verb *know*, but there is a range of forms, such as *indeed, I like, I know, no doubt, I am afraid*, or *I daresay*, which may also appear (see Biber et al. 1999 for a typology of these stance expressions). We also find *yes*- and *no*-particles, and elliptic sentences. These features are so characteristic of DS/FDS that they can be seen as a set of parameters that need to be fulfilled for a stretch of discourse to be labeled as DS/FDS. It would appear, therefore, that the presence of quotation marks is but the starting point in the identification of speech categories.

For those stretches of discourse presentation with direct speech, thought, or writing that are not free, it is assumed that usually a reporting stretch/clause is present, which in turn facilitates their automatic searching. The presence of reporting clauses also enables the analyst to differentiate between direct *speech* (DS) presentation that is not free and direct *thought* (DT) presentation that is not free, because the reporting clauses are different. The step of detecting surrounding reporting clauses should thus follow the step of searching for interactional and transactional characteristics in the direct versions of speech presentation (also to possibly distinguish the free from the not-free direct passages).

For 19th-century narrative fiction, an inventory of reporting verbs introducing speech, writing, or thought presentation can be established (see section 7.1 in Chapter 7). Keeping in mind that some of these reporting constructions only seem to have validity for 19th-century English (because of language change), reporting verbs for speech presentation have been categorized following Caldas-Coulthard's (1994) typology (an annotation that could also be done for other types of verbs and could be incorporated in the automatic algorithms for annotation). For speech, these are all verbs that denote verbal activities. A modified and historically informed semantic tagging, already partly realizable in *Wmatrix*, would be able to enhance this kind of search. Other reporting constructions begin with a form of *be* and are followed by another reference to verbal activities, such as *words* or the rejoinder in "were her words."

Reporting clauses, as seen in section 7.1 in Chapter 7, may interrupt a pres entation of DS after one word, for instance in order to identify the speaker, as in "'Come on,' said he, 'you are anxious for a compliment,'" and to insert what some have called "suspensions" (Mahlberg and Smith 2010). It was possible to measure the average length of reporting stretches (see section 7.1 in Chapter 7). These interruptions of a stretch of DS realized as reporting clauses can be put in relation to the length of the reported clause, as well as the use of commas if one uses modern editions, where DS is frequently marked by quotation marks and reporting clauses are separated by commas (which can be seen in my corpus as well as in 19th-century grammars). Length of both the reported and the reporting clauses can then be included in the automatic annotation process, because they could be defined as stretches that are not allowed to be longer than four to five words. In addition, as will be further detailed in Chapter 7, there is a striking interplay between stretches of reporting clauses and paralinguistic features—that is, references to the speaker's eye and body movements or bodily reactions. These paralinguistic features frequently follow the finite stretch of the reporting verb by means of a nonfinite participle construction as in "said Emma, laughing" (*Emma* 1985 [1816]). These observations concerning a more systematic analysis of reporting clauses can serve as a further guide for automatic annotation. Here I will include Mahlberg's (2007a, 2007b, 2013) observations about repetitive three- to five-word clusters, which may also appear in reporting clauses (see also CLiC, i.e., *Corpus Linguistics in Context*, Mahlberg 2016, http://clic.bham.ac.uk/).

A note on *say* as the most ubiquitous reporting verb is in order because in its past-tense form it is also the most frequent verb prospecting speech presentation; that is, it is the default marker and could be programmed that way. Sometimes, however, we also find constructions like *said to himself* where the *said to*-construction is followed by a reflexive pronoun and hence seen as diagnostic of NRT.

The automatic annotation of stretches of DS and FDS should be followed by the identification of stretches of NV and NRSA. In NV, references are made to verbal activities with, for instance, the lexeme *word* at the center (as in *said these words*, or *to have a word or two*). Three other keywords that are identified as indicating NV are *voice(s)*, *spoke*, and *conversation*. These again represent guidelines for programming the algorithms.

While NV only reports about minimal verbal activities, NRSA mentions the speech act as well as the subject (realized as a nominal group) that is talked about. Therefore, speech act verbs and other linguistic realizations of speech acts can be used as diagnostics for the identification of NRSA. Among them are verbs that indicate a turn in, or that structure, a conversation. These are, for instance, verbs like *commence*, followed by a noun phrase such as *his story*. Some of these forms also contain a reference to phatic communion, realized through a greeting such as *welcome*, for instance. Other keywords are the verb *called*, and the nouns *answer* and *question*. *Say* also introduces NRSA when it is followed by a nominal group.

Another diagnostic feature of stretches of NRSA are (coordinating) conjunctions, such as *and, but,* and *after,* which can be used as clear linguistic markers for the script.

Moving from NV and NRSA to IS, we can say that the identification of reporting clauses introducing (direct or indirect) speech now needs to be modified, because the reporting verb is generally followed by quotation marks (to indicate DS) or complementizers, such as *if, that,* or *whether* (to indicate IS). In the 19th-century corpus of narrative fiction the complementizer *that* is far more frequent in stretches of IS than *if* or *whether,* for instance. In addition, *that* is typically followed by a pronoun, existential *there,* the determiner *this,* a proper noun, or a *wh*-pronoun. The reported clause of IS will also contain pronouns like *his, her, them, it,* or *mine* followed by a modal verb like *would* or a past form of *be* and *have.* Further, third-person pronouns are key (being overrepresented when compared to first-person singular or plural pronouns). Another diagnostic feature that marks IS is the use of the past tense.

The automatic identification of FIS seems to be a challenging task because it is not easy to differentiate it from stretches of FIT and sometimes even from IT. For instance, in the sentence "She thought it was improper" (*Cranford* 2007 [1853]: 38) contextual information is needed to identify this stretch as FIS rather than as consisting of a reporting clause "she thought" and the reported clause "it was improper." Because of the few examples of FIS in the corpus it is difficult to form any generalizations. Yet, it can be said that the past-tense form of verbs as well as the use of auxiliaries in the past-tense form are characteristic of FIS. Another striking feature is the repetition of some constructions such as that beginning with the *to*-particle, or the repetition of similar syntactic structures such as noun phrases. In the following I will elaborate on the ways these diagnostics can be discriminated against their use to encode FIT.

The step of identifying and tagging stretches of writing presentation should follow the step of identifying speech presentation. For automatically identifying the different modes of writing presentation, it is particularly helpful to draw on semantic fields that denote writing. I suggest to begin the automatic tagging process with labeling stretches of DW presentation that are marked by quotation marks, but—compared to DS/FDS and DT/FDT—the surrounding reporting clauses are of a different kind. They contain verbs such as *wrote* or references to a letter, a message, or a note (see section 7.1 in Chapter 7).

Stretches of DW are usually rather long, with a mean length of about 21 words, and they typically include references to proper nouns (personal names and place names), which can be automatically searched for in a POS-tagged corpus. FDW is rather rare in my corpus because usually the narrator uses a reporting clause for reasons of prospecting to the reader that a stretch of writing presentation follows.

NW simply mentions that some writing process has taken place without reference to the writing act. In the 19th-century corpus, the mean length of these stretches is 7.1 words per tag. Nouns like *note, letter,* and *message* are key and can be used as guidelines for the automatic identification of these stretches.

The mean length of NRWA stretches is 8.8 words per tag. Representative realizations are "accepting" and "thanking for an invitation" or "receiving news." To identify stretches of IW, the reporting stretches need to be labeled first. Stretches of IW usually contain past-tense forms and a surrounding reporting stretch. FIW instances are as difficult to identify as stretches of FIT and FIS. However, FIW is frequently introduced or prospected by a stretch of NV and therefore it makes sense to investigate the surrounding sentences, too.

The final step of the automatic annotation is the identification of the different modes of thought presentation. Although instances of DT and FDT are not particularly frequent, the tagging should begin with stretches of DT and FDT, as these can frequently be identified by means of quotation marks. Note also that, despite the fact that stretches of DS/FDS and of DT/FDT will by now have been identified, the problem remains as to how to distinguish stretches of FDT from stretches of FDS and FDW, respectively. Instances of DT are surrounded by reporting clauses, which are marked by keywords such as *thought, felt,* or *think.* In addition, these reporting stretches indicating thought presentation can also be introduced by verbs of communication co-occurring with a reflexive pronoun in examples such as *said to himself.*

Except for the different reporting clauses that introduce DT and FDT as opposed to DS/DW and FDS/FDW another way of discriminating these direct modes of speech and thought presentation against one another is also their length. In my corpus, stretches of FDT are much shorter (with a mean length of 9.6 words per tag) than stretches of FDS and DS.

To achieve an accurate reading of NI instances, it makes sense to draw on some of the semantic domains identified by the *Wmatrix* tagger. Because of its functions, NI ensues that special attention should be paid to the semantic fields of *fear* and *shock, sadness, contentment, happiness,* and those referring to the display of interest. Such an analysis will have to be adjusted to account for historical data. Other semantic domains which will be of help are those referring to psychological and emotional experiences, *liking* and *dislike.*

Stretches of NT are realized by constructions like *began to think,* but they may also be more metaphorically realized by formulations like *so active were her thoughts,* which include a reference to the semantic domains of motion and activity. Verbs to search for are *verba sentiendi.* In addition, the nouns *thought* and *reflections* are further diagnostic markers, with *thought* typically occurring in such constructions as *lost in thought.*

NRTA can be identified when the algorithm searches for *verba sentiendi* and accompanying noun phrases. Verbs classified as *verba sentiendi* are, for instance, *think, feel, imagine, conceive, consider, suppose, believe,* or *trust.* The construction *thought of* is key and therefore also diagnostic of NRTA. Adjectival constructions containing *excited* or *impressed* can be searched for as well. As described earlier, Toolan (2009) suggests a rather comprehensive list of diagnostics inclusive of, for instance, the verbs *thought, knew,* and *wondered,* or relevant modalizing verbs such as *know, think, seem, appear, suspect, expect, want, need, see, look, wonder*, and *believe*.

IT is easiest to identify if the reporting clause occurs at the beginning of the sentence and literally introduces the reported stretch of IT. It is especially the complementizer *that* which is diagnostic of the reported clause in IT.

Stretches of FIT contain the highest number of words of all instances of thought presentation in the corpus. Their mean length is 22.3 words per tag. Earlier I have described in detail Toolan's (2009: 135) three-stage procedure for the identification of FIT, as well as the fact that he stresses that these procedures do not necessarily help to distinguish FIT from FIS (see sections 2.1.6 in Chapter 2 and 5.2.4.2 in Chapter 5). Some of the diagnostics he describes are, for instance, the presence of a pronoun co-occurring with a modal (which must be in direct proximity), but he also highlights that certain constructions should be excluded from being diagnostics of FIT, such as instances of non-inverted subject plus modal plus *not* or *n't*.

Mention has been made of the fact that in my corpus the past-tense forms of *be, seem*, and *have* are key, which suggests that they can be used as clear diagnostic markers for FIT. In contrast to DT and FDT, instances of FIT are marked by reference to a third-person (possessive) pronoun (with the first-person pronouns being underrepresented, see section 5.2.4.2 in Chapter 5). Further constructions that can be searched for are *it was* [. . .], *it seemed* [. . .], and *there was* [. . .].

The co-occurrence of a personal pronoun in direct proximity with a past-tense modal like *can, could, should, might*, and *must* is also diagnostic of FIT in the 19th-century corpus. However, complementizers, such as *if, that*, or *whether*, need to be excluded. Stance adverbials indicating attitude will also serve as further markers of FIT alongside discourse markers and interjections, such as *oh, alas, god help me, yes*, or *no*. Furthermore, in the 19th-century corpus, nonfinite constructions beginning with initial *to*, as in "to receive so flattering an invitation" can equally be searched for, especially because these constructions are also often repeated.

It has been mentioned that in FIT nominal group structures are often repeated (see section 5.2.4.2 in Chapter 5). It would therefore be useful to be able to search for incomplete sentences that consist of repetitions of noun phrases. Such a search will also account for the fact that nominal groups are often topicalized in stretches of FIT in so-called header-tail constructions (Carter and McCarthy 2006: 782), such as "The Tilneys, they [. . .]" (*Northanger Abbey* 1985 [1818]: 149). For identifying header-tail constructions, a nominal group can be searched that co-occurs with the anaphorical personal pronoun. Further, instances of FIT most likely occur with flanking sentences that report a thinking process.

This section has proposed a number of formal diagnostic features for the identification of discourse presentation and some procedures to help to automatically detect stretches of discourse presentation in a corpus of narrative fiction. It has to be kept in mind, however, that the procedures suggested here do not capture all relevant instances of discourse presentation and that manual checking that includes contextual information is paramount to achieve full coverage. Further, the suggested procedures may not always reliably indicate the scope of a stretch of discourse presentation, for instance, if it stretches out over more than one sentence. However, the procedures described in the preceding may serve as starting points for a new tool that allows for the automatic identification of discourse presentation or which can be adopted to programs like *Wmatrix* (Rayson 2018) and *WordSmith Tools* (Scott 2017; see also Toolan 2009: 143).

CHAPTER 7 Narrative Progression and Characterization

The Functional Interplay between Narration and Discourse Presentation

THIS CHAPTER FOCUSES ON the functional interplay between passages of narration in close proximity to and therefore interplaying with different modes of discourse presentation. My aim is to show how the interplay between narrative stretches and speech, writing, and thought presentation may be linguistically realized in 19th-century narrative fiction and what functional potential for narrative progression (Toolan 2009, 2016) and characterization (Culpeper 2001; McIntyre 2015) this interchange may have. A focus will be on (a) the lexico-grammatical variety of reporting verbs that accompany direct and indirect forms of speech, writing, and thought presentation; (b) what I will call paralinguistic narration, that is, on those narrative stretches that describe mime, gesture, and body movement, as well as moments of silence, and interact with discourse presentation modes; and (c) foregrounded occurrences of passages of visual narration and discourse presentation.

Sinclair's (2004) concept of "trusting the text," as outlined in section 2.4.1 of Chapter 2, serves as the theoretical basis for the description of the interplay between context/narration, on the one hand, and discourse presentation, on the other. In this chapter, I illustrate how the interaction between these two complex modes is structured by encapsulation and prospection and how it contributes to narrative progression. Narrative progression is the way in which readers are guided by specific lexico-grammatical choices and how these may also prompt suspense, surprise, and secrecy that are also included in reader's expectations (Mahlberg 2012; Toolan 2009, 2016). This interplay not only informs the reader about the narrator's controlling comments, but also illustrates how this is influenced by, for instance, guiding and leading readers' evaluation of the characters, or by overseeing characters' communicative interactions and thoughts, by what is summarized or constitutes a reference to what has already been there. In turn, what comes next in fictional texts

Speech, Writing, and Thought Presentation in 19th-Century Narrative Fiction. Beatrix Busse, Oxford University Press (2020). © Oxford University Press.
DOI: 10.1093/oso/9780190212360.001.0001

is constrained by some structural, lexical, contextual, and functional principles and parameters, if coherence is safeguarded. Due to the fact that particular grammatical, syntactic, and pragmatic patterns prime narrative stretches, the reader is able to identify them as such and use them as anchor points for the processing of the narrative in general. Via recourse to quantitative methodology, that is, for instance, the identification of keywords in these stretches, it is possible to draw some conclusions about particular 19th-century strategies of world creation.

7.1. Reporting Strategies of NRS, NRT, and NRW and Discourse Presentation

I start by briefly summarizing issues related to the formal structure of reporting verbs and reporting clauses and then elaborate on their functional potential. Reporting verbs or other linguistic realizations of signaling reports are usually tied to the direct and indirect scales and categories of discourse presentation, but not to the free modes of discourse presentation, such as FIT. As mentioned before, the relation between the reporting clause—also called "inquit clause" or "framing clause" (Toolan 2001: 120)—and the reported clause differs between indirect and direct discourse. In indirect discourse, their syntactic connection is realized by hypotaxis, whereas in direct discourse, the two stretches are paratactically connected (Toolan 2001: 126; Halliday and Matthiessen 2014: 446). As explained in section 6.2 of Chapter 6, I have tagged reporting clauses separately—not only in order to facilitate their analysis and that of the categories they "introduce" (especially with regard to word counts and the adoption of tags), but also because of the function of reporting verbs as a way to evaluate or to describe the speech of others. Thus, reporting verbs "do not constitute part of the SW&TP scales themselves, but are effectively part of the narration which introduces adjacent discourse presentation categories" (Semino and Short 2004: 36).

There are other ways of indicating that the reporting stretch and reporting clauses can vary in their grammatical structure, as Thompson (1996) and others (e.g., Jucker 2006) have observed: "The ways in which the reporter can signal that the hearer or reader is to understand a stretch of language as a report are far more varied than simply the traditional reporting clause" (Thompson 1996: 518). Thompson includes here reporting clauses, reporting adjuncts, reporting nouns, reporting adjectives, and reporting verbs (Thompson 1996: 518). This variability can also be found in reporting clauses introducing DS or IS in the 19th-century corpus. Thus, we find, for instance, "'Dear Miss Woodhouse'—and 'Dear Miss Woodhouse,' *was all that Harriet*, with many tender embraces *could articulate at first*" (*Emma* 1985 [1816]: 99, my emphasis), which is a deviation from the usual reporting verb because it contains a form of the copula verb *be* almost "delaying" the reporting, and a complex NP inclusive of a relative clause containing the verb *articulate*, which signals to the reader that the preceding stretch is actually direct speech presentation. By ridiculing Harriet's failure in articulating her feelings properly, it also foregrounds Emma's natural belief in the sincerity of people's words, in this case Mr. Elton's charade.

In Brontë's *Jane Eyre*, "'Madam, I should like some tea,' was the sole rejoinder she got" (*Jane Eyre* 1985 [1847]: 152) illustrates Mr. Rochester's wish to silence Mrs. Fairfax as well as to stress his authority. In both cases the copula verb *be* is connected to a nominal group or a noun, and it is the combination of *be* and the subsequent NP, whose semantic content must include some reference to an act of uttering in some shape or form, that really functions in place of a reporting verb.

NRS, NRT, and NRW tags were counted by separating the stretches of reporting from those stretches in which discourse is reported in either direct or indirect discourse presentation. A prototypical example of a reporting verb as part of a reporting clause in direct speech (DS) presentation can be found in Austen's *Emma* (1985 [1816]) in "'Emma knows I never flatter her,' said Mr. Knightley" (*Emma* 1985 [1816]: 42). The reporting clause "said Mr. Knightley" is a finite clause containing the prototypical reporting verb *say*. In this example, the reporting clause follows the reported clause.

Reporting clauses can also occur in the middle or at the beginning of a stretch of discourse presentation. In the conventional case of indirect speech (IS) presentation, the position of the reporting clause is usually more restricted to the beginning, as in "Once more, I stammered with difficulty that I had no objection" (*Great Expectations* 1999 [1860]: 109). The reporting clause contains the finite verb *stammer*, and the reported clause is introduced by the conjunction *that*.

Table 7.1 illustrates the number of tags that account for the distribution of reporting signals in my corpus. NRS tags are the most frequent reporting signals (12.4%), followed by NRT tags with 6.2%. Only 0.7% of all identified tags are stretches of NRW. As previously stated, these results confirm that speech presentation in general and DS in particular are the most frequent discourse presentation modes in this corpus.

Comparing the stretches of identified NRS with the nonfictional subcorpus of CONCE allows me to identify keywords in 19th-century stretches of reporting clauses that mark speech presentation, and it also allows me to contextualize these statistics further. One particular form, the past tense form of the reporting verb *say* (that is, *said*), stands out with a keyness value of 450.56. A second key form is *replied*, with a keyness value of 166.77. Further key verbs are:

- *cried* (95.19)
- *inquired* (94.15)
- *asked* (61.08)
- *returned* (47.88)
- *continued* (46.23)

TABLE 7.1 Percentages and Raw Figures Identified for NRS, NRT, NRW, Narration, and Ambiguous Categories

DISCOURSE PRESENTATION MODE	NARRATION	NRS	NRT	NRW	TOTAL
Pure	594	498	194	24	1,310
Embedded	2	98	67	8	175
Hypothetical	0	6	7	0	13
Hypothetical / inferred	0	0	4	0	4
Embedded / hypothetical	0	18	12	4	34
Embedded / hypothetical / inferred	0	0	1	0	1
Inferred	0	1	9	0	10
Embedded / inferred	0	1	18	0	19
Total	596	622	312	36	1,566
Percentages within corpus	11.9%	12.4%	6.2%	0.7%	35.2%
Percentages among narration categories	33.7%	35.2%	17.7%	2%	100%

– *answered* (42.72)
– *added* (39.34)
– *faltered* (37.52)
– *growled* (37.52)
– *retorted* (37.52)
– *remarked* (31.53)
– *resumed* (24.66).

Stretches of NRS appear to occur more frequently than the copula constructions mentioned before. Segundo (2016) illustrates both the type and token number of reporting verbs for DS in selected works of Dickens's narrative fiction. He shows that Dickens shows a preference for the reporting verbs *replied* and *returned* to embrace DS. In my corpus, which contains two of Dickens's novels, *replied* is key on second position, following *cried*. *Returned* is key, too. *Answered*, being infrequent in Dickens's work, is nevertheless frequent in my corpus.

Caldas-Coulthard (1988, 1994) devises a typology of reporting verbs which is based on Modern English. Her taxonomy consists of the following categories:

1) neutral structuring verbs such as *say*, *tell*, or *ask*;
2) metapropositional verbs which label and categorize the contribution of a speaker. These consist of (1) assertives such as *agree*, (2) directives such as *urge*, and (3) expressives such as *confess*.
3) metalinguistic verbs such as *narrate*, *quote* or *recount*;
4) descriptive verbs, which are either prosodic, such as *cry*, *intone*, *shout*, or paralinguistic, such as *whisper*, *murmur*, and *groan*, and function as voice qualifiers or voice qualification;

5) transcript verbs which are discourse-signaling rather than speech-reporting; they accompany DS and mark the relationship of a quote to other parts of the discourse.

Applying Caldas-Coulthard's categorization with due caution, I find that most of the key verbs identified for stretches of NRS in 19th-century narratives can be classified either as neutral verbs (*said* or *asked*) or transcript verbs, that is, they are discourse signaling rather than speech reporting (e.g., *returned, continued,* or *added*). This shows that reporting verbs are mainly used to identify the speaker, to attribute turn-taking characteristics to the discourse that is presented, and, at times, also to identify the illocutionary force of the reported clause. The verbs listed earlier may thus be classified as follows:

- *cried*: descriptive
- *inquired*: neutral
- *asked*: neutral
- *returned*: transcript
- *continued*: transcript
- *answered*: neutral
- *added*: transcript
- *faltered*: transcript
- *growled*: descriptive
- *retorted*: transcript
- *remarked*: neutral
- *resumed*: transcript.

In the comparison of the stretches of NRS with the fictional sub-corpus of CONCE, the keyness of the reporting verb *said* interestingly increases from 450.56 (when compared to the nonfictional sub-corpus) to 861.14. This allows me to tentatively argue that—in comparison to the CONCE corpus—*said* is used frequently. It also testifies to the high occurrence of DS in my corpus. It could also be tentatively argued that the texts in my corpus seem to not only proportionally use more examples of DS, but also accompany these with the reporting verb *said*.

Further reporting verbs with high keyness value are:

- *replied* (77.41)
- *asked* (70.49)
- *inquired* (62.16)
- *exclaimed* (46.28)
- *cried* (39.46)
- *answered* (37.93)
- *returned* (31.32)
- *continued* (36.30)
- *remarked* (26.01).

These comparisons show two more interesting features that highlight the ways that reference is made to the respective speaker in reporting clauses introducing DS and IS. When the stretches of NRS are compared with the non-fictional sub-corpus of CONCE, personal names or titles are key:

- *Bumble* (212.76)
- *Mann* (150.15)
- *Wopsle* (125.12)
- *Utterson* (87.57)
- *Mr.* (83.90).

In addition, references to personal pronouns in subjective case are equally key:

- *she* (132.04)
- *he* (85.97).

When the stretches of NRS are compared with the fictional sub-corpus of CONCE, the following remain key:

- *Mr.* (110.63)
- *Mrs.* (50.28)
- *Bumble* (106.62)
- *Mann* (75.23)
- *Wopsle* (62.68)
- *Mary* (50.14)
- *Utterson* (43.87).

These key terms therefore seem to illustrate a trend toward personalization in my corpus. Furthermore, they highlight person deixis in the reporting stretches, with pronouns in subjective case being key and serving to identify the speaker. Admittedly, it could be argued that the proper names in the preceding list are key in the target corpus simply because they are absent from the two reference sub-corpora. Yet, there is no denying that, first, personal names and titles are generally frequent and that with their help, direct reference is made to the speakers of the various DS/IS stretches; second, it would also appear that readers are expected to recognize speakers by means of referential cohesion when a personal pronoun is used.

Identification of the verbal constructions that constitute NRS and that collocate with either personal names or personal pronouns is of crucial importance for the automatic annotation of stretches of discourse presentation and narrative contextual information. It also allows us to draw some general conclusions about the characteristic patterns of NRS.

The following list contains samples of linguistic constructions for NRS in my corpus and the raw token frequencies with which they occur:

said 232	*was* 13	*exclaimed* 10
replied 20	*cried* 12	*returned* 10
asked 16	*inquired* 11	*say* 9

continued 8
added 7
answered 7
had 6
says 6
remarked 5
began 4
repeated 4
reply 4
asking 3
crying 3
faltered 3
growled 3
observed 3
paused 3
pursued 3
resumed 3
retorted 3
telling 3
told 3
assured 2
beginning 2
bellowed 2
demanded 2
is 2
looking 2
may 2
pleaded 2
question 2
rejoined 2
requested 2
rising 2
saying 2
wanted 2
went 2
addressing 1
affirmed 1
agree 1
allowed 1
appeared 1
arrived 1
bade 1
begged 1
begun 1
bid 1
blushing 1
breaking 1
brought 1
calling 1
coined 1
command 1
commenced 1
conjecture 1
considered 1
cry 1
daresay 1
declare 1
declared 1
declined 1
determined 1
directed 1
discerned 1
drawing 1
elevating 1
embarrassed 1
emphasis 1
fated 1
feigning 1
found 1
giving 1
have 1
hearing 1
hesitate 1
holding 1
interjected 1
interposed 1
interrupting 1
judged 1
kept 1
known 1
means 1
muttered 1
offered 1
opening 1
ordered 1
persuaded 1
pointing 1
pressing 1
promise 1
put 1
questioned 1
quoth 1
rage 1
reflected 1
reflectively 1
refused 1
rejoinder 1
relaxing 1
running 1
show 1
shrill 1
shutting 1
sighs 1
silence 1
smiles 1
smiling 1
soothe 1
speaking 1
spoke 1
stammered 1
starting 1
striking 1
suggesting 1
talk 1
tell 1
threatened 1
tone 1
tried 1
turning 1
used 1
venturing 1
waggish 1
walked 1
warrant 1
whimpering 1
whispered 1
withdrawing 1
wondering 1
worked 1
wrinkles 1

There are a number of studies of Present-Day English that have analyzed which functions reporting verbs have for discourse presentation, mostly for (direct) speech presentation (Caldas-Coulthard 1988; Goossens 1990; Kissine 2010; Klamer 2000; Mahlberg 2013; Rudzka-Ostyn 1988; Urban and Ruppenhofer 2001; Segundo 2016; Zwicky 1971). The identified functions comprise individualization of characters in general, or their voices, mime, gesture, or movement in particular, further specification of narrator's stance, exemplification of the faithfulness claim, and marking of narrative progression.

With recourse to an example from Austen's *Emma* (1985 [1816]), the qualitative functional potential of *say* is used in the following to illustrate that—despite its ubiquity, which might be used as an argument for its functional frozenness—*say* may occur at stylistically prominent turns (which go beyond the function of re-identifying the speaker) to foreground[1] (Douthwaite 2000) the respective framing clause in relation to the reported clause and thus behaves like a vocative (Busse 2006). The relationship between the different discourse modes, the speech act accompanying DS, and its interaction with the reporting verb is crucial. It appears as if the narrator playfully compensated for a lack of a variety of reporting verbs by introducing the speech act verb *say*. Thus, in this example, Mr. Knightley ironically praises Emma's achievements to educate and upgrade Harriet's social performance:

> "Come," said he, "you are anxious for a compliment, so I will tell you that you have improved her. You have cured her of her school-girl's giggle; she really does you credit." (*Emma* 1985 [1816]: 85)

The example is part of the initial verbal fencing between Emma and Mr. Knightley. The reporting clause interrupts the exclamative "Come" and—apart from identifying the speaker—also prepares for and foregrounds what he has to say, namely that he looks through Emma and that he knows how sure she is of her success. Furthermore, the reporting verb *say* stresses the expressive speech act in "Come" (Searle 1976).

The reporting clause in the example just quoted is foregrounded (Douthwaite 2000), because its role goes beyond that of the ostensive—that is, to show that the projected clause follows. It adds an additional interpersonal dimension which goes beyond speaker identification and rather underlines the fact that the reported clause retains all the interactive features of the clause as exchange (the full mood potential, etc.). Hence the functional orientation of the overall effect is also relevant to the indication of perspectives as used by the narrator or reporter and the speaker, and as transferred to the recipient who perceives both reporting clause and reported clause.

An example from Austen's *Pride and Prejudice* (1994 [1813]) may further illustrate the complex functionality of reporting verbs:

> "Mr. Darcy is all politeness," said Elizabeth, smiling. (*Pride and Prejudice* 1994 [1813]: 23)

This example illustrates that the posterior position of the frequently occurring reporting verb *say* appears to add the narrator's ironic tone to the declarative; not only because it is Elizabeth who has now politely denied Mr. Darcy's wish to dance with her, but also because, after a set of uncommented free direct speech (FDS) utterances, it is the narrator again who comments—as part of the narration—on the discourse presentation and on how Elizabeth phrases her evaluation of Mr. Darcy. Simultaneously, the narrator reinforces both the fact that the direct string exactly reports the structures as well as the words used by the character and the speech act value, the propositional content, the words and the grammatical structures, which are claimed to have been used to utter the propositional content and associated speech act. Hence, the degree of faithfulness is particularly high and the presentation chosen contributes to the vividness and dramatization of the speech act, but also to its irony.

So far, many of the studies that analyze reporting clauses have looked at reporting stretches for direct and indirect speech presentation that is not free. In contrast to this, the tagging system in my corpus allows me to analyze reporting clauses for thought presentation as well. Direct forms of thought and speech show a character's words without internal amendment, and it seems that the narrator moves away from the quoted utterance, which expresses purely the character's viewpoint. However, since the framing clause unambiguously anchors or attributes the clause to a particular character as the source of that speech or thought, that particular character is also identified. Hence, the controlling teller stands always behind it, especially if stretches of DS are set in sharply evaluative framing contexts (Toolan 2001: 129).

When compared with the fictional sub-corpus of CONCE, the following keywords are identified in stretches of NRT that embrace both DT and IT:

- *thought* (257.23)
- *felt* (56.34)
- *seemed* (49.32)
- *thinkest* (39.93)
- *think* (39.30)
- *wished* (38.45)
- *knew* (35.39)
- *resolved* (35.32)
- *remembered* (34.37)
- *determined* (33.57)
- *convinced* (26.17).

When compared to the nonfictional sub-corpus of CONCE, the following words are key:

- *thought* (207.60)
- *think* (49.64)
- *wished* (39.87)
- *seemed* (32.00)
- *felt* (26.27).

It is obvious that only particular verbs of feeling are key and are frequently used in 19th-century discourse presentation, while others seem to refer to verbal processes that are turned into reporting stretches to introduce thought presentation. The following list shows linguistic constructions of stretches of NRT that embrace DT or IT, together with their raw numbers of occurrences in the corpus:

thought 45
think 18
could 12
felt 11
seemed 10
knew 9
know 8
wished 7
determined 6
might 6
suppose 6
remember 5
remembered 5
convinced 4
doubt 4
hope 4
resolved 4
began 3
fancied 3
like 3
said 3
saw 3
seeing 3
thinkest 3
appeared 2
believe 2
believed 2
considered 2
cried 2
desired 2
expected 2
feel 2
find 2
finding 2
help 2
hoping 2
knowing 2
led 2

let 2
liked 2
made 2
mind 2
perceive 2
preferred 2
see 2
seems 2
sure 2
surprised 2
suspect 2
uncertain 2
wish 2
wonder 2
wondering 2
acknowledge 1
added 1
appears 1
asked 1
asking 1
aware 1
begin 1
beginning 1
belongs 1
bid 1
came 1
change 1
compelled 1
compels 1
completed 1
composed 1
conjectured 1
consider 1
decided 1
delighted 1
*deny*1
deplored 1
doubting 1

dread 1
dreamt 1
endeavoured 1
express 1
failed 1
favoured 1
fear 1
feeling 1
foresaw 1
forgetting 1
granted 1
guessed 1
hold 1
imagine 1
imagining 1
informed 1
intended 1
intending 1
interested 1
intimation 1
learn 1
learns 1
leave 1
left 1
longed 1
marvelled 1
may 1
mock 1
moved 1
observed 1
observing 1
persuaded 1
pray 1
prepared 1
prophesied 1
raised 1
recognised 1
recollect 1

recollection 1
reflecting 1
refrained 1
rejoice 1
relieved 1
remarked 1
remembering 1
remembers 1
replied 1
return 1
say 1
says 1
scrip 1
seen 1
signified 1
sought 1
startled 1
stood 1
striving 1
strong 1
taken 1
taking 1
tempted 1
thinking 1
touch 1
trained 1
understand 1
urged 1
use 1
wanted 1
wanting 1
warned 1
wishing 1
wondered 1

Here are two examples that illustrate how NRT stretches embrace DT or IT. In the example from *Emma*, it is interesting that the position of the reporting clause appears to be less fixed than in the indirect version:

> "To fall in with each other on such an errand as this," *thought Emma*; "to meet in a charitable scheme; this will bring a great increase of love on each side. I should not wonder if it were to bring on the declaration. It must, if I were not here. I wish I were anywhere else." (*Emma* 1985 [1816]: 112, my emphasis)

The NRT stretch "thought Emma" separates the initial passage of DT from the following, which is longer than the first part of the infinitival passage of DT. The function of the NRT stretch is to show the reader that these are Emma's thoughts and not her words.

The following example is more complex in that the position of the reporting clause appears to have the function of foregrounding Emma's thought process. It is preceded by a number of rather more summarizing stretches of DS from Mr. Knightley, who condescendingly muses about typical characteristics of a ball:

> "[. . .] Fine dancing, I believe, like virtue, must be its own reward. Those who are standing by are usually thinking of something very different."
>
> *This Emma felt was aimed at her*; and it made her quite angry. It was not in compliment to Jane Fairfax however that he was so indifferent, or so indignant; he was not guided by *her* feelings in reprobating the ball, for *she* enjoyed the thought of it to an extraordinary degree. It made her animated—open hearted—she voluntarily said. (*Emma* 1985 [1816]: 262–263, first italics my emphasis, second in the original)

The question arises as to whether the sentence "This Emma felt was aimed at her" is indirect thought (IT) or free indirect thought (FIT), a mixture of both, or simply the narrator speaking. The reporting clause is "Emma felt" and it is in medial position. It foregrounds the demonstrative deictic pronoun *this*, which appears to be stranded—anaphoric and therewith encapsulating Mr. Knightley's utterance. The rephrasing to "This was aimed at her, Emma felt" helps understand the meaningful choice that is made. "This" would be part of IT and "Emma felt" a stretch of NRT. Because of its unusual position, the stretch "was aimed at her" is either IT or FIT in the original. The annotation process highlights the effect of interpreting IT and FIT pragmatically. It allows the reader to zoom into her thinking process, first through FIT and only then the reader is informed that it is Emma thinking—and no longer Mr. Knightley.

In the following (already discussed) example from *Emma*, the initial reporting clause "was her immediate exclamation" interrupts Emma's initial vocatival outburst and, as a textual caesura, foregrounds her indignation and her emotional restlessness:

> "Insufferable woman!" *was her immediate exclamation.* "Worse than I had supposed. Absolutely insufferable! Knightley!—I could not have believed it. Knightley!—never seen him in her life before, and call him Knightley!—and discover that he is a gentleman! A little upstart, vulgar being, with her Mr. E., and her *caro sposo*, and her resources, and all her airs of pert pretension and underbred finery. Actually to discover that Mr. Knightley is a gentleman! I doubt whether he will return the compliment, and discover her to be a lady. I could not have believed it! And to propose that she and I should unite to form a musical club! One would fancy we were bosom friends! And Mrs. Weston!—Astonished that the person who had brought me up should be a gentlewoman! Worse and worse. I never met with her equal. Much beyond my hopes. Harriet is disgraced by any comparison. Oh! what would Frank Churchill say to her, if he were here? How angry and how diverted he would be! Ah! there I am—thinking of him directly. Always the first person to be thought of! How I catch myself out! Frank Churchill comes as regularly into my mind!"—
>
> *All this ran so glibly through her thoughts*, that by the time her father had arranged himself, after the bustle of the Eltons' departure, and was ready to speak, she was very tolerably capable of attending. (*Emma* 1985 [1816]: 280–281, first and third italics my emphasis, second in the original)

Finally, other examples illustrate the summary function of Emma's thoughts by using NRT, as in, "These were her reasons" (*Emma* 1985 [1816]: 180); the copula verb *to be* and a nominal group occur in NRT, as in " 'This would soon have led to something better, of course,' *was her consoling reflection*; 'any thing interests between those who love; and any thing will serve as introduction to what is near the heart. If I could but have kept longer away' " (*Emma* 1985 [1816]: 113, my emphasis).

I end this section by focusing on writing presentation; unlike with speech and thought presentation, it is difficult to identify keywords in this group, because stretches of NRW occur very rarely in the corpus (0.6%). Stretches of NRW are characterized by reference to a letter or a message, but also by verbs of communication. Writing presentation is also made by means of the verb *write* in present or past tense. Indirect writing (IW) is used in the following quotation, where the reporting clause consists of "This letter tells us:"

> *This letter tells us*—it is a short letter—written in a hurry, merely to give us notice—it tells us that they are all coming up to town directly, on Mrs. Churchill's

account—she has not been well the whole winter, and thinks Enscombe too cold for her—so they are all to move southward without loss of time. (*Emma* 1985 [1816]: 305, my emphasis)

From the point of view of today, the following example of NRW and IW would count as a deviation from the norm, because a conventional reporting verb for NRW does not occur: "A letter arrived from Mr. Churchill to urge his nephew's instant return" (*Emma* 1985 [1816]: 263). It would need to be investigated, however, what the norms for 19th-century English were in order to be able to determine whether Jane Austen intentionally creates a deviation from the norm. NRW may also be realized by the copula verb *to be* and a nominal group, as in "was her reply," "was the answer," or "was Lord Henry's answer." NRW may also be realized by a complete sentence as in "An express arrived at Randalls to announce the death of Mrs. Churchill" (*Emma* 1985 [1816]: 379).

Although it cannot be statistically verified, stretches of NRW are frequently introduced by the coordinating conjunction *and*, as in "and it signified, briefly enough" or another cohesive adjective, such as in the following stretch from Charles Dickens's *Oliver Twist* (1993 [1837]), where an advertisement that promises a reward for the person who finds Oliver Twist is directly quoted:

> The first paragraph upon which Mr. Bumble's eye rested, was the following advertisement; "FIVE GUINEAS REWARD [. . .] ." (*Oliver Twist* 1993 [1837]: 122)

To conclude, the textual force of the reporting signal reminds the reader of the textual function of vocatives (see also Busse 2006). Like vocatives, reporting signals which embrace direct or indirect discourse presentation stretches that are not free may also represent an interruption to the direct flow of speech or thought in order to highlight the preceding discourse, to encapsulate or prospect what is to come. In order to capture the meaningful potential of reporting verbs, the interplay between reporting verbs and the following features must be stressed by

a) the form of the reporting construction chosen;
b) the accompanying reported clause, its scale and category of discourse presentation, and the speech act it may be expressing;
c) the position of the reporting clause.

As regards their functional import, reporting clauses further outline the narrator's stance and as such they identify the character. Further, as shall be illustrated in more detail in the next section, they add more directly and locally to characterization or to outlining the character's body movements, mime, or gesture.

7.2. *Paralinguistic Narration*

This section will focus on the interplay between so-called paralinguistic narrative stretches with discourse presentation. Paralinguistic narration is the description of facial expressions, bodily expressions or movements, mime, gesture, or pitch of voice, as well as descriptions of silence. When paralinguistic narration appears in close proximity to the presentation of speech, writing, and thought presentation, it is meaning-making and functional in furthering narrative progression and characterization.

Brown (1996) and Person (1999) are two of the few people to transfer their observations of paralinguistic features to the analysis of literature. Brown (1996) discusses such features as pitch span, placing in voice range, tempo, voice setting, lip setting, and pausing. According to Brown (1996: 112), paralinguistic features "contribute to the expression of attitude by a speaker," and the meaning contributed by the paralinguistic features is the affective meaning of the utterance, where the feeling and the attitudes of the speaker are to some extent revealed. Recently, Mahlberg (2013: 165) has implemented an extensive analysis of lexical bundles, focusing on the interaction of linguistic clusters and body movement in stretches of reporting clauses of DS. Segundo (2016) analyzes reporting verbs in Dickens's narrative fiction.

Paralinguistic narration may be realized by different lexico-grammatical strategies. With regard to the strategies' functions of both encapsulation and prospecting discourse presentation, paralinguistic narration helps to inform the reader about the multimodal simultaneity of communication and body movement—a practice that is necessary in order to depict in vivid narrative what must be conventionally narrated in a linear fashion. This functional potential is realized by paralinguistic narration, functioning also as turn-taking practices through, for instance, the description of nodding or the description of pause or silence. By these means, the narrator additionally contributes to the vivid creation of fictional personae and their interactions, which also leaves impressions on the reader of being "in the scene" him/herself. This process of characterization is forcefully underlined by the specific patterned lexico-grammatical constructions of reporting clauses.

In the following excerpt from Jane Austen's *Emma* (1985 [1816]), paralinguistic information realized by three paratactically combined material clauses precedes stretches of DS. It creates the impression of the simultaneity of speech and body movement and further contributes to characterization to help the reader understand the atmosphere of the situation. Frank Churchill has just told Emma that, due to the illness of Mrs. Churchill, he cannot be part of the ball. FDS is interrupted by contextual information about how he, after a moment of hesitation, moves his body to the window:

> *He hesitated, got up, walked to a window.* "In short," said he, "perhaps, Miss Woodhouse —I think you can hardly be quite without suspicion"—*He looked at her,* as if wanting to read her thoughts. She hardly knew what to say. It seemed like the forerunner of something absolutely serious, which she did not wish. Forcing herself to speak, therefore, in the hope of putting it by, she calmly said "You are quite in the right; it was most natural to pay your visit, then"— (*Emma* 1985 [1816]: 265, my emphasis)

The paralinguistic description of Frank's movement to a window prospects the gravity as well as importance of what he is about to say. The narrative progression is furthered through imitation of the reader's meaning inference with Emma's thoughts and the switch of the discourse presentation mode: "It seemed like the forerunner of something absolutely serious."

In Oscar Wilde's *The Picture of Dorian Gray* (1994 [1891]), Dorian is described as utterly embarrassed when he mistakes Lady Harry's entrance for that of Lord Harry in his salon:

> "I am afraid it is not Harry, Mr. Gray," answered a *shrill voice*.
>
> *He glanced quickly round, and rose to his feet.* "I beg your pardon. I thought—"
>
> "You thought it was my husband. It is only his wife. You must let me introduce myself. I know you quite well by your photographs. I think my husband has got seventeen of them." (*The Picture of Dorian Gray* 1994 [1891]: 55–56, my emphasis)

The embarrassment is highlighted by the elaboration on the reporting clause "answered [. . .]" with an adjectival specification referring to his voice: "shrill." The description of his body movement is also highlighted by two material clauses. Functionally, these add to the characterization of Dorian as insecure and they prospect the DS stretch in which Dorian apologizes for his mistaken assumption. Lady Harry is similarly characterized as a dissatisfied, unloved woman, which is also disclosed through the paralinguistic and contextual narratological resumption in:

> "Yes; it was at dear 'Lohengrin.' I like Wagner's music better than anybody's. It is so loud that one can talk the whole time without other people hearing what one says. That is a great advantage, don't you think so, Mr. Gray?" *The same nervous staccato laugh broke from her thin lips, and her fingers began to play with a long tortoise-shell paper-knife.* (*The Picture of Dorian Gray* 1994 [1891]: 56, my emphasis)

Adding to the characterization of fictional personae, paralinguistic narration may also be meticulously described, such as, for instance, by means of a description of a character's aura, which is followed by a description of how he positions himself close to the fire and, finally, a description of the position of his hands. This is the case in Dickens's *Great Expectations* (1999 [1860]), in the scene already quoted before at length but in a different context, where the words with which the lawyer announces his search for Joe Gargery need introduction before the narrator chooses to modulate toward the character again:

> The strange gentleman, with an air of authority not to be disputed, and with a manner expressive of knowing something secret about every one of us that would effectually do for each individual if he chose to disclose it, left the back of the settle, and came into the space between the two settles, in front of the fire, where he remained standing, *his left hand in his pocket, and he biting the forefinger of his right.*

> "From information I have received," said he, looking round at us as we all quailed before him, "I have reason to believe there is a blacksmith among you, by name Joseph—or Joe—Gargery. Which is the man?" (*Great Expectations* 1999 [1860]: 107, my emphasis)

This is not only a very lively description to construe a character's authority, but it also heightens the atmosphere of tension. Pip feels like a startled fawn because of the constant fear of being found out. This is also reinforced by a recurrent lexico-grammatical cluster, "his left hand in his pocket" (Mahlberg 2007a, 2007b, 2013), which prospects the authoritative statement to come.

Paralinguistic narrative intervention does not always have to be intertwined with the presentation of speech. Thought and writing presentation can be foregrounded and therewith prospected or encapsulated through paralinguistic contextual narration as well. One rather theatrical example of introducing paralinguistic movement as a replacement of speech that interplays with thought presentation can be found in George Meredith's *The Ordeal of Richard Feverel* (1968 [1859]), where two lovers are described. FIT, which makes the reader feel very close to the characters, is constantly interrupted by narration, which explains the body movements that are performed:

> Before her playfully imperative injunction was fairly spoken, *Richard had glanced at the document* and discovered a Griffin between two Wheatsheaves: his crest in silver: and below—O wonderment immense! His own handwriting! *He handed it to her. She took it, and put it in her bosom.* Who would have thought, that, where all else perished, Odes, Idyls, Lines, Stanzas, this one Sonnet to the stars should be miraculously reserved for such a starry fate—passing beatitude! (*The Ordeal of Richard Feverel* 1968 [1859]: 121, my emphasis)

In another example from Brontë's *Jane Eyre* (1985 [1847]), the first-person narrator Jane describes her first meeting with Mr. Rochester. The reader is allowed access to her inferred thoughts about Mr. Rochester's attitude toward her in FIT, when she tries to describe Mr. Rochester's passivity and alleged disinterest in her presence when she enters the room. Her inference is based on or encapsulated in the fact that Mr. Rochester does not lift his head:

> Mr. Rochester must have been aware of the entrance of Mrs. Fairfax and myself; but it appeared he was not in the mood to notice us, for *he never lifted his head* as we approached. (*Jane Eyre* 1985 [1847]: 152, my emphasis)

For the reader, this paralinguistic information foregrounds Jane's gentle, but sharp perception and Mr. Rochester's alleged authority. At the same time, it serves as a prelude to the interrogation game that Mr. Rochester sets up for Jane and which is presented to the reader in FDS (see also section 5.2.2.5 in Chapter 5). Following Mrs. Fairfax's verbal announcement that Jane has entered the room to finally be introduced in person to him, Mr. Rochester flouts Grice's (1975) maxim of quality and is impolite by neither replying to Mrs. Fairfax nor welcoming Jane. Instead he takes a paralinguistic turn, which is to signify his acknowledgment of Jane's arrival.

> "Here is Miss Eyre, sir," said Mrs. Fairfax, in her quiet way. He bowed, still not taking his eyes from the group of the dog and child. (*Jane Eyre* 1985 [1847]: 152)

Only then does he reply to Mrs. Fairfax (but not to Jane) and demands that Jane be offered a place to sit. As such, the paralinguistic narrative intervention is foregrounded and at the same time highlights his peculiar authoritative style of communication and his somewhat belated decision to use his voice:

> "Let Miss Eyre be seated," said he: and there was something in *the forced stiff bow*, in the *impatient yet formal tone*, which seemed further to express, "What the deuce is it to me whether Miss Eyre be there or not? At this moment I am not disposed to accost her." (*Jane Eyre* 1985 [1847]: 152, my emphasis)

Paralinguistic narration may also function as a visual presentation of a turn. In Dickens's *Oliver Twist* (1993 [1837]), Mr. Brownlow signals to his interlocutors to be silent by shaking his head. The narrator even further explains the projected purpose of this gesture:

> "Of course," observed Mr. Grimwig aside to his friend, "I knew he was. A beadle all over!" Mr. Brownlow *gently shook his head* to impose silence on his friend, and resumed: "Do you know where this poor boy is now?" (*Oliver Twist* 1993 [1837]: 123, my emphasis)

The narrative description of silence must also be paid attention to in a study that investigates the forms and functions of discourse presentation. In my corpus, silence plays a variety of roles. It may, for instance, occur in response to DS and thereby indicate disbelief in what was previously said: It may also indicate a reflective thought or be used to indicate power. Further, there are cases in which silence may be used to describe a situation of discomfort. Structurally, the description of silence—or of the "disnarrated"—is a narratological turn in order to describe the simultaneity of speech, silence, and other paralinguistic activities in a linear narrative.

The presentation of silence is, for instance, foregrounded in Emma's and Mr. Knightley's mutual love declaration in Austen's *Emma* (1985 [1816]). Following Emma's declarative speech, in which she denies having had any sincere feelings for Mr. Churchill, the insertion of the description of silence on Mr. Knightley's part is highly effective:

> *He listened in perfect silence.* She wished him to speak, but he would not. She supposed she must say more before she were entitled to his clemency; but it was a hard case to be obliged still to lower herself in his opinion. (*Emma* 1985 [1816]: 414, my emphasis)

After Emma and Mr. Knightley decide to go for another walk, the narrator prepares for the confession of their mutual feelings. But they are not given voice without some of the narrator's intruding comments, in which Emma's silence is foregrounded:

"My dearest Emma," said he, "for dearest you will always be, whatever the event of this hour's conversation, my dearest, most beloved Emma—at once. Say 'No,' if it is to be said."—*She could really say nothing.*—"You are silent," *he cried, with great animation;* "absolutely silent! At present I ask no more." *Emma was almost ready to sink under the agitation of this moment. The dread of being awakened from the happiest dream, was perhaps the most prominent feeling.* "I cannot make speeches, Emma": *he soon resumed; and in a tone of such sincere, decided, intelligible tenderness as was tolerably convincing.*—"If I loved you less, I might be able to talk about it more. But you know what I am.—You hear nothing but truth from me.—I have blamed you, and lectured you, and you have borne it as no other woman in England would have borne it. Bear with the truths I would tell you now, dearest Emma, as well as you have borne with them. The manner, perhaps, may have as little to recommend them. God knows, I have been a very indifferent lover.—But you understand me.—Yes, you see, you understand my feelings—and will return them if you can. At present, I ask only to hear, once to hear your voice." (*Emma* 1985 [1816]: 417, my emphasis)

The high proliferation of this contextual narrative commenting on Emma's speechlessness builds up the narrator's ridiculing the agitation of this moment.[2]

In Jane Austen's *Northanger Abbey* (1985 [1818]), the presentation of silence is used to express Catherine's boredom and insecurity about Mrs. Allen:

She began first to be sensible of this, and to sigh for her conversation, as she walked along the pump-room one morning, by Mrs. Allen's side, *without anything to say or to hear;* and scarcely had she felt a five minutes' longing of friendship, before the object of it appeared, and inviting her to a secret conference, led the way to a seat. (*Northanger Abbey* 1985 [1818]: 151, my emphasis)

An example of the presentation of silence foregrounding the authority of the character who does not speak comes from Charles Dickens's *Oliver Twist* (1993 [1857]):

Mr. Bumble stopped not to converse with the small shopkeepers and others who spoke to him, deferentially, as he passed along. He merely returned their salutations *with a wave of his hand,* and relaxed not in his dignified pace, until he reached the farm where Mrs. Mann tended the infant paupers with parochial care. (*Oliver Twist* 1993 [1837]: 118, my emphasis)

The ambiguity here stems from the position of the negating particle "not" as either qualifying the main finite verb "stop" or the nonfinite infinitival construction "to converse."

The first-person narrator in Brontë's *Jane Eyre* (1985 [1847]) describes Mr. Rochester's authoritative silence and relates this to his body movement. Both paralinguistic details and the narrative description of silence prospect the tenseness of the situation and the foregrounded character of his entering the conversation:

> He went on as a statue would, that is, *he neither spoke nor moved.* Mrs. Fairfax seemed to think it necessary that some one should be amiable, and she began to talk. Kindly, as usual—and, as usual, rather trite—she condoled with him on the pressure of business he had had all day; on the annoyance it must have been to him with that painful sprain: then she commended his patience and perseverance in going through with it. (*Jane Eyre* 1985 [1847]: 152, my emphasis)

In Brontë's *Wuthering Heights* (2009 [1847]), Catherine reports about Linton's authoritative silence through an embedded narration of silence in DS:

> However, the dogs gave notice of my approach. Zillah received me, and saying "the lad was mending nicely," showed me into a small, tidy, carpeted apartment, where, to my inexpressible joy, I beheld Linton laid on a little sofa, reading one of my books. *But he would neither speak to me nor look at me,* through a whole hour, Ellen: he has such an unhappy temper. And what quite confounded me, when he did open his mouth, it was to utter the falsehood that I had occasioned the uproar, and Hareton was not to blame! (*Wuthering Heights* 2009 [1847]: 223, my emphasis)

Another example from Elizabeth Gaskell's *North and South* (2003 [1854]) invokes silence to show that Mrs. Thornton is apparently dissatisfied with her daughter's suggestion and needs some reflection of how to proceed:

> "I don't know—the weather, I think. It is so relaxing. Couldn't you bring nurse here, mamma? The carriage could fetch her, and she could spend the rest of the day here, which I know she would like." *Mrs. Thornton did not speak;* but she laid her work on the table, and seemed to think. "It will be a long way for her to walk back at night!" she remarked, at last. (*North and South* 2003 [1854]: 95, my emphasis)

A further example can be found in Elizabeth Gaskell's *Cranford* (2007 [1853]), in which the first-person intradiegetic narrator, Mary, presents a conversation with Miss Pole about the illness of Mr. Holbrooke and Miss Matty's knowledge of it. Mary finds out that Miss Matty knew about the fact that he is on the verge of dying after his return from Paris, but that she did not talk to anybody about it. Miss Pole is surprised by the fact that Miss Matty has not told Mary. This act of surprise is presented in DS and then follows the narrative move, which is—Mary being the narrator—both narrator- and character-oriented, but here her thoughts are presented in IT and NRS: "Not at all, I thought." Then she moves to the paralinguistic description of silence:

> Not at all, I thought; *but I did not say anything.* I felt almost guilty of having spied too curiously into that tender heart, and I was not going to speak of its secrets—hidden, Miss Matty believed, from all the world. (*Cranford* 2007 [1853]: 47, my emphasis)

Another example comes from Charles Kingsley's *Alton Locke* (1967 [1859]), in which the first-person narrator prefers silence over an expression of false belief and infidelity. Therewith, a comment is also made on the doubtable statements made by his cousin:

> "My good cousin, it is the only method yet discovered for turning a snob (as I am, or was) into a gentleman; except putting him into a heavy cavalry regiment. My brother, who has no brains, preferred the latter method. I, who flatter myself that I have some, have taken the former." The thought was new and astonishing to me, *and I looked at him in silence while he ran on—*
>
> *[. . .]*
>
> I was very near confessing that it had: but a feeling came over me, I knew not why, that my cousin would have been glad to get me into his power, and would therefore have welcomed a confession of infidelity. *So I held my tongue.* (*Alton Locke* 1967 [1859]: 133–135, my emphasis)

To conclude, this section has illustrated how paralinguistic narration in combination with descriptions of silence may serve as a means of prospection and encapsulation in the interplay with discourse presentation. Further, paralinguistic narration may have the function of a reporting signal. This points to the necessity to embrace discourse presentation and narration as interactive modes of reflecting and creating a social mind in interaction. Palmer (2004: 212) quotes Wittgenstein's question (1958: 179): "Is this a report about his behaviour or a state of mind?" which shows how closely interlinked both processes are. The discussion of the use of silence has illustrated the meaning-making interplay in which it can stand with discourse presentation in general, and with FDS or DS in particular. Although it is a purely narrative mode, it needs to be incorporated into an analysis of discourse presentation.

7.3. Imagination and Observation: Thought Presentation and Visual Narration in 19th-Century Narrative Fiction

My view of historical linguistics, outlined in the introduction in Chapter 1, embraces a necessary interplay between quantitative and qualitative investigations, between linguistic and literary critical approaches and the contextualization of respective results within contemporaneous writing. This form of contextualization also illustrates the need for a cultural understanding of the modes of discourse presentation and the narrative stretches that embrace them (Moore 2011; Vološinov (1973 [1929]). This section illustrates this complex exchange by analyzing thought presentation and stretches of paralinguistic narration in their 19th-century cultural context.

In the following I address narrative stretches that make reference to aspects of vision and movement as they interact with the different modes of thought presentation. From the point of view of information organization, these reveal that in 19th-century narrative fiction paralinguistic information is often given by the narrator to create as well as to foreshadow what is going to come, on the one hand, or to encapsulate what has been described (Sinclair 2004: 52), on the other. Thought presentation is also used to foreground a character's state of mind or to highlight imaginative processes which follow or precede the narrative stretch. As mentioned, according to Brown (1996: 112), paralinguistic features "contribute to the expression of attitude by a speaker," and the meaning contributed by the paralinguistic features is the affective meaning of the utterance, where the feeling and the attitudes of the speaker are to some extent revealed.

My annotation of the stretches of discourse presentation in 19th-century narrative fiction, on the one hand, and narration, on the other, has revealed (a) an interplay between thought presentation and narrative reference to the thinker's eyes, (b) thought presentation and its co-occurrence with a metaphorical expression in which thought is seen as movement and activity, and (c) paralinguistic narrative passages which construe or stand for a character's thinking process. They represent a linguistic evocation of a multimodal and sensual world in which reference is often made to the movements or status of the thinker's eyes, which fulfill a variety of roles. For instance, it is used to announce or summarize a character's introspection, to describe a state of mind which is not overtly expressed or discussed, or to interrupt in order to express the visual role of the "blinking of eyes" as discourse markers to initiate a turn. At the same time, these discoursal phenomena have to be situated within the "Victorian delight in the technologies of vision" (Flint 2000: xiii) and their interest in the roles of eyes to construe imagination and to observe. In what follows I discuss these functions by illustrating them with examples from my corpus.

A description of the movement of a character's eyes or gaze can be used to describe a character's state of mind. In *Dr. Jekyll and Mr. Hyde* (Stevenson 2003 [1886]), Utterson uses "the look in the eye" to determine Dr. Lanyon's well-being and his current state of mind:

> The rosy man had grown pale; his flesh had fallen away; he was visibly balder and older; and yet it was not so much these tokens of a swift physical decay that arrested the lawyer's notice, *as a look in the eye and quality of manner that seemed to testify to some deep-seated terror of the mind.* (*Dr. Jekyll and Mr. Hyde* 2003 [1886]: 128, my emphasis)

It is a well-worn trope that eyes are windows to the soul. In this example, this connection is directly expressed because Utterson's gaze and Dr. Lanyon's expression "seemed to testify to some deep-seated terror of the mind."

The difference between saying and thinking, on the one hand, and the function of one's eyes to indicate one's real feelings/thoughts, on the other, is romantically transferred in the following example:

> "Then I am old Blaize's niece." She tripped him a soft curtsey. The magnetized youth gazed at her. By what magic was it that this divine sweet creature could be allied with that old churl! "Then what—what is your name?" said his mouth,

> *while his eyes added,* "O wonderful creature! How came you to enrich the earth?" "Have you forgot the Desboroughs of Dorset, too?" she peered at him from a side-bend of the flapping brim. "The Desboroughs of Dorset?" A light broke in on him. "And have you grown to this? That little girl I saw there!" (*The Ordeal of Richard Feverel* 1968 [1859]: 123, my emphasis)

The reporting clause "while his eyes added" introduces a stretch of DT, beginning with "O wonderful creature." It stands in contrast to the narrator's report of speech in "said his mouth" and the stretch of DS in "Then what—what is your name?" Through a lexical antithesis between the reporting stretches "his mouth said" and "his eyes added," the narrator obviously underlines the discrepancy between Richard's words and what he really thinks (but is not allowed to say). In Text World Theory (Werth 1999: 221; Gavins 2007: 50), this move from the actual words uttered between the two characters, Richard and old Blaize's niece, to the former's thoughts represents a move into a deictic subworld (Werth 1999) or modal world (Gavins 2007) in which Richard's thinking is temporarily the deictic center. Eyes can only speak paralinguistically, but they represent a conventional reference to the mind and as such add the notion of faithfulness to the presentation of the character's thoughts. The mentioning of his eyes is a key marker that foreshadows a narratological switch to the presentation of his direct thoughts.

As we have seen in previous chapters, a similar contrast between changing states of minds is expressed by means of the narrator's reference to the movement of Mr. Bumble's eyes in Dickens's *Oliver Twist* (1993 [1837]):

> When Mr. Bumble had laughed a little while, *his eyes again encountered the cocked hat*; and he became grave. "We are forgetting business, ma'am," said the beadle; "here is your porochial stipend for the month." (*Oliver Twist* 1993 [1837]: 120)

Mr. Bumble's eye movement causes him to spot his hat, which, in turn, reminds him of the business he has to undertake. This foreshadows the change of mood that takes place in him, and he switches from laughing to becoming "grave."

A further example from Jane Austen's *Emma* (1985 [1816]), having been mentioned before, may be re-cited in this context. In this example Emma is described as being satisfied with Frank Churchill's assertion that he is still willing to arrange the ball. Her gratefulness is not presented through discourse, but—with an entertaining and ironic effect—through narration that also ridicules Emma's constant attempt at being the center of attention. This strategy shows that Emma implies rather than voices her assertion before Frank Churchill is given another stretch of DS:

> "If I can come again, we are still to have our ball. My father depends on it. Do not forget your engagement." *Emma looked graciously.* (*Emma* 1985 [1816]: 264, my emphasis)

The short, three-word narratological insertion of contextual and paralinguistic information in "Emma looked graciously" focuses on the expression of Emma's face and eyes. The omission of the presentation of a proper turn uttered by Emma foregrounds Emma's consciousness and her emotional reliance on what Frank says; that is, as Brown (1996) discusses, paralinguistic description allows for Emma's emotional state to be revealed alongside her actual thinking process. It furthers her characterization to the reader, which, in this case, portrays her as not only grateful but also spoiled. The reader further experiences a rather swift move to Emma's thoughts before Frank's text-world is presented again in DS. The fact that her reaction is not portrayed as verbal turn-taking but paralinguistically shows that these narrative stretches surrounding speech and thought presentation function as markers of the dialogic structure of conversation and also illustrate that at times verbal turn-taking that is articulated with words is not necessary. They represent an attempt at describing faithfully the verbal and nonverbal characteristics of conversation. The reference to Emma's facial expressions is attitudinal because its foregrounding in "Emma looked graciously" signals her attempt at being cordial. It also gives the reader an understanding of the narrator's ironic comment on the stereotypical atmosphere between two people who are almost in love.

Getting back again to Brontë's *Jane Eyre* (1985 [1847]) and the scene in which Jane has entered the room to finally be introduced in person to Mr. Rochester (see section 7.2), Mr. Rochester's impoliteness is in not replying to Mrs. Fairfax's statement or welcoming Jane. Instead, as mentioned before, he takes a paralinguistic turn—bowing—which is to signify his acknowledgment of Jane's presence. Yet, he does not move his eyes toward them and therefore does not grant her a polite look at her face:

> "Here is Miss Eyre, sir," said Mrs. Fairfax, in her quiet way. *He bowed, still not taking his eyes from the group of the dog and child.* (*Jane Eyre* 1985 [1847]: 152, my emphasis)

The negative polarity in "still not taking his eyes from the group of the dog and child" implies the positive, namely, that he should have done so to be polite or cordial (Nørgaard 2007). His persistent look at the dog and the child furthermore calls his alleged disinterest in Jane's arrival into question.

In *Dr. Jekyll and Mr. Hyde* (2003 [1886]), Utterson's sadness about Dr. Lanyon's death is reinforced by a letter that he receives after the funeral. His stretch of DT—"'I have buried one friend to-day,' he thought: 'what if this should cost me another?'" (*Dr. Jekyll and Mr. Hyde* 2003 [1886]: 129)—is then followed by a descriptive passage of him opening the seal of Lanyon's letter:

> And then he condemned the fear as a disloyalty, and broke the seal. Within there was another enclosure, likewise sealed, and marked upon the cover as "not to be opened till the death or disappearance of Dr. Henry Jekyll." *Utterson could not trust his eyes.* Yes, it was disappearance; here again, as in the mad will which he had long ago restored to its author, here again were the idea of a disappearance and the name of Henry Jekyll bracketed. But in the will, that idea had sprung

from the sinister suggestion of the man Hyde. (*Dr. Jekyll and Mr. Hyde* 2003 [1886]: 129, my emphasis)

The narrator describes Utterson's astonishment at Lanyon's words (hinting at Dr. Jekyll's possible disappearance) through reference to Utterson's eyes: "Utterson could not trust his eyes." This foreshadows a shift back to Utterson's feelings.

The visual movement of eyes is stereotypically used to announce a character's introspection. This strategy is employed in the example from Wilde's *The Picture of Dorian Gray* (1994 [1891]), where Lord Henry—after his conversation with Dorian about love and marriage—is left alone to think. As we have seen, the narrator's report of thought in "he began to think" is used to frame the reader's mind toward the presentation of Lord Henry's thought in FIT (see section 5.2.4.2 in Chapter 5). But before, reference is also made paralinguistically to the movement of his eyes in "his heavy eyelids drooped" to signal that he is now falling into introspection:

> As he left the room, *Lord Henry's heavy eyelids drooped,* and *he began to think.* Certainly few people had ever interested him so much as Dorian Gray, and yet the lad's mad adoration of some one else caused him not the slightest pang of annoyance or jealousy. He was pleased by it. It made him a more interesting study. (*The Picture of Dorian Gray* 1994 [1891]: 68–69, my emphasis)

The description of what a character does with his or her eyes not only introduces the character's thought presentation or embeds it, but also represents a means of depicting cognitive detail and prompts a switch from the narratological description to the character and what she or he might be thinking. The visual stands for a thought process that is going on in the character's mind.

In Gaskell's *Cousin Phillis* (2006 [1963]), the first-person narrator uses the reporting clause "I felt" to introduce his IT. Yet embedded in his thoughts is also a description of what Phillis does with "those deep grey eyes [. . .] upon me:"

> Her daughter Phillis took up her knitting—a long grey worsted man's stocking, I remember—and knitted away without looking at her work. I felt that *the steady gaze of those deep grey eyes was upon me,* though once, when I stealthily raised mine to hers, she was examining something on the wall above my head. (*Cousin Phillis* 2006 [1863]: 379, my emphasis)

The narrator's ongoing thinking process begins to focus on speculations about what Phillis might be thinking. Here the paralinguistic reference to the "steady gaze" and "those deep grey eyes" illustrates to the reader that Phillis is both observing and, at the same time, thinking about him. In Text World Theory (Werth 1999: 221), the move from the narrative description of her knitting to his thoughts, introduced by the reporting clause "I felt," projects a new modal world in which paralinguistic descriptions are mixed with the narrator's thought presentation. This is done in an embedded way, with Phillis's thought process alluded to by the way she directs her visual camera.

In the following example from Brontë's *Jane Eyre* (1985 [1847]), Jane's answer to Mr. Rochester's question about whether she is fond of presents is described by a paralinguistic narratological intervention that refers to what Mr. Rochester does with his eyes: "and he searched my face with eyes that I saw were dark, irate and piercing":

> "Who talks of cadeaux?" said he gruffly. "Did you expect a present, Miss Eyre? Are you fond of presents?" *and he searched my face with eyes that I saw were dark, irate, and piercing.* "I hardly know, sir; I have little experience of them: they are generally thought pleasant things." (*Jane Eyre* 1985 [1847]: 152, my emphasis)

The pronounced focalization on Mr. Rochester's paralinguistic movements portrays him as a vigilant observer and underlines his interest in Jane's psyche, and vice versa, we also see him through her eyes as she is a good observer, too. At the same time, the narrator immediately shifts back to Jane's thoughts, because the way she perceives those eyes as "dark, irate, and piercing" is described. Mr. Rochester attempts to see with his eyes what Jane is thinking and, at the same time, to visually force her to reply to his question. The prepositional phrase "with eyes that I saw were dark, irate, and piercing" is chosen by the first-person narrator to foreground the color and force of Mr. Rochester's eyes. At the same time, these adjectives serve as a further means of characterization of Mr. Rochester's psyche—"dark" might foreshadow his morals as well as the depth of his emotions, "irate" his attitude toward himself and "the world" that has done him wrong, and "piercing" his energy and intellect (Möhlig-Falke p.c.).

Following Oatley (2001, 2009), that is, to argue that literature offers its readers a simulation of everyday situations and experience, the qualitative narratological reference to the eyes serves at least as a trigger to announce a state of mind or thought processing within the intratextual frame or the text-world. Readers may experience within themselves the emotion that is announced via recourse to the eyes, or they may have experienced the qualitative force of this paralinguistic movement. This leads to the question of whether this is also a form of "narrative progression" (Toolan 2009). In reconstructing some of the contextual frameworks that might have led to this precise and detailed narratological description of the complex interplay between paralinguistic narration and thought presentation in 19th-century literature, one needs to take a closer look at 19th-century psychological, biological, and literary statements about vision and the psyche.

As mentioned before (see section 5.1 in Chapter 5), the 19th century saw a rise of research in psychological consciousness and optical inventions which is reflected in 19th-century literature. Thus, in *Daniel Deronda* (1998 [1876]), George Eliot draws the reader's attention to the mysteries of the human psyche: "There is a great deal of unmapped country within us which would have to be taken into account in the explanation of our guts and storms" (*Daniel Deronda* 1998 [1876]: 235). The idea of vision, introspection, and seeing, which can be related to the famous metaphor of UNDERSTANDING IS SEEING (Lakoff and Johnson 2003), also corresponds to 19th-century research into the perception of colors and optical inventions as well as to the way literature reacted to them (Kern-Stähler 2005: 108). Notions of agency, perception, and looking find their complex pragmatic expression in the interplay between narrative and discourse presentation and provide a narrator with means of displaying cognitive processes in ways that perhaps had not been seen before. The focalized characters' eyes play a crucial role as markers of stance (Biber et al. 1999: 967), indicating an additional attitudinal comment on the part of the narrator and prospecting introspection to the reader. At the same time, they are a means of indicating to the reader that observation and imagination are prevalent.

Henry James's (1905) concept of the "house of fiction," quoted in length in section 5.1 in Chapter 5, explicitly stresses the fact that in fiction the narrator is able to portray a number of individuals by looking through a "million" (James 1975 [1905]: 7) number of windows. It is the narrator's "individual vision" (James 1975 [1905]: 7), and also that of the reader, which helps create the "human scene" (James 1975 [1905]: 7). James draws on a number of metaphors from the field of vision:

> But they have this mark of their own that at each of them stands a figure with a pair of eyes, or at least with a field glass, which forms, again and again, for observation a unique instrument, insuring to the person making use of it an impression distinct from every other. He and his neighbors are watching the same show, but one seeing more where the other sees less, one seeing black where the other sees white, one seeing big where the other sees small [. . .]. The spreading field, the human field, is "the choice of subject"; [. . .] but they are, singly or together, as nothing without the posted presence of the watcher—without, in other words, the consciousness of the artist. (James 1975 [1905]: 7).

Furthermore, it becomes obvious that the presentation of thought in general is frequent—and complex in the display of the variety of modes that realize it and in the way they interact with narrative elements and create consciousness. Following the quantitative and qualitative analysis of stretches of discourse presentation in the novels and the respective functions they assume, it becomes even more obvious why Richter (2009) argues that narrating in 19th-century novels is an evolutionary adaption and a creation of a room of imagination in order to preserve what Darwin (1996 [1859]) destroyed in his Theory of Natural Selection outlined in *The Origin of Species*.

Thought presentation is also a means of describing cognitive processing and characters' complex thoughts, which often cannot be expressed for reasons of social decorum. As such, thought presentation is addressed to the reader to inform him/her of what is going on in the minds of the characters. To quote Flint (2000),

> [t]he Victorians were fascinated with the act of seeing, with the question of reliability—or otherwise—of the human eye, and with the problems of interpreting what they saw. These problems extended from the observation of the natural world and the urban environment, to the more specialist interpretation demanded by actual works of art. In each case, the act of seeing was something performed by individuals, each with their particular subjectivities, and their own ocular physiology. Simultaneously, what was seen was necessarily selected, stressed, described and filtered through many cultural conventions. (Flint 2000: 2)

In relation to narrative fiction, this quotation illustrates that the author is in control of what is described, and that the discussion about vision and the role of eyes goes beyond subjectivity and the social (Flint 2000: 2; Palmer 2010). It also includes an outward and inward dimension of observation and imagination, which is also referred to by Palmer (2004: 62) when he stresses the already mentioned interplay between what is reported as an activity of the mind and how this is accompanied by action.

Corpus-stylistic methodology may give substance to all of these considerations. Consider, for instance, the following concordance of the word *eyes* from my 19th-century corpus of narrative fiction:

. . . way, and her blue	**eyes**	lightened laughter . . .
. . . As her blue	**eyes**	shine through her golden hair. . . .
. . . Here were two blue	**eyes**	and golden hair; and by some strange chance, . . .
. . . Tears, unrestrained, fell from my brother's	**eyes**	; a sense of . . .
. . . cheeks! sweet mouth! strange sweet brows!	**eyes**	of softest fire! . . .
. . . So they stood a moment, changing	**eyes**	, and then Miranda spoke, . . .
. . . So to each other said their changing	**eyes**	in the moment they stood together; . . .
. . . devouring us with their eager	**eyes**	. I love one woman more than all . . .
. . . while with gloating	**eyes**	and extended arms he again set to at the half . . .
. . . those deep grey	**eyes**	was upon me, though once . . .
. . . Guest's	**eyes**	brightened, and he sat down at once . . .
. . . with plaited coils of dark-brown hair,	**eyes**	that were violet wells of passion, . . .
. . . gazing between her	**eyes**	"Good-bye," . . .
. . . something from her	**eyes**	, she looked up in her husband's face with a smile. . . .

. . . Carabas would give her	**eyes**	for her! A prodigy of accomplishments! . . .
. . . there was a frightened light in her	**eyes**	. Could it be that Sue had acted with . . .
. . . wistfulness in her	**eyes**	, I knew that there had been more . . .
. . . and kept her	**eyes**	fixed obstinately on an open book. . . .
. . . the clearness of her	**eyes**	, bore witness to the body's virtue; . . .
. . . and the constant rubbing she inflicted on her	**eyes**	. The following night she . . .
. . . her neck, and the circles round her	**eyes**	dark with watching. "What a fright I . . .
. . . shading her	**eyes**	from the sinking sun with her hand. . . .
. . . drinking her in with all his	**eyes**	, and young Love has a thousand. . . .
. . . his mouth agape, and his	**eyes**	fixed on the savage baron with . . .
. . . his cheeks were sunken; and his	**eyes**	large and bright. The scanty parish dress, . . .
. . . His face was purple and his	**eyes**	dim, as he put her down and left her. . . .
. . . with that passage before his	**eyes**	, can lay his head upon his pillow after having . . .
. . . but his	**eyes**	would not be gainsaid, and checked her lips. . . .
. . . away from his	**eyes**	. And away with her went the wild . . .
. . . She looked into his	**eyes**	with her own tearful ones, and her lips suddenly . . .
. . . not daring to lift his	**eyes**	from the floor; and dreading even to . . .
. . . He touched her hand, not moving his	**eyes**	from her, nor speaking, and she, . . .
. . . no more laugh off the piercing fervour of his	**eyes**	. Her volubility . . .
. . . Mr. Bumble opened his	**eyes**	; read the advertisement, slowly and carefully, . . .
. . . gathering over his	**eyes**	, as if uncertain . . .
. . . raised his	**eyes**	, and encountered those of Mr. Bumble. . . .
. . . The minister shifted his	**eyes**	to Phillis's face; it mutely gave him . . .
. . . still not taking his	**eyes**	from the group of the dog and child. . . .

. . . Mr. Bumble had laughed a little while, his	**eyes**	again encountered the . . .
. . . Richard, with his	**eyes**	still intently fixed on her, returned, . . .
. . . that Isabella's	**eyes**	were continually bent towards one door or the . . .
. . . that Jude's	**eyes**	were even wetter than hers as he . . .
. . . there were some illusions under Mary's	**eyes**	which were not quite comic to . . .

As these concordances show, *eyes* collocates with terms that refer to color, but also with words that highlight their observing function, as in "not moving his eyes from her" or "the minister shifted his eyes." At the same time, eyes are described as offering access to the imagination, as in "there were some illusions under Mary's eyes."

To further underline the activity of the mind as a tool for the imagination as well as the complexity involved in the human psyche, I refer again to the fact that in 19th-century narrative fiction thought is—following a long tradition going back to Old English—also presented by means of a metaphor that conceptualizes it as movement and sees the thinker as active. In the following example, already quoted before (see section 7.1), Emma's thoughts are presented as DT:

> "And Mrs. Weston!—Astonished that the person who had brought me up should be a gentlewoman! Worse and worse. I never met with her equal. Much beyond my hopes. Harriet is disgraced by any comparison. Oh! what would Frank Churchill say to her, if he were here? How angry and how diverted he would be! Ah! there I am—thinking of him directly. Always the first person to be thought of! How I catch myself out! *Frank Churchill comes as regularly into my mind!*" (*Emma* 1985 [1816]: 280–281, my emphasis)

Emma's thoughts are then summarized as follows:

> *All this ran so glibly through her thoughts*, that by the time her father had arranged himself, after the bustle of the Eltons' departure, and was ready to speak, she was very tolerably capable of attending. (*Emma* 1985 [1816]: 280–281, my emphasis)

Furthermore, through the quantitative clash between the words used to report her direct thoughts and those used in the encapsulating NRTA/NI, her real feelings for Mr. Knightley are foregrounded. *Glibly* usually collocates with speech (OED s.v. *glibly* adj. 1), but here the transfer is made to stress the agility of her active mind illustrated by the verb *run*. The mind is here metaphorically conceptualized as a SPACE through which Emma's thoughts travel, just like a physical object would travel through concrete space (Möhlig-Falke p.c.).

Another manifestation of the movement metaphor is employed to encapsulate the speed with which Emma, almost theatrically, reveals to herself that she and Mr. Knightley should be married. In this case, IT presentation is used: "It darted through her, with the speed of an arrow, that Mr. Knightley must marry no one but herself" (*Emma* 1985 [1816]: 398). The verb *dart,* as well as the appositively positioned prepositional phrase functioning as an adverbial ("with the speed of an arrow"), stresses the suddenness or abruptness with which she realizes that she is in love with Mr. Knightley. Nevertheless, it could be argued that the effect for the reader is rather different. Emma's sudden realization does, in fact, take place toward the end of the novel, so readers are aware of how much "textual time" Emma has taken to make this discovery while they themselves have suspected this long before. Hence, the irony is reinforced by a foregrounded emphasis on the speed of her thoughts (she is a quick thinker, but not when it comes to her own feelings).[3]

A further characteristic of 19th-century narration, which alludes to another of the inventions of the period in addition to the illustrated press, is photography (Flint 2000: 3). A literary reflection of this is found in what could be considered a "narratological camera." Like a real camera, the narratological camera gazes like humans do, but this gaze is always mitigated: "Language gives a fuller image, which is all the better for being vague. After all the true seeing is within" (*Middlemarch* 1986 [1871–1872]: 186). There is this interplay between the seen and the unseen:

> The sight of the eye, the most precious of all man's physical gifts, is only a parable of that truer sight of the world which makes a man a poet, an artist, a lover, a spiritual creature. To "see the unseen" is the paradox of religion as it is the crowning glory of man [. . .] Properly speaking, Sight and Insight are not two antagonistic tendencies, but opposite poles of one and the same magnet. (Wood 1880: 225)

To conclude, there is a complex interplay between a variety of modes of thought presentation and narrative descriptions of or reference to the thinkers' eyes—vision as well as mind. These references may either announce a stretch of thought presentation or summarize it and, at the same time, can also serve as turn-taking markers. The presentation of thought and its introduction through stretches of narration including paralinguistic aspects can thus be seen to be related to 19th-century ideas and theories of vision and the psyche in complex ways. This chapter has also illustrated the usefulness of combining a corpus-assisted methodological approach to discourse presentation with qualitative investigation. This triangulation has identified the large share of paralinguistic description in its interplay with discourse presentation modes to further narrative progression.

CHAPTER 8 | Conclusion

> The use of language is not confined to its being the medium through which we communicate our ideas to one another; it fulfils a no less important function as an instrument of thought, not being merely its vehicle, but giving it wings for flight. Metaphysicians are agreed that scarcely any of our intellectual operations could be carried on to any considerable extent without the agency of words. None but those who are conversant with the philosophy of mental phenomena can be aware of the immense influence that is exercised by language in promoting the development of our ideas, in fixing them in the mind, and detaining them for steady contemplation.
>
> —Roget (1992 [1852]: vii)

THIS QUOTATION FROM THE mid-19th century illustrates the contemporary preoccupation with discourse presentation. Issues discussed embrace the general functions of language to report, present, and create speech—but also thinking and thought. It also raises questions about the relation of faithfulness between the antecedent and the reported discourse, as well as addressing epistemological and ideological concerns about how the mind works and how this can be presented (Palmer 2004: 243). The reporter/narrator seems to be the powerful guiding force in his/her role as being a "fair narrator" (Brontë 2009 [1847]: 136).

My study has illustrated that discourse presentation in 19th-century narrative fiction indeed works on all different scales and in a variety of modes. It can be seen to play a crucial role in establishing, reflecting, and construing a social mind in action. This construal affects both intra- and intertextual dimensions, including readers and their processing as well as theoretical concerns of interpretation and methodological issues of analysis. Therefore, in this study, discourse presentation in 19th-century narrative fiction has been surveyed from a variety of angles and approaches: (Modern) historical linguistics, stylistics, historical pragmatics, corpus linguistics, cognitive linguistics, narratology, and literary criticism.

Speech, Writing, and Thought Presentation in 19th-Century Narrative Fiction. Beatrix Busse, Oxford University Press (2020). © Oxford University Press.
DOI: 10.1093/oso/9780190212360.001.0001

Based on a theoretical concept that the presentation of discourse is an engaged, social process of interaction, this study has investigated the historical development of forms and functions of discourse presentation and how they relate to one another. This diachronization of narratology (Fludernik 2003a) is a necessary step to explore the relationship between stability and change of discourse presentation in general—and in 19th- and 20th-century discourse presentation in particular—within a number of theories available. Palmer (2004: 240) asks for a book that shows more fully "the social mind in action" and that goes beyond the verbal norm (cf. Fludernik's [1993: 281] "discourse fallacy"). This study is a contribution to his call. Despite the small size of the corpus used here, the corpus-based approach and the manual annotation of stretches of speech, writing, and thought presentation allow for a systematic investigation of the frequencies of forms of discourse presentation and their functions, which is based on the model developed by Semino and Short (2004). The categories are robust for an analysis of 19th-century narrative fiction, although this study retains a distinction between the free direct and non-free direct forms on all scales, also drawing the reader's attention to paralinguistic phenomena and their interplay with narration and discourse presentation modes. The proposed annotation system has been developed to better distinguish between formal and functional aspects. Despite Fludernik's (1993) critical prospects of a corpus-based approach to the investigation of literature, this study has guaranteed a rigorous, retrievable annotation procedure, which is based on explicit definitions of the different categories of speech, writing, and thought presentation. Sets of formal and structural criteria which contain graphological, syntactic, and deictic parameters have been employed. In addition, however, pragmatic and contextual inferencing is indispensable for determining whether somebody might have said, thought, or written something, especially in cases where embedded discourse presentation occurs or where distinguishing between FIT and FIS is difficult.

My view of New Historical Stylistics and Historical Linguistics, as presented in Chapter 1, where I outline, among other matters, the interplay between quantitative and qualitative investigation and the need for an inclusion and reading of contemporary sources, accounts for the functional identification of the variety of discourse presentation modes in a historical framework. It is necessary to determine whether the content and the lexical choices in a narrative text reflect antecedent views, writings, or the verbal repertoire of particular individuals—or whether a refunctionalization of a particular mode or the introduction of a new function is paramount. To this end, the 20th-century results have been used as a base of comparison. And yet, a reanalysis of some categories—especially NI viewed as a separate category that moves between discourse presentation and narration—as well as the interplay between paralinguistic narration and speech, writing, and thought presentation should be considered.

My in-depth analysis has revealed several similarities but also differences between 19th- and 20th-century narrative fiction. All scales and all modes of discourse presentation identified by Semino and Short (2004) also feature in the 19th-century corpus of narrative fiction. In describing how they relate to one another, my findings show that despite the fact that the distribution of the scales of discourse presentation is similar for 19th- and 20th-century narrative fiction, there is still a considerable number of speech presentation in the 19th century. In addition, thought presentation categories feature rather prominently in the 19th century while writing presentation is comparatively scarce, but nevertheless functional in context as a means of narrative progression.

As section 4.2 of Chapter 4 has illustrated, direct speech (DS) is the most frequent form of speech presentation in the 19th-century corpus, both in terms of the number of words employed to linguistically realize this category and in terms of the number of identified tags. As far as thought presentation is concerned, the narrator's report of a thought act (NRTA) is the most frequent category in the 19th-century corpus, followed by indirect thought (IT), whereas the category employing the highest number of words is free indirect thought (FIT). Thus, in contrast to speech presentation, the direct forms of thought presentation are not the most frequent ones, although these are the categories of discourse presentation which receive most attention in the literature.

Thought report is much more prevalent in the 19th-century corpus and follows Palmer's (2004) more theoretical observations of the fictional mind in action. The notion of "internal speech" to explain thought presentation processes does not, however, fully account for the complexities of thought presentation displayed in 19th-century narrative fiction. The distribution of tags among the thought presentation modes in interplay with the other modes of speech and writing presentation illustrates that, in 19th-century fiction, the mind is active and social. As such, the more mimetic and at times more "glamorous" (Palmer 2004: 57) forms of thought presentation, such as FIT, should not be privileged over the more diegetic forms of thought (as well as speech) report. It has been especially difficult to determine whether NI should be seen as part of narration or as part of discourse presentation, because in the 19th-century corpus it contains not only internal activities that characters are not consciously aware of, but also more conscious cognitive activities. Especially the speech, thought, or writing reports contribute to the social mind in action and to characterization. This line of interpretation could be outlined through the systematic annotation, the historicized approach, and the identification of features—lexical, syntactic, pragmatic, and textual. These results were embedded in 19th-century cultural historical findings about vision and the psyche and their contextualization within claims made in 19th-century grammars, illustrating contemporary preoccupations with how the mind and communication function and whether this should—and if so, how—be (faithfully) represented. The fact that all modes of discourse presentation on the different scales occur in my corpus illustrates that the presentation of the mind in 19th-century narrative fiction was not unusual. This furthermore reflects an ideological as well as an epistemological concern about what cannot be reported, portrayed, or narrated.

Discourse presentation categories fulfill the function of prospection and encapsulation and mark narrative progression, which—through specific lexico-grammatical choices and the ways these are repetitively dispersed through the texts and in the corpus—shapes the reader's expectations, for instance, as to suspense or surprise. This finding could be obtained through the analysis of the individual incidents of the respective modes of discourse presentation.

This study has done pioneer work in the way it uses the analysis of keywords and repetitive patterns as basis for a—yet to be developed—tool that automatically annotates speech, writing, and thought presentation. Repetitive patterns could be observed on all levels of discourse, that is, on the word, phrase, sentence, and pragmatic level. These patterns contribute to characterization, that is, the individualization of a fictional persona. They also function as a means of narrative progression (Toolan 2009), that is, as linguistic cues for readers to understand that, for instance, modal auxiliaries are characteristic of FIT. Through discourse presentation we may empathize with a character. Discourse presentation may be realistic or entertaining, or may function as a trigger for a character's speech, thought, or writing about the past, the present, and the future, as well as even about something imagined. All this means that work on the topic of discourse presentation is far from finished. Further studies need to go back in time and also investigate further genres, such as newspaper reports.

NOTES

Chapter 1

1. It is beyond the scope of this study to revisit the various approaches to point of view, but see Chapter 2, section 2.6.3. The term "point of view" is deemed to be problematic because, as Toolan (2001: 60) highlights, "it does nothing to discourage the conflation and confusion of two distinct aspects of narrative practice: 1. The orientation we infer to be that from which what gets told is told. 2. The individual we judge to be the immediate source and authority for whatever *words* are used in telling" (emphasis in the original). Genette's (1980, 1988) theory of focalization, which describes the direction from which a narrative can be seen and differentiates between external and internal focalization, was further developed by Bal (1997). Virtually all existing proposals (e.g., Uspensky 1973; Fowler 1986; Simpson 1993) attempt to look at the different relationships of narration and the reader in an orderly and systematic way. Matters of orientation or deixis, to use the linguistic term, in presenting a narrative can also take on different modes.

2. I follow Semino and Short (2004: 3) in their use of the label *discourse presentation* to refer to how the discourse of others is presented. The term *report* is often used as a default by grammarians (e.g., Huddleston and Pullum 2002: 1023–1030; Quirk et al., 1985: 1020–1033) and other linguists who tend to invent examples when discussing discourse presentation. The term *report* suggests an unproblematic relationship between the discourse presentation and the anterior discourse that is presented, as if "faithful report" could simply be assumed. I do not want to use the term *representation* as a default either, as this tends to be used by linguists (e.g., critical discourse analysts such as Caldas-Coulthard 1994 and Fairclough 1988) who concentrate mainly on distortions and misrepresentations in the reporting of anterior discourses.

3. Whenever the term *discourse* is used, it generally refers to the discourse presentation modes of speech, writing, and thought presentation.

4. See Leech (2008) and Toolan (2009) for the challenges involved in choosing the right reference corpus.

5. See Fitzmaurice and Taavitsainen (2007a: 7; 2007b) on what the denominator *pragmatics* means in historical pragmatic studies.

6. Beal (2004) also pays attention to structural aspects of "Later Modern English." Likewise, Bailey (1996) focuses on "writing," "sounds," and "words," but also "slang."

7. The title of this section echoes and was inspired by Wolfgang Teubert's (2005) article "My Version of Corpus Linguistics."

8. See Leech (2008: 187) for other approaches to text and his reasoning as to why he follows the basic linguistic notion of a text.

9. See also Douthwaite (2000) and van Peer (1986, 2007).

10. From a linguistic point of view, I would not like to overemphasize the specific status of literary language, and rather follow Leech (2008: 7) and see the denominator *literature or literary language* as a prototype concept. There are common criteria which seem to define literary language—such as linguistic, sociocultural, or aesthetic ones. In terms of linguistic criteria, Leech sees foregrounding, the autotelic nature of literature, as well as its richness in the multiplicity of significance, as determining factors.

Chapter 2

1. The acronym NRSA has remained, but Semino and Short (2004) have renamed this category, as the "R" now stands for presentation and no longer for "representation/report," as it used to.

2. Semino and Short (2004: 44) regard Page's (1973: 32) idea of "submerged speech," McHale's (1978) notion of "diegetic summary," and Short's (1996) "Narrator's Representation of Speech" as similar concepts.

3. Toolan (2001: 119, 142) does not subsume NV and NI under the heading of discourse presentation but sees it as narration.

4. Readers are encouraged to also check work by Allen (1994), Bell (1991), Carter and McCarthy (2006), Dancygier (2007a, 2007b), Dodgson (1995), Guadagnin (1994), Halliday and Matthiessen (2014), Ikeo (2007), Semino (2007), and Short (1988, 1994).

5. Contemporaneous studies of grammatical aspects can be found in Anderson (1892), who focuses on relative clauses; Ljunggren (1893–1894), who considers the use of the modals *shall* and *will*; Koch (1863–1869) and Mätzner's (1860–1865) general grammars; and Sweet's (1891–1898) *A New English Grammar.*

6. Authors like Stitt (1998) focus on the use of metaphorical language in 19th-century English fiction, too.

7. Some of the topics discussed in Kytö, Rydén, and Smitterberg (2006) are the use of the passive in 19th-century writing (Gustafsson 2006), the use of relativizers and the distribution of *that* and *wh*-forms (Johansson 2006), as well as more pragmatically oriented topics, such as an investigation of modifiers of common nouns with female and male reference (Bäcklund 2006), and Grund and Walker's (2006) study of the subjunctive.

8. See Mahlberg (2013) for a discussion of the differences between corpus linguistics and corpus stylistics concerns.

9. Hoey (2005) is a corpus-based project which stands in the Firthian (1957a, 1957b) tradition. The concept of collocational priming does not refer to an automatic

or strict sequence of words, but refers to "a looser bonding of discoursal chunks such that, when we hear or read part of that chunk, the remainder is expectable" (Toolan 2009: 17). A collocation may be defined as the far-greater-than-chance tendency of particular words to co-occur (adjacently or within a few words of another). These co-occurrence tendencies have text-constructional and semantic implications. Proficient native language users are equipped, by their communicational experience, with the commoner collocational tendencies and implications (Toolan 2009: 19).

The tendencies of particular units to co-occur in particular grammatical constructions are often summarized under the heading of "colligation." Further, "collocation" and "colligation" are often mentioned in unison. Colligation describes the tendency of grammatical units to co-occur with specific lexical items.

10. *WordSmith Tools* (Scott 2017) uses a statistical calculation to bring out statistically significant words and to calculate their ranks both in terms of over-recurrence and under-use with respect to the reference corpus, in my case CONCE. This statistical analysis and further comparison go beyond the selection of allegedly frequent or recurrent words and the correlation of those items to the construction of particular imagery as is used in certain literary texts, a practice that has often been pursued in literary criticism, especially in Shakespeare studies, as a means of identifying general themes (Clemen 1951; Kolbe 1930). Also, using comparative keyword analysis further serves as a test-bed for the critic's intuition about a particular sequence of words occurring in more than regular frequency or being relevant to the "style" of a text. Software such as *WordSmith Tools* (Scott 2017) is capable of identifying frequent words and multi-word units (or clusters, lexical bundles, or n-grams) on a more objective basis, because these programs do not pre-select, but "simply list and count all multi-word sequences" (Toolan 2009: 41). However, different reference corpora may lead to different keyword lists and key clusters (see Fischer-Starcke 2009; Leech 2008; Toolan 2009), something that also needs bearing in mind. Another reason which will generate discrepant results is the adoption of different p-values.

Chapter 3

1. The term *annotation* is also used in editorial criticism. Here it will be used interchangeably with the term *tagging* and it refers to the categories (following Semino and Short 2004) that are ascribed to each instance of discourse presentation occurring in the respective text.

2. It should be stressed that the existing software used in corpus-driven approaches has been created by humans, who have also used their own (informed) intuition and knowledge, so those analyses can, by no means, be described as solely objective or mechanic.

3. For further details on these tagging tools, see the UCREL website at Lancaster University: http://www.comp.lancs.ac.uk/ucrel/. I would like to thank Paul Rayson for giving me access to *Wmatrix* (Rayson 2008) and for his useful advice.

4. *Wmatrix* is a tool widely used by corpus stylisticians. As an example, check Leech (2008), Montoro (2012), or Walker (2010). For examples of how *Wordsmith Tools* has been exploited, see Archer (2009) and Culpeper (2002).

5. A word significantly overused in a text will appear at the top of the list. In other words, the words in the keyness list are ordered according to their unusual frequency

which endows them with a higher keyness value; this value is calculated as a positive score of log-likelihood. Log-likelihood (LL) is a measure of significance which can be compared to the chi-square test in the following way: "Any score at or above 3.8 is significant to the level of $p<0.05$ in chi-square terms; any score at or above 6.6 is significant to the level of $p<0.01$" (Leech 2008: 165).

6. CONCE is *A Corpus of Nineteenth-Century English*, compiled at the universities of Uppsala and Tampere in the mid-1990s (Kytö et al. 2000). It roughly contains one million words and is divided into periods of several decades. It is also genre-specific, containing debates, trials, drama, fiction, letters, and historical and scientific monographs (Kytö et al. 2000; Kytö et al. 2006).

7. Although some of them published under pseudonyms.

Chapter 4

1. I do not claim that this is the case for *all* 19th-century fiction, though. As I have repeatedly stated throughout this book, I am aware of the issues related to my corpus size. Having said that, my quantitative analysis provides evidentiary support to my suggestions, something which is missing from other, less quantitatively oriented, studies.

Chapter 5

1. As my corpus consists of narrative fiction only, it is necessary for the identification of keywords to initially take out the fictional sub-corpus from the reference corpus CONCE, as otherwise I would compare like with like, that is, similar text types.

2. *Embedding* here means that the discourse presentation mode is positioned within another discourse presentation mode (see Busse 2010c).

3. It is beyond the scope of this book to draw conclusions that go beyond the main focus of my study, which is 19th-century fiction. However, the analysis of a bigger corpus inclusive of a fuller diachronic spread might prove that the effects I mention here are, in fact, prototypical of DS and FDS in narrative fiction in general.

4. It remains to be seen whether this claim would, in fact, apply to all fictional writing, but that task falls well outside the remit of this book.

5. These features are identified for Joyce's short story "Two Gallants." They were subsequently tested against other short stories in Toolan's (2009) 20th-century corpus of short stories, and adjusted accordingly. Toolan explicitly stresses that the features identified may be different for historical data.

6. By *host* I mean here that although the discourse presented is hypothetical, the mode of the discourse presentation (as speech, writing, or thought) can still be identified as a source or host.

7. In *Text World Theory* (Werth 1999), hypotheticals are a means of expressing an epistemic modal-world which is distant or remote because it is not realized.

Chapter 7

1. "Foregrounding" is not to be understood as a synonym of "emphasizing" but, as mentioned, needs to be related to the Theory of Foregrounding (Douthwaite 2000,

Short 1996), which is crucial to stylistics. The psychological effect of signaling importance, salience, or prominence may be achieved through two fundamental higher-order techniques: deviation and parallelism. In the linguistic sense, deviation is the breaking of a rule or norm. Parallelism occurs in repetition (Douthwaite 2000: 181), which can be either literal or non-literal.

2. In order to further stress the heavy weight of the lovers' feelings, on the one hand, as well as to ridicule them, on the other, the non-use of speech is foregrounded through a high proliferation of prospective silence, as in "He was silent" (*Emma* 1985 [1816]: 412), "For a moment or two nothing was said" (*Emma* 1985 [1816]: 413), "He listened in perfect silence" (*Emma* 1985 [1816]: 414), "She wished him to speak, but he would not" (*Emma* 1985 [1816]: 414), "but he was silent; and, as far as she could judge, deep in thought" (*Emma* 1985 [1816]: 415), "Emma could say no more" (*Emma* 1985 [1816]: 416), and "She could really say nothing" (*Emma* 1985 [1816]: 417). In order to process the use of non-speech, or that of the disnarrated or the negative, we have to imagine a world which takes into account what is said and what is not said.

3. There is a controversy about when and how metaphors like THINKING IS MOVEMENT are processed because not all metaphors activate some underlying cross-domain mappings in people's minds, but are rather too conventional and therefore are processed by (simple) lexical disambiguation. Yet, more reference to thinking being conceptualized as movement can be found in the 19th-century corpus of narrative fiction. Further examples are: "But so active were her thoughts" (*Northanger Abbey* 1985 [1818]: 150), "The multitude of feelings that crowded into my mind" (*Frankenstein* 2003 [1818]: 76), or "Various ideas rushed through her mind as to what the burning of a second will might imply. She had to make a difficult decision in a hurry" (*Middlemarch* 1986 [1871–1872]: 234).

BIBLIOGRAPHY

Primary Literature

Austen, Jane. 1994 [1813]. *Pride and Prejudice.* London: Penguin.

Austen, Jane. 1985 [1816]. *Emma,* ed. Ronald Blythe. London: Penguin.

Austen, Jane. 1985 [1818]. *Northanger Abbey,* ed. Anne Henry Ehrenpreis. London: Penguin.

Brontë, Charlotte. 1985 [1847]. *Jane Eyre,* ed. Queenie D. Leavis. London: Penguin.

Brontë, Emily. 2009 [1847]. *Wuthering Heights,* ed. Ian Jack. Oxford: Oxford University Press.

Chandler, Raymond. 1993. *"The Big Sleep" and Other Novels.* London: Penguin.

Collins, Wilkie. 1998 [1868]. *The Moonstone,* ed. Sandra Kemp. London: Penguin.

De Quincey, Thomas. 1864 [1845]. *Suspiria de Profundis* (published in one volume with *Confessions of an English Opium-Eater*). Boston: Ticknor and Fields.

Dickens, Charles. 1993 [1837]. *Oliver Twist.* New York and London: W. W. Norton.

Dickens, Charles. 1999 [1860]. *Great Expectations,* ed. Edgar Rosenberg. New York: Norton.

Disraeli, Benjamin. 2004 [1826]. *Vivian Grey, By the Earl of Beaconsfield.* Whitefish, MT: Kessinger Publishing's Rare Reprints.

Edgeworth, Maria. 2008 [1802]. *The Grateful Negro.* Gloucester: Dodo Press.

Eliot, George. 1996 [1859]. *Adam Bede,* ed. Valentine Cunningham. Oxford: Oxford University Press.

Eliot, George. 1986 [1871–1872]. *Middlemarch,* ed. David Carroll. Oxford: Oxford University Press.

Eliot, George. 1998 [1876]. *Daniel Deronda,* ed. Graham Handley. Oxford: Oxford University Press.

Gaskell, Elizabeth. 2007 [1853]. *Cranford,* ed. Jenny Uglow Watson. London: Bloomsbury.

Gaskell, Elizabeth. 2003 [1854]. *North and South,* ed. Patricia Ingham. London: Penguin.

Gaskell, Elizabeth. 2006 [1863]. *Cousin Phillis.* Fairford: Echo Library.

Godwin, William. 1991 [1794]. *Caleb Williams.* World's Classics. Oxford: Oxford University Press.

Hardy, Thomas. 1975 [1891]. *Jude the Obscure*, ed. Philip N. Furbank. The New Wessex Edition 2. London: Macmillan.

James, Henry. 1975 [1905]. *A Portrait of a Lady*, ed. Robert D. Bamberg. London: Norton.

Kingsley, Charles. 1967 [1859]. *Alton Locke: Tailor and Poet: An Autobiography*, vol. 1 and 2. London: Cassell.

Lewes, George H. 1874–1879. *Problems of Life and Mind*. Boston: Houghton, Osgood.

Meredith, George. 1968 [1859]. *The Ordeal of Richard Feverel*. New York: Russell & Russell.

Oliphant, Margarete. 2000 [1879]. *A Beleaguered City*. Edinburgh: Canongate.

Rymer, James M. 2015 [1845–1847]. *Varney the Vampire; or The Feast of Blood*. Mineola: Dover Publications.

Scott, Sir Walter. 1998 [1819]. *Ivanhoe*, ed. Graham Tulloch. The Edinburgh Edition of the Waverley Novels 8. Edinburgh: Edinburgh University Press.

Scott, Sir Walter. 1973 [1822]. *The Fortunes of Nigel*. St. Albans, England: Panther.

Shakespeare, William. 1997. *King Lear*. The Riverside Shakespeare, 2nd ed., ed. Gwynne B. Evans. Boston: Houghton Mifflin.

Shakespeare, William. 1997. *Romeo and Juliet*. The Riverside Shakespeare. 2nd ed., ed. Gwynne B. Evans. Boston: Houghton Mifflin.

Shelley, Mary. 2003 [1818]. *Frankenstein or the Modern Prometheus*, ed. Maurice Hindle. London: Penguin.

Spencer, Herbert R. 1877 [1855]. *Principles of Psychology*. New York: D. Appleton.

Spencer, Herbert R. 1857. Progress: Its Law and Cause. In *Victorian Prose. An Anthology*, ed. Rosemary J. Mundhenk and Luann McCracken Fletcher, 295–303. New York: Columbia University Press.

Spencer, Herbert R. 1860. The Social Organism. *Westminster Review* 17: 90–121.

Stevenson, Robert L. 2003 [1886]. *The Strange Case of Dr Jekyll and Mr Hyde*, ed. Richard Dury. Edinburgh: Edinburgh University Press.

Thackeray, William M. 1910 [1846–1847]. The Book of Snobs. In *The Works of William Makepeace Thackeray*. The Centenary Biographical Edition. London: Smith, Elder, 1–220.

Thackeray, William M. 1994 [1847]. *Vanity Fair*, ed. Peter Shillingsburg. New York and London: Northon.

Trollope, Anthony. 1988 [1863]. *Rachel Ray*, ed. P. D. Edwards. Oxford: Oxford University Press.

Wilde, Oscar. 1997 [1891]. The Critic as Artist. In *The Artist as Critic: Critical Writings of Oscar Wilde*, ed. Richard Ellmann, n.p. Los Angeles: Green Integer.

Wilde, Oscar. 1994 [1891]. *The Picture of Dorian Gray*. London: Penguin.

Wordsworth, William. 1992 [1798]. *Lyrical Ballads*, ed. Michael Mason. London: Longman.

Secondary Literature

Adamson, Sylvia. 1994. From Empathetic Deixis to Empathetic Narrative: Stylisation and (De-)Subjectivisation as Processes of Language Change. *Transactions of the Philological Society* 92 (1): 55–88. Reprinted in *Subjectivity and Subjectivisation*, ed. Sarah Wright and Dieter Stein, 195–224. Cambridge: Cambridge University Press, 1995.

Adamson, Sylvia. 2001. The Rise and Fall of Empathetic Narrative. In *New Perspectives on Narrative Perspective*, ed. Willie van Peer and Seymour Chatman, 83–99. Albany: State University of New York Press.

Aikhenvald, Alexandra Y. 2004. *Evidentiality*. Oxford: Oxford University Press.

Alford, Henry. 1866. *A Plea for the Queen's English: Stray Notes on Speaking and Spelling*. London: Strahan; Cambridge: Deighton, Bell.

Allen, Rosamund. 1994. *The Presentation of Speech and Thought in Popular Fiction*. Lancaster: Lancaster University.

Altick, Richard D. 1957. *The English Common Reader: A Social History of the Mass Reading Public 1800–1900*. Chicago and London: University of Chicago Press.

Andersson, Herman. 1892. *Some Remarks on the Use of Relative Pronouns in Modern English Prose*. Lund: Gleerup.

Anderwald, Lieselotte. 2016. *Language between Description and Prescription: Verbs and Verb Categories in Nineteenth-Century Grammars of English*. Oxford: Oxford University Press.

Andrew, James. 1817. *Institutes of Grammar*. London: Black, Parbury and Allen.

Archer, Dawn, ed. 2009. *What's in a Word-List: Investigating Word Frequency and Keyword Extraction*. Oxon: Ashgate.

Arnaud, René. 1973. *La forme progressive en anglais du XIXe siècle*. Lille.

Arnovick, Leslie K. 1999. *Diachronic Pragmatics: Seven Case Studies in English Illocutionary Development*. Amsterdam: John Benjamins.

Austin, John L. 1962. *How to Do Things with Words*. Oxford: Oxford University Press.

Axelsson, Karin. 2009. Tag Questions in Fiction Dialogue vs. Spoken Conversation. Paper presented at the 30th annual conference of the International Computer Archive of Modern and Medieval English (ICAME 30), Lancaster University, May 27–31, 2009.

Bäcklund, Ingegerd. 2006. Modifiers Describing Women and Men in Nineteenth-Century English. In *Nineteenth-Century English: Stability and Change*, ed. Merja Kytö, Mats Rydén, and Erik Smitterberg, 17–66. Cambridge: Cambridge University Press.

Bailey, Richard W. 1996. *Nineteenth-Century English*. Ann Arbor: University of Michigan Press.

Bailey, Richard W. 2003. The Ideology of English in the Late Eighteenth Century. In *Insights into Late Modern English*, ed. Marina Dossena and Charles Jones, 21–44. Linguistic Insights 7. Bern: Peter Lang.

Bakhtin, Mikhail M. 1981. Discourse in the Novel. In *The Dialogic Imagination: Four Essays by M. M. Bakhtin*, 12th ed., ed. Michael Holquist, tr. Caryl Emerson and Michael Holquist, 259–442. Austin: University of Texas Press.

Bakhtin, Mikhail M. 1984. *Problems of Dostoevsky's Poetics*. Trans. Caryl Emerson. Manchester: Manchester University Press.

Bal, Mieke. 1997. *Narratology: Introduction to the Theory of Narrative*, 2nd ed. Toronto: Toronto University Press.

Bally, Charles. 1912a. Le style indirect libre en français moderne I. *Germanisch-Romanische Monatsschrift* 4: 549–556.

Bally, Charles. 1912b. Le style indirect libre en français moderne II. *Germanisch-Romanische Monatsschrift* 4: 597–606.

Banfield, Ann. 1973. Narrative Style and the Grammar of the Direct and Indirect Speech. *Foundations of Language* 10: 1–39.

Banfield, Ann. 1982. *Unspeakable Sentences: Narration and Representation in the Language of Fiction*. Boston: Routledge & Kegan Paul.

Barber, Charles. 1964. *Linguistic Change in Present-Day English*. Edinburgh: Oliver and Boyd.

Barry, Peter. 2002. *Beginning Theory: An Introduction to Literary and Cultural Theory*, 2nd ed. Manchester: Manchester University Press.

Bauer, Brigitte L. M. 1996. The Verb in Indirect Speech in Old French: System in Change. In *Reported Speech: Forms and Functions of the Verb*, ed. Theo A. J. M. Janssen and Wim van der Wurff, 75–96. Amsterdam and Philadelphia: John Benjamins.

Bauer, Laurie. 1994. *Watching English Change: An Introduction to the Study of Linguistic Change in Standard Englishes in the Twentieth Century*. London: Longman.

Baynham, Mike, and Stef Slembrouck. 1999. Speech Representation and Institutional Discourse. *Text* 19 (4): 439–457.

Beal, Joan C. 2004. *English in Modern Times: 1700–1945*. London: Arnold.

Bednarek, Monika. 2006a. Epistemological Positioning and Evidentiality in English News Discourse: A Text-Driven Approach. *Text and Talk* 26 (6): 635–660.

Bednarek, Monika. 2006b. *Evaluation in Media Discourse: Analysis of a Newspaper Corpus. Corpus and discourse. Research in corpus and discourse.* London and New York: Continuum.

Bell, Allan. 1991. *The Language of News Media*. Oxford: Blackwell.

Bell, Alice. 2007. "Do You Want to Hear About It?" Exploring Possible Worlds in Michael Joyce's Hyperfiction, Afternoon, a Story. In *Contemporary Stylistics*, ed. Marina Lambrou and Peter Stockwell, 43–55. London: Continuum.

Benveniste, Emile. 1977. *Probleme der allgemeinen Sprachwissenschaft*. Frankfurt am Main: Syndikat.

Berger, Peter, and Luckmann, Thomas. 2000. *Die gesellschaftliche Theorie der Wirklichkeit: Eine Theorie der Wissenssoziologie*, 17th ed. Frankfurt: Fischer.

Bertuccelli Papi, M. 2000. Is a Diachronic Speech Act Theory Possible? *Journal of Historical Pragmatics* 1: 57–66.

Biber, Douglas. 1988. *Variation across Speech and Writing*. Cambridge: Cambridge University Press.

Biber, Douglas. 1990. Methodological Issues Regarding Corpus-Based Analyses of Linguistic Variation. *Literary and Linguistic Computing* 5 (1): 257–269.

Biber, Douglas. 1993. Representativeness in Corpus Design. *Literary and Linguistic Computing* 8 (4): 243–258.

Biber, Douglas. 1995. *Dimensions of Register Variation: A Cross-Linguistic Comparison*. Cambridge: Cambridge University Press.

Biber, Douglas, and Jena Burgess. 2000. Historical Change in Language Use of Women and Men. *Journal of English Linguistics* 28: 21–37.

Biber, Douglas, Susan Conrad, and Viviana Cortes. 2004. "If You Look At . . .": Lexical Bundles in University Teaching and Textbooks. *Applied Linguistics* 25 (3): 371–405.

Biber, Douglas, Susan Conrad, and Randi Reppen. 1998. *Corpus Linguistics: Investigating Language Structure and Use*. Cambridge: Cambridge University Press.

Biber, Douglas, and Edward Finegan. 1989. Styles of Stance in English: Lexical and Grammatical Marking of Evidentiality and Affect. *Text* 9 (1): 93–124.

Biber, Douglas, and Edward Finegan. 1997. Diachronic Relations among Speech-based and Written Registers in English. In *To Explain the Present: Studies in the Changing English Language in Honour of Matti Rissanen*, ed. Terttu Nevalainen and Leena Kahlas-Tarkka, 253–275. Mémoires de la Société Néophilologique de Helsinki 52. Helsinki: Société Néophilologique.

Biber, Douglas, Edward Finegan, and Dwight Atkinson. 1994a. ARCHER and Its Challenges: Compiling and Exploring a Representative Corpus of Historical English Registers. In *Creating and Using English Language Corpora: Papers from the Fourteenth International Conference on English Language Research on Computerized Corpora, Zürich 1993*, ed. Udo Fries, Gunni Tottel, and Peter Schneider, 1–11. Language and Computers: Studies in Practical Linguistics 11. Amsterdam and Atlanta, GA: Rodopi.

Biber, Douglas, Edward Finegan, Dwight Atkinson, Ann Beck, Dennis Burges, and Jena Burges. 1994b. The Design and Analysis of the ARCHER Corpus: A Progress Report. In *Corpora across the Centuries: Proceedings of the First International Colloquium of English Diachronic Corpora, St Catharine's College Cambridge, 25–27 March 1993*, ed. Merja Kytö, Matti Rissanen, and Susan Wright, 3–6. Language and Computers: Studies in Practical Linguistics 11. Amsterdam and Atlanta, GA: Rodopi.

Biber, Douglas, Stig Johansson, Geoffrey Leech, Susan Conrad, and Edward Finegan. 1999. *The Longman Grammar of Spoken and Written English*. London: Longman.

Blackwell, Natalia, and Jean E. Fox Tree. 2012. Social Factors Affect Quotative Choice. *Journal of Pragmatics* 44: 1150–1162.

Blakemore, Diane, and Fabrizio Gallai. 2014. Discourse Markers in Free Indirect Style and Interpreting. *Journal of Pragmatics* 60: 106–120.

Blinova, Olga A. 2015. Speech and Thought Representation in Hemingway: The Case of Free Indirect Discourse. *Mediterranean Journal of Social Sciences* 6 (1): 458–464.

Borsley, Robert D., and Richard Ingham. 2002. Grow Your Own Linguistics? On Some Applied Linguists' Views of the Subject. *Lingua* 112: 1–6.

Bortolussi, Marisa, and Peter Dixon. 1996. Literary Communication: Effects of Reader-Narrator Cooperation. *Poetics* 23: 405–430.

Bortolussi, Marisa, and Peter Dixon. 2003. *Psychonarratology: Foundations for the Empirical Study of Literary Response*. Cambridge: Cambridge University Press.

Bray, Joe. 2002. Embedded Quotations in Eighteenth-Century Fiction: Journalism and the Early Novel. *Journal of Literary Semantics* 31: 61–75.

Bright, William. 1982. Literature: Written and Oral. In *Analyzing Discourse: Text and Talk*, ed. Deborah Tannen, 271–283. Washington, DC: Georgetown University Press.

Brinton, Laurel J. 1980. "Represented Perception": A Study in Narrative Style. *Poetics* 9: 363–381.

Brinton, Laurel J. 1996. *Pragmatic Markers in English: Grammaticalization and Discourse Functions*. Berlin and New York: Mouton de Gruyter.

Brinton, Laurel J. 2001. Historical Discourse Analysis. In *Handbook of Discourse Analysis*, ed. Deborah Schiffrin, Deborah Tannen, and Heidi E. Hamilton, 138–160. Oxford: Blackwell.

Britain, David. 2002. Sociolinguistic Variation. In *A Web Guide to Teaching and Learning in Languages, Linguistics and Area Studies*, ed. David Bickerton. Southampton: Subject Centre for Languages, Linguistics and Area Studies, 2002. Online at: <http://www.lang.ltsn.ac.uk/resources/goodpractice.aspx?resourceid=1054>

Brittain, Lewis. 1788. *Rudiments of English Grammar*. London.

Brorström, Sverker. 1963. *The Increasing Frequency of the Preposition About during the Modern English Period: With Special Reference to the Verbs Say, Tell, Talk and Speak*. Stockholm Studies in English 9. Stockholm: Almqvist and Wiksell.

Brosch, Renate, ed. 2008. *Victorian Visual Culture*. Anglistik und Englischunterricht 71. Heidelberg: Winter.

Brown, Gillian. 1996. *Listening to Spoken English: Applied Linguistics and Language Study*, 2nd ed. London and New York: Longman.

Brown, Goold. 1860. *The Institutes of English Grammar, Methodically Arranged*. New York: Samuel & William Wood.

Brown, Penelope, and Stephen C. Levinson. 1987. *Politeness: Some Universals in Language Usage*. Cambridge: Cambridge University Press.

Brunner, Annelen. 2013. Automatic Recognition of Speech, Thought, and Writing Representation in German Narrative Texts. *Literary and Linguistic Computing* 28 (4): 563–575.

Brunner, Annelen. 2015. *Automatische Erkennung von Redewiedergabe in literarischen Texten. Ein Beitrag zur quantitativen Narratologie*. Berlin: de Gruyter.

Bublitz, Wolfram. 2001. *Englische Pragmatik: Eine Einführung*. Berlin, Germany: Schmidt.

Busse, Beatrix. 2006. *Vocative Constructions in the Language of Shakespeare*. Amsterdam: John Benjamins.

Busse, Beatrix. 2010a. Adverbial Expressions of Stance in Early Modern "Spoken" Language. In *Anglistentag 2009 Klagenfurt—Proceedings*, ed. Jörg Helbig, 47–64. Trier: WVT.

Busse, Beatrix. 2010b. Recent Trends in New Historical Stylistics. In *Language and Style: In Honour of Mick Short*, ed. Dan McIntyre and Beatrix Busse, 32–54. Houndmills: Palgrave Macmillan.

Busse, Beatrix. 2010c. Analysing Embedded Discourse Presentation: Bridging Disciplines. *Zeitschrift für Anglistik und Amerikanistik* 58 (3): 229–255.

Busse, Beatrix. 2014. (New) Historical Stylistics. In *The Routledge Handbook of Stylistics*, ed. Michael Burke, 101–117. London and New York: Taylor and Francis.

Busse, Beatrix. 2015. New Historical Stylistics. In *The Bloomsbury Companion to Stylistics*, ed. Violeta Sotirova, pp. 177–188. London: Bloomsbury.

Caldas-Coulthard, Carmen R. 1988. *Reporting Interaction in Narrative: A Study of Speech Representation in Written Discourse*. Unpublished PhD Thesis, University of Birmingham, UK.

Caldas-Coulthard, Carmen R. 1994. On Reporting Reporting: The Representation of Speech in Factual and Factional Narratives. In *Advances in Written Text Analysis*, ed. Malcolm Coulthard, 295–308. London: Routledge, 1994.

Cannon, Charles D. 1959. A Survey of the Subjunctive Mood in English. *American Speech* 34: 11–19.

Carroll, Noël. 2001. On the Narrative Connection. In *New Perspectives on Narrative Perspective*, ed. Willie van Peer and Seymour Chatman, 21–41. Albany: State University of New York Press.

Carter, Ronald, and Michael McCarthy. 2006. *The Cambridge Grammar of English: A Comprehensive Guide: Spoken and Written English, Grammar and Usage.* Cambridge: Cambridge University Press.

Chatman, Seymour. 1978. *Story and Discourse.* Ithaca, NY: Cornell University Press.

Chatman, Seymour. 2001. Ironic Perspective: Conrad's Secret Agent. In *New Perspectives on Narrative Perspective*, ed. Willie van Peer and Seymour Chatman, 117–131. Albany: State University of New York Press.

Claridge, Claudia, and Terry Walker. 2001. Causal Clauses in Written and Speech-Related Genres in Early Modern English. *ICAME Journal* 25: 31–63.

Clark, Herbert H., and Richard J. Gerrig. 1990. Quotation as Demonstration. *Language* 66: 784–805.

Clemen, Wolfgang. 1951. *The Development of Shakespeare's Imagery.* London: Methuen.

Cohn, Dorrit C. 1978. *Transparent Minds: Narrative Modes for Presenting Consciousness in Fiction.* Princeton, NJ: Princeton University Press.

Coleridge, Samuel T. 1975. *Biographia Literaria*, ed. George Watson. London: Dent.

Collins, Daniel E. 2001. *Reanimated Voices. Speech Reporting in a Historical Pragmatic Perspective.* Amsterdam and Philadelphia: John Benjamins.

Collins, Daniel E. 2009. Indirectness in Legal Speech Acts: An Argument against the Out of Ritual Hypothesis. *Journal of Pragmatics* 41:427–439.

Comrie, Bernard. 1986. Tense in Indirect Speech. *Folia Linguistica* 20: 265–296.

CONCE = *A Corpus of Nineteenth-Century English*, compiled by Merja Kytö (Uppsala University) and Juhani Rudanko (University of Tampere).

Cook, Chris, and John Stevenson. 1996. *The Longman Handbook of Modern British History 1714–1995.* 3rd ed. London and New York: Longman.

Coulmas, Florian, ed. 1986a. *Direct and Indirect Speech.* Berlin and New York: de Gruyter.

Coulmas, Florian. 1986b. Reported Speech: Some General Issues. In *Direct and Indirect Speech*, ed. Florian Coulmas, 1–28. Berlin and New York: de Gruyter.

Cruse, Alan. 2000. *Meaning in Language: An Introduction to Semantics and Pragmatics.* Oxford: Oxford University Press.

Culpeper, Jonathan. 2001. *Language and Characterisation: People in Plays and Other Texts.* Harlow: Longman.

Culpeper, Jonathan. 2002. A Cognitive Stylistic Approach to Characterization. In *Cognitive Stylistics: Language and Cognition in Text Analysis*, ed. Elena Semino and Jonathan Culpeper, 251–277. Amsterdam: John Benjamins.

Culpeper, Jonathan. 2011. *Historical Sociopragmatics.* Amsterdam: John Benjamins.

Culpeper, Jonathan, and Jane Demmen. 2012. Nineteenth-Century English Politeness: Negative Politeness, Conventional Indirect Requests and the Rise of the Individual Self. In *Understanding Historical (Im)Politeness: Relational Linguistic Practice over Time and across Cultures*, ed. Marcel Bax and Dániel Kádár, 49–80. Amsterdam: John Benjamins.

Culpeper, Jonathan, and Merja Kytö. 2000. Data in Historical Pragmatics: Spoken Interaction (Re)cast as Writing. *Journal of Historical Pragmatics* 1: 175–199.

Curme, George O. 1977. *A Grammar of the English Language: Syntax*, vol. 2. Essex, CT: Verbatim Printing.

Dancygier, Barbara. 2006. What Can Blending Do for You? *Language and Literature* 15 (1): 5–15.

Dancygier, Barbara. 2007a. Narrative Anchors and the Processes of Story Construction: The Case of Margaret Atwood's The Blind Assassin. *Style* 41 (2): 133–152.

Dancygier, Barbara, Jose Sanders, and Lieven Vandelanotte, eds. 2012. *Textual Choices in Discourse.* Amsterdam: John Benjamins.

Dancygier, Barbara, and Radoslava Trnavac. 2007b. Conjunctions, Verb Forms, and Epistemic Stance in Polish and Serbian Predictive Conditionals. *Cognitive Paths into the Slavic Domain*, ed. Dagmar Divjak and Agata Kochańska, 181–120. Berlin: Mouton de Gruyter.

Dancygier, Barbara, and Lieven Vandelanotte. 2009. Judging Distances: Mental Spaces, Distance, and Viewpoint in Literary Discourse. In *Cognitive Poetics: Goals, Gains and Gaps*, ed. Geert Brône and Jeroen Vandaele, 319–369. Berlin: Mouton de Gruyter.

Darwin, Charles. 1996 [1859]. *The Origin of Species*, ed. Gillian Beer. Oxford: Oxford University Press.

Davis, Lennard J. 1983. *Factual Fictions: The Origins of the English Novel.* New York: Columbia University Press.

Dekeyser, Xavier. 1975. *Number and Case Relations in 19th-Century British English: A Comparative Study of Grammar and Usage.* Antwerp and Amsterdam: Uitgeverij De Nederlandsche Boekhandel.

Denison, David. 1993. *English Historical Syntax: Verbal Constructions.* London and New York: Longman.

Denison, David. 1998. Syntax. In *The Cambridge History of the English Language*, vol.4, ed. Suzanne Romaine, 92–329. Cambridge: Cambridge University Press.

Dixon, Peter, and Marisa Bortolussi. 1996. Literary Communication: Effects of Reader-Narrator Cooperation. *Poetics: Journal of Empirical Research on Culture, the Media and the Arts* 23 (6): 405–430.

Dixon, Peter, and Marisa Bortolussi. 2003. *Psychonarratology: Foundations for the Empirical Study of Literary Response.* Cambridge: Cambridge University Press.

Dodgson, Martyn. 1995. *Computer Recognition of Speech Presentation in Text: Project Report.* Computing Department, Lancaster University, 1995.

Doležel, Lubomir. 1998. *Heterocosmica: Fiction and Possible Worlds.* Baltimore, MD, and London: John Hopkins University Press.

Douthwaite, John. 2000. *Towards a Linguistic Theory of Foregrounding.* Alessandria: Edizioni dell'Orso.

Duchan, Judith F., Gail A. Bruder, and Lynne E. Hewitt, eds. 1995. *Deixis in Narrative: A Cognitive Science Perspective.* Hillsdale, NJ: Lawrence Erlbaum Associates.

Eagleton, Terry. 1994. *Literary Theory: An Introduction.* Oxford: Blackwell.

Eco, Umberto. 1990. *The Limits of Interpretation.* Bloomington and Indianapolis: Indiana University Press.

Ehrlich, Susan. 1990. *Point of View: A Linguistic Analysis of Literary Style.* London: Routledge.

Elliott, Ralph W. V. 1984. *Thomas Hardy's English Grammar.* Oxford: Blackwell.

Elson, David K., and Kathleen R. McKeown. 2010. Building a Bank of Semantically Encoded Narratives. In *Proceedings of the Seventh International Conference on Language Resources and Evaluation (LREC 2010), 17–23 May 2010*, Valletta, Malta.

Emmott, Catherine. 1997. *Narrative Comprehension: A Discourse Perspective.* Oxford: Oxford University Press.

Evans, Mel. 2017. Royal Language and Reported Discourse in Sixteenth-Century Correspondence. *Journal of Historical Pragmatics* 18: 30–57.

Evans, Vyvyan, and Melanie Green. 2006. *Cognitive Linguistics: An Introduction.* Edinburgh: Edinburgh University Press.

Eysenck, Michael W., and Mark T. Keane. 2000. *Cognitive Psychology: A Student's Textbook.* Hove: Psychology Press.

Fairclough, Norman. 1988. Discourse Representation in Media Discourse. *Sociolinguistics* 17: 125–139.

Fairclough, Norman. 1992. *Discourse and Social Change.* London: Polity Press.

Fairclough, Norman. 1994. Conversationalization of Public Discourse and the Authority of the Consumer. In *The Authority of the Consumer,* ed. Russell Keat, Nigel Whiteley, and Nicolas Abercrombie, 253–268. London: Routledge.

Fairclough, Norman. 1995. *Media Discourse.* London and New York: Arnold.

Fairman, Tony. 2006. Words in English Record Office Documents of the Early 1800s. In *Nineteenth-Century English: Stability and Change,* ed. Merja Kytö, Mats Rydén, and Erik Smitterberg, 56–88. Cambridge: Cambridge University Press.

Fanego, Teresa. 1996. On the Historical Development of English Retrospective Verbs. *Neuphilologische Mitteilungen* 97: 71–79.

Fauconnier, Gilles, and Mark Turner. 2002. *The Way We Think: Conceptual Blending and the Mind's Hidden Complexities.* New York: Basic Books.

Ferrara, Kathleen, and Barbara Bell. 1995. Sociolinguistic Variation and Discourse Function of Constructed Dialogue Introducers: The Case of Be + Like. *American Speech* 70: 265–290.

Fillmore, Charles. 1992. "Corpus Linguistics" or "Computer-Aided Armchair Linguistics." In *Directions in Corpus Linguistics,* ed. Jan Svartvik, 35–60. Berlin: Mouton de Gruyter.

Finegan, Edward. 1998. English Grammar and Usage. In *The Cambridge History of the English Language,* Vol. IV: *1776–1997,* ed. Suzanne Romaine, 536–588. Cambridge: Cambridge University Press.

Firth, John R. 1957a. Modes of Meaning. In *Papers in Linguistics 1934–51.* London: Oxford University Press.

Firth, John R. 1957b. A Synopsis of Linguistic Theory 1930–55. *Studies in Linguistic Analysis, special volume of the Philological Society,* 1–32. Oxford: Blackwell. Reprinted in *Selected Papers of J. R. Firth 1952–59,* ed. Frank R. Palmer, 168–205. London: Longman, 1968.

Fischer-Starcke, Bettina. 2009. Keywords and Frequent Phrases of Jane Austen's *Pride and Prejudice*: A Corpus-Stylistic Approach. *International Journal of Corpus Linguistics* 14 (4): 492–523.

Fish, Stanley. 1980 [1973]. *Is There a Text in This Class? The Authority of Interpretative Communities.* Cambridge, MA: Harvard University Press.

Fitzmaurice, Susan. 2000. Remarks on the Rhetoric of Historical Pragmatics. *Journal of Historical Pragmatics* 2: 1–6.

Fitzmaurice, Susan, and Irma Taavitsainen. 2007a. Introduction. In *Methods in Historical Pragmatics,* ed. Susan Fitzmaurice and Irma Taavitsainen, 1–10. Berlin: Mouton de Gruyter.

Fitzmaurice, Susan, and Irma Taavitsainen. 2007b. Historical Pragmatics: What It Is and How to Do It. In *Methods in Historical Pragmatics*, ed. Susan Fitzmaurice and Irma Taavitsainen, 11–36. Berlin: Mouton de Gruyter.

Fitzmaurice, Susan, and Irma Taavitsainen, eds. 2007c. *Methods in Historical Pragmatics*. Berlin: Mouton de Gruyter.

Flavin, Louise. 1987. Mansfield Park: Free Indirect Discourse and the Psychological Novel. *Studies in the Novel* 19: 137–159.

Fleischmann, Suzanne. 1990. *Tense and Narrativity: From Medieval Performance to Modern Fiction*. Austin: University of Texas Press.

Flint, Kate. 2000. *The Victorians and the Visual Imagination*. Cambridge: Cambridge University Press.

Fludernik, Monika. 1993. *The Fictions of Language and the Languages of Fiction*. London and New York: Routledge.

Fludernik, Monika. 1996. *Towards a "Natural" Narratology*. London: Routledge.

Fludernik, Monika. 2003a. The Diachronization of Narratology. *Narrative* 11 (3): 331–348.

Fludernik, Monika. 2003b. Metanarrative and Metafictional Poetry. *Poetica* 35: 1–39.

Fludernik, Monika. 2006. *An Introduction to Narratology*, tr. Patricia Häusler-Greenfield and Monika Fludernik. London and New York: Routledge.

Fludernik, Monika. 2007. Letters as Narrative: Narrative Patterns and Episode Structure in Early Letters, 1400 to 1650. In *Methods in Historical Pragmatics*, ed. Susan Fitzmaurice and Irma Taavitsainen, 241–267. Berlin: Mouton de Gruyter.

Fludernik, Monika. 2009. *An Introduction to Narratology*. London: Routledge.

Fowler, Henry Watson. 1926. *A Dictionary of Modern English Usage*. Oxford: Clarendon.

Fowler, Roger. 1986. *Linguistic Criticism*. Oxford: Oxford University Press.

Fowler, Roger. 1996. *Linguistic Criticism*, 2nd ed. Oxford: Oxford University Press.

Fraser, Bruce. 1975. *Hedged Performatives. In Syntax + Semantics*, Vol 3: *Speech Acts*, ed. Peter Cole and Jerry L. Morgan, 187–210. New York: Academic Press.

Gadamer, Hans-Georg. 1976. *Philosophical Hermeneutics*, ed. and tr. David E. Linge. Berkeley: University of California Press.

Galbraith, Mary. 1995. Deictic Shift Theory and the Poetics of Involvement in Narrative. In *Deixis in Narrative: A Cognitive Science Perspective*, ed. Judith F. Duchan, Gail A. Bruder, and Lynne E. Hewitt, 19–59. Hillsdale, NJ: Lawrence Erlbaum Associates.

Garside, Roger, Geoffrey N. Leech, and Anthony McEnery, eds. 1987. *Corpus Annotation*. London: Longman.

Gavins, Joanna. 2007. *Text World Theory: An Introduction*. Edinburgh: Edinburgh University Press.

Genette, Gérard. 1972. *Figures III*. Paris Seuil.

Genette, Gérard. 1980. *Narrative Discourse*. Ithaca, NY: Cornell University Press.

Genette, Gérard. 1988. *Narrative Discourse Revisited*. Ithaca, NY: Cornell University Press.

Ginsburg, Michal Peled. 1970. Free Indirect Course: Theme and Narrative Voice in Flaubert, George Eliot, and Vega. *DAI* 39: 2236A.

Ginsburg, Michal Peled. 1982. Free Indirect Discourse: A Reconsideration. *Language and Style* 15 (2): 133–149.

Goatly, Andrew. 1997. *The Language of Metaphors*. London: Routledge.

Gold, Victor R., Thomas L. Hoyt, Jr., Sharon H. Ringe, Susan Brooks Thistlethwaite, Burton H. Throckmorton, Jr., and Barbara A. Withers, eds. 1995. *The New Testament and Psalms: An Inclusive Version.* New York and Oxford: Oxford University Press.

Goossens, Louis. 1990. Metaphtonymy: The Interaction of Metaphor and Metonymy in Expressions for Linguistic Action. *Cognitive Linguistics* 1 (3): 323–340.

Görlach, Manfred. 1999. *English in Nineteenth-Century England: An Introduction.* Cambridge: Cambridge University Press.

Gottschall, Jonathan. 2008. Measure for Measure. *Boston Globe,* May 11. Accessed April 4, 2009 <http://www.boston.com/bostonglobe/ideas/articles/2008/05/11/measure_for_measure>

Greenblatt, Stephen. 1980. *Renaissance Self-Fashioning.* Chicago: University of Chicago Press.

Greenblatt, Stephen. 1988. *Shakespearean Negotiations: The Circulation of Social Energy in Renaissance England.* Berkeley: University of California Press.

Greisler, Christer. 2002. Investigating Register Variation in Nineteenth-Century English: A Multi-Dimensional Comparison. In *Using Corpora to Explore Linguistic Variation,* ed. Randi Reppen, Susan M. Fitzmaurice, and Douglas Biber, 249–271. Amsterdam and Philadelphia: John Benjamins.

Greisler, Christer. 2003. Gender-Based Variation in Nineteenth-Century English Letter Writing. In *Corpus Analysis: Language Structure and Language Use,* ed. Pepi Leistyna and Charles F. Meyer, 87–106. Amsterdam and New York: Rodopi.

Grice, Herbert P. 1975. Logic and Conversation. *In Syntax and Semantics III: Speech Acts,* ed. Peter Cole and Jerry Morgan, 41–58. New York: Academic Press.

Gruber, Helmut. 1993. Evaluation Devices in Newspaper Reports. *Journal of Pragmatics* 19: 469–486.

Grund, Peter J. 2012. The Nature of Knowledge: Evidence and Evidentiality in the Witness Depositions from the Salem Witch Trials. *American Speech* 87 (1): 7–38.

Grund, Peter J. 2017. Description, Evaluation and Stance: Exploring the Forms and Functions of Speech Descriptors in Early Modern English. *Nordic Journal of English Studies* 16: 41–73.

Grund, Peter, and Terry Walker. 2006. The Subjunctive in Adverbial Clauses in Nineteenth-Century English. In *Nineteenth-Century English: Stability and Change,* ed. Merja Kytö, Mats Rydén, and Erik Smitterberg, 89–109. Cambridge: Cambridge University Press.

Guadagnin, M. 1994. *A Corpus-Based Analysis of Speech and Thought Presentation Categories in 20th Century British Prose Fiction.* Lancaster: Lancaster University Press.

Gunn, Daniel P. 2004. Free Indirect Discourse and Narrative Authority in *Emma. Narrative* 12 (1): 35–54.

Gustafsson, Larisa Oldireva. 2006. The Passive in Nineteenth-Century Scientific Writing. In *Nineteenth-Century English: Stability and Change,* ed. Merja Kytö, Mats Rydén, and Erik Smitterberg, 110–135. Cambridge: Cambridge University Press.

Haan, Pieter de. 1996. More on the Language of Dialogue in Fiction. *ICAME Journal* 20: 23–40.

Haan, Pieter de. 1997. Syntactic Characteristics of Dialogue and Non-Dialogue Sentences in Fiction Writing. In *Corpus-Based Studies in English,* ed. Magnus Ljung, 101–117. Amsterdam: Rodopi.

Haberland, Hartmut. 1986. *Reported Speech in Danish: In Direct and Indirect Speech*, ed. Florian Coulmas, 219–253. Berlin: Mouton de Gruyter.

Halliday, M. A. K. 1985. *An Introduction to Functional Grammar*. London: Arnold.

Halliday, M. A. K. 1991. Corpus Studies and Probabilistic Grammar. In *English Corpus Linguistics*, ed. Karin Ajimer and Bengt Altenberg, 30–43. London and New York: Longman.

Halliday, M. A. K. 1992. New Ways of Meaning: The Challenge to Applied Linguistics. In *Thirty Years of Linguistic Evolution: Studies in Honour of René Dirven*, ed. Martin Pütz. Philadelphia and Amsterdam: John Benjamins, 59–95. Reprinted in *The Ecolinguistics Reader: Language, Ecology, and Environment*, ed. Alwin Fill and Peter Mühlhäusler, 175–202. London and New York: Continuum, 2001.

Halliday, M. A. K. 1994. *An Introduction to Functional Grammar*, 2nd ed. London: Arnold.

Halliday, M. A. K., and Christian Matthiessen. 2004. *An Introduction to Functional Grammar*, 3rd ed. London: Arnold.

Halliday, M. A. K., and Christian Matthiessen. 2014. *Halliday's Introduction to Functional Grammar*, 4th ed. London: Routledge.

Hamburger, Kate. 1973. *The Logic of Literature*, tr. Marilyn J. Rose. Bloomington: Indiana University Press.

Herman, David. 1994. Hypothetical Focalization. *Narrative* 2 (3): 230–253.

Hickmann, Maya. 1993. The Boundaries of Reported Speech in Narrative Discourse: Some Developmental Aspects. In *Reflexive Language: Reported Speech and Metapragmatics*, ed. John A. Lucy, 63–90. Cambridge: Cambridge University Press.

Hoey, Michael 2005. *Lexical Priming: A New Theory of Words and Language*. London: Routledge.

Holt, Elizabeth, and Rebecca Clift, eds. 2007. *Reporting Talk: Reported Speech in Interaction*. Cambridge: Cambridge University Press.

Holt, Jim. 1999. Talking Heads: Speaking out of Both Sides of Your Brain. *Lingua Franca: The Review of Academic Life* 9 (2): 68.

Hoover, David L., Jonathan Culpeper, and Kieran O'Halloran. 2014. *Digital Literary Studies: Corpus Approaches to Poetry, Prose and Drama*. New York and Abingdon: Routledge.

Hori, Masahiro. 2004. *Investigating Dickens' Style: A Collocational Analysis*. London: Palgrave.

Huddleston, Rodney, and Geoffrey K. Pullum. 2002. *The Cambridge Grammar of the English Language*. Cambridge: Cambridge University Press.

Hunston, Susan, and Gill Francis. 2000. *Pattern Grammar: A Corpus-Driven Approach to the Lexical Grammar of English*. Amsterdam: John Benjamins.

Ikeo, Reiko. 2001. The Positions of Reporting Clauses of Speech Presentation with Special Reference to the Lancaster Speech, Thought and Writing Presentation Corpus. In *Proceedings of the Corpus Linguistics 2001 Conference*, ed. Paul Rayson, Andrew Wilson, Tony McEnery, Andrew Hardie and Shereen Khoja, 281–288. University Centre for Computer Corpus Research on Language, Technical Papers 13. Lancaster University.

Ikeo, Reiko. 2007. Unambiguous Free Indirect Discourse? A Comparison between "Straightforward" Free Indirect Speech and Thought Presentation and Cases

Ambiguous with Narration. *Language and Literature: Journal of the Poetics and Linguistics Association* 16 (4): 367–387.

Ikeo, Reiko. 2009. An Elaboration of the Faithfulness Claims of Direct Writing. *Journal of Pragmatics* 41 (5): 999–1016.

Ikeo, Reiko. 2015. Speech and Thought Presentation with a Case Study of Woolf's *To The Lighthouse*. In *Bloomsbury Companion to Stylistics*, ed. Violeta Sotirova, 356–379. London: Bloomsbury.

Iser, Wolfgang. 1978. *The Act of Reading: A Theory of Aesthetic Response*. Baltimore, MD: John Hopkins University Press.

Jacobs, Andreas, and Andreas H. Jucker. 1995. The Historical Perspective in Pragmatics. In *Historical Pragmatics: Pragmatic Developments in the History of English*, ed. Andreas Jucker, 3–33. Amsterdam and Philadelphia: John Benjamins.

Jahn, Manfred. 1992. Contextualizing Represented Speech and Thought. *Journal of Pragmatics* 17: 347–367.

Jakobson, Roman. 1960. Closing Statement: Linguistics and Poetics. In *Style in Language*, ed. Thomas A. Sebeok, 250–377. Cambridge, MA: MIT Press.

Jakobson, Roman. 1971. *Word and Language: Selected Writings*, vol. 2. The Hague and Paris: Mouton.

Janssen, Theo A. J. M., and Wim van der Wurff. 1996. *Reported Speech: Forms and Functions of the Verbs*. Amsterdam and Philadelphia: John Benjamins.

Jefferson, Ann. 1981. The Place of Free Indirect Discourse in the Poetics of Fiction: With Examples from Joyce's "Eveline." *Essays Poetics* 5 (1): 36–47.

Jespersen, Otto. 1927. *A Modern English Grammar on Historical Principles. Part 3*. Heidelberg: Carl Winters.

Jespersen, Otto. 1931. *A Modern English Grammar on Historical Principles. Part 4*. Heidelberg: Carl Winters.

Jespersen, Otto. 1949. *A Modern English Grammar on Historical Principles. Part 7*. Copenhagen: Ejnar Munksgaard.

Johansson, Christine. 2006. Relativizers in Nineteenth-Century English. In *Nineteenth-Century English: Stability and Change*, ed. Merja Kytö, Mats Rydén, and Erik Smitterberg, 139–182. Cambridge: Cambridge University Press.

Jucker, Andreas H., ed. 1995. *Historical Pragmatics: Pragmatic Developments in the History of English*. Amsterdam and Philadelphia: John Benjamins.

Jucker, Andreas H. 2000. English Historical Pragmatics: Problems of Data and Methodology. In *English Diachronic Pragmatics*, ed. Gabriella di Martino and Maria Lima, 17–55. Naples: Cuen.

Jucker, Andreas H. 2002. Discourse Markers in Early Modern English. In *Alternative Histories of English*, ed. Richard Watts and Peter Trudgill, 210–230. London: Routledge.

Jucker, Andreas H. 2004. Contrastive Analysis across Time: Issues in Historical Dialogue Analysis. In *Contrastive Analysis in Language: Identifying Linguistic Units of Comparison*, ed. Dominique Willems, Bart Defrancq, Timothy Colleman, and Dirk Noel, 197–212. Basingstoke: Palgrave Macmillan.

Jucker, Andreas H. 2006a. "But 'tis believed that . . .": Speech and Thought Presentation in Early English Newspapers. In *News Discourse in Early Modern Britain*, ed. Nicholas Brownlees, 105–125. Bern: Peter Lang.

Jucker, Andreas H. 2006b. Historical Pragmatics. In *Encyclopedia of Language and Linguistics*, 2nd ed., ed. Keith Brown, 329–332. Oxford: Elsevier.

Jucker, Andreas H., and Manuel Berger. 2014. The Development of Discourse Presentation in *The Times*, 1833–1988. *Media History* 20 (1): 67–87.

Jucker, Andreas H., Gerd Fritz, and Franz Lebsanft, eds. 1999. *Historical Dialogue Analysis*. Pragmatics and Beyond 66. Amsterdam and Philadelphia: John Benjamins.

Jucker, Andreas H., and Irma Taavitsainen. 2000. Diachronic Speech Act Analysis: Insults from Flyting to Flaming. *Journal of Historical Pragmatics* 1: 67–95.

Kamenade, Ans van, and Bettelou Los, eds. 2006. *The Handbook of the History of English*. Oxford: Blackwell.

Kaunisto, Mark. 2006. Anaphoric Reference in the Nineteenth Century: That/those + of Constructions. In *Nineteenth-Century English: Stability and Change*, ed. Merja Kytö, Mats Rydén, and Erik Smitterberg, 183–193. Cambridge: Cambridge University Press.

Kern-Stähler, Annette. 2005. Homer and the Evolutionary Scale: Interrelations between Biology and Literature in the Writings of William Gladstone and Grant Allen. In *Unmapped Countries: Biological Visions in Nineteenth-Century Literature and Culture*, ed. Anna-Julia Zwierlein, 107–115. London: Anthem Press.

Kissine, Mikhail. 2010. Metaphorical Projection, Subjectification and English Speech Act Verbs. *Folia Linguistica* 44 (2): 339–370.

Klamer, Marian. 2000. How Report Verbs Become Quote Markers and Complementisers. *Lingua* 110: 69–98.

Koch, C. Friedrich. 1863–1869. *Historische Grammatik der englischen Sprache*. 3 Vols. Weimar: Hermann Böhlau.

Kohnen, Thomas. 2000a. Corpora and Speech Acts: The Study of Performatives. *In Corpus Linguistics and Linguistic Theory: Papers from the Twentieth International Conference on English Language Research on Computerized Corpora (ICAME 20)*, ed. Christian Mair and Marianne Hundt, 177–186. Amsterdam and Atlanta: Rodopi.

Kohnen, Thomas. 2000b. Explicit Performatives in Old English. *Journal of Historical Pragmatics* 1 (2): 301–321.

Kohnen, Thomas. 2006a. Variability of Form as a Methodological Problem in Historical Corpus Analysis: The Case of Modal Expressions in Directive Speech Acts. In *Corpora and the History of English: Papers Dedicated to Manfred Markus on the Occasion of His Sixty-Fifth Birthday*, ed. Christian Mair and Reinhard Heuberger, 221–233. Anglistische Forschungen, 363. Heidelberg: Winter.

Kohnen, Thomas. 2006b. Introduction. *Anglistik* 17 (2): 7–10.

Kolbe, Frederick C. 1930. *Shakespeare's Way*. London: Sheed & Ward.

Kövecses, Zoltán. 2000. *Metaphor and Emotion*. Cambridge: Cambridge University Press.

Kripke, Saul. 1972. *Naming and Necessity*. Oxford: Blackwell.

Kruger, Haidee, and Bertus van Rooy. 2016. Syntactic and Pragmatic Transfer Effects in Reported-Speech Constructions in Three Contact Varieties of English Influenced by Afrikaans. *Language Sciences* 56: 118–131.

Kullmann, Dorothea. 1992. Zur Wiedergabe des Style Indirect Libre durch die Deutschen Übersetzer von *Madame Bovary*. In *Geschichte, System, Literarische*

Übersetzung/Histories, Systems, Literary Translations, ed. Harald Kittel, 323–333. Berlin: Erich Schmidt Verlag.

Kullmann, Dorothea. 1995. Beobachtungen zum Style Indirect Libre in den Romanen *Madame Bovary* und *L'Assommoir* sowie zu einer Wiedergabe im Deutschen. In *Erlebte Rede und Impressionistischer Stil. Europäische Erzählprosa im Vergleich mit ihren Deutschen Übersetzungen*, ed. Dorothea Kullmann, 89–135. Göttingen: Wallstein.

Kvantaliani, Nino. 2014. Variations and Effects of Speech and Thought Presentation Categories on the Basis of Short Stories by Contemporary Women Writers in English. *International Journal of Humanities and Social Science* 4.8 (1): 30–36.

Kytö, Merja. 1996a. "The Best and Most Excellentest Way": The Rivalling Forms of Adjective Comparison in Late Middle and Early Modern English. In *Words: Proceedings of an International Symposium, Lund, 25–26 August 1995*, ed. Jan Svartvik, 123–144. Konferenser 36. Stockholm: Kungl. Vitterhets Historie och Antikvitets Akademien.

Kytö, Merja. 1996b. *Manual to the Diachronic Part of the Helsinki Corpus of English Texts: Coding Conventions and Lists of Source Texts*, 3rd ed. Helsinki: Department of English, University of Helsinki.

Kytö, Merja, and Suzanne Romaine. 2006. Adjective Comparison in Nineteenth-Century English. In *Nineteenth-Century English: Stability and Change*, ed. Merja Kytö, Mats Rydén, and Erik Smitterberg, 194–214. Cambridge: Cambridge University Press.

Kytö, Merja, Juhani Rudanko, and Erik Smitterberg. 2000. Building a Bridge between the Present and the Past: A Corpus of Nineteenth-Century English. *ICAME Journal* 24: 85–97.

Kytö, Merja, Mats Rydén, and Erik Smitterberg, eds. 2006. *Nineteenth-Century English: Stability and Change*. Cambridge: Cambridge University Press.

Kytö, Merja, Terry Walker, and Peter Grund. 2007. English Witness Depositions 1560–1760: An Electronic Edition. *ICAME Journal* 31: 65–85.

Labov, William. 1972. The Transformation of Experience in Narrative Syntax. In *Language in the Inner City*, ed. William Labov, 354–396. Philadelphia: University of Philadelphia Press.

Labov, William. 1982. Speech Actions and Reactions in Personal Narrative. In *Analyzing Discourse: Text and Talk*, ed. Deborah Tannen, 219–247. Washington, DC: Georgetown University Press.

Lakoff, George, and Mark Johnson. *Metaphors We Live By*. 1980. Chicago: Chicago University Press.

Lakoff, George, and Mark Johnson. 1999. *Philosophy in the Flesh: The Embodied Mind and Its Challenge to Western Thought*. New York: Basic Books.

Lambert, Mark. 1981. *Dickens and the Suspended Quotation*. New Haven, CT: Yale University Press.

Lass, Roger. 1997. *Historical Linguistics and Language Change*. Cambridge: Cambridge University Press.

Leech, Geoffrey. 1985. Stylistics. In *Discourse and Literature*, ed. Teun A. van Dijk, 39–57. Amsterdam: John Benjamins.

Leech, Geoffrey. 2007. Style in Fiction Revisited: The Beginning of Great Expectations. *Style* 41 (2): 117–132.

Leech, Geoffrey. 2008. *Language in Literature: Style and Foregrounding*. London: Longman.

Leech, Geoffrey, Tony McEnery, and Martin Wynne. 1997. Further Levels of Annotation. In *Corpus Annotation*, ed. Roger Garside, Geoffrey Leech, and Tony McEnery, 85–101. London: Longman.

Leech, Geoffrey, and Mick Short. 1981. *Style in Fiction*, 1st ed. London: Longman.

Leech, Geoffrey, and Mick Short. 2007a. *Style in Fiction*, 2nd ed. London: Longman.

Leech, Geoffrey, and Mick Short. 2007b. Style in Fiction: New Directions for Research. *Style* 41 (2): 115–116.

Leskiv, Alina. 2009. The Literary Phenomenon of Free Indirect Speech. *Seria Filologiczna Zeszyt* 60: 51–58.

Levinson, Stephen C. 1979. Activity Types in Language. *Linguistics* 17 (5–6): 365–399.

Lewis, David. 1973. *Counterfactuals*. Cambridge: Cambridge University Press.

Linnell, Per. 1982. *The Written Language Bias in Linguistics*. Linköping, Sweden: University of Linköping Press.

Ljunggren, Wilhelm P. F. 1893–1894. *On the Auxiliaries Will and Shall in the English Language, Especially with Regard to Modern English*, vols. 1–2. Lund: Carlskrona, printed at Länsboktryckeriet.

Louw, Bill. 1993. Irony in the Text or Insincerity in the Writer? The Diagnostic Potential of Semantic Prosodies. In *Text and Technology: In Honour of John Sinclair*, ed. Mona Baker, Gill Francis, and Elena Tognini-Bonelli, 157–176. Amsterdam: John Benjamins.

Louw, Bill. 1997. The Role of Corpora in Critical Literary Appreciation. In *Teaching and Language Corpora*, ed. Anne Wichmann, Steven Figlestone, Tony McEnery, and Gerry Knowles, 240–252. London and New York: Longman.

Louw, Bill. 2000. Contextual Prosodic Theory: Bringing Semantic Prosodies to Life. In *Words in Context*, ed. Chris Heffer and Helen Sauntson, 48–94. Birmingham: Birmingham University Press.

Louw, Bill. 2006. Literary Worlds as Collocation. In *Literature and Stylistics for Language Learners: Theory and Practice*, ed. Greg J. Watson and Sonia Zyngier, 91–105. London: Palgrave.

Lubbock, Percy. 1921. *The Craft of Fiction*. London: Jonathan Cape.

Lucy, John A., ed. 1993. *Reflexive Language: Reported Speech and Metapragmatics*. Cambridge: Cambridge University Press.

Lutzky, Ursula. 2015. Quotations in Early Modern English Witness Depositions. In *The Pragmatics of Quoting Now and Then*, ed. Jenny Arendholz, Wolfram Bublitz, and Monika Kirner-Ludwig, 343–368. Berlin: Mouton de Gruyter.

Macaulay, Ronald. 2001. You're like "why not?": The Quotative Expressions of Glasgow Adolescents. *Journal of Sociolinguistics* 5 (1): 3–21.

Mahlberg, Michaela. 2006. Lexical Cohesion: Corpus Linguistic Theory and Its Application in English Language Teaching. *International Journal of Corpus Linguistics* 11 (3): 227–247.

Mahlberg, Michaela. 2007a. Corpus Stylistics: Bridging the Gap between Linguistics and Literary Studies. In *Text, Discourse and Corpora: Theory and Analysis*, ed. Michael Hoey, Michaela Mahlberg, Michael Stubbs, Wolfgang Teubert, and John Sinclair, 219–246. London: Continuum.

Mahlberg, Michaela. 2007b. A Corpus Stylistic Perspective on Dickens' Great Expectations. In *Contemporary Stylistics*, ed. Marina Lambrou and Peter Stockwell, 19–31. London: Continuum.

Mahlberg, Michaela. 2013. *Corpus Stylistics and Dickens's Fiction*. London and New York: Routledge.

Mahlberg, Michaela, and Catherine Smith. 2010. Corpus Approaches to Prose Fiction: Civility and Body Language in Pride and Prejudice. In *Language and Style*, ed. Beatrix Busse and Daniel McIntyre, 449–67. Basingstoke: Palgrave.

Mahlberg, Michaela, et al. 2016. CLiC Dickens: Novel Uses of Concordances for the Integration of Corpus Stylistics and Cognitive Poetics. In *Corpora* 11 (3): 433–463.

Maingueneau, Dominique. 1991. *A l'analyse du discours*. Paris: Hachette.

Mair, Christian. 2006a. Grammatical Change in 20th-Century English. *Anglistik* 17 (2): 11–34.

Mair, Christian. 2006b. Nonfinite Complement Clauses in the Nineteenth Century: The Case of Remember. In *Nineteenth-Century English: Stability and Change*, ed. Merja Kytö, Mats Rydén, and Erik Smitterberg, 215–228. Cambridge: Cambridge University Press.

Mair, Christian. 2006c. *Twentieth-Century English*. Cambridge: Cambridge University Press.

Mair, Christian, and Reinhard Heuberger, eds. 2006. *Corpora and the History of English*. Heidelberg: Universitätsverlag Winter.

Mamede, Nuno, and Pedro Chaleira. 2004. Character Identification in Children Stories. In *Advances in Natural Language Processing: 4th International Conference (EsTAL 2004), Alicante, Spain, October 20–22, 2004, Proceedings*, ed. José Luis Vicedo, Patricio Martínez-Barco, Rafael Muñoz, and Maximiliano Saiz Noeda, 82–90. Berlin and Heidelberg: Springer.

Margolin, Uri. 2000. Telling in the Plural: From Grammar to Ideology. *Poetics Today* 21 (3): 591–618.

Marnette, Sophie. 2005. *Speech and Thought Presentation in French: Concepts and Strategies*. Amsterdam and Philadelphia: John Benjamins.

Mätzner, Eduard. 1860–1865. *Englische Grammatik*. 3 vols. Berlin: Weidmann.

McCarthy, Michael, and Anne O'Keeffe. 2012. Analysing Speech Corpora. In *The Encyclopedia of Applied Linguistics*, ed. Thomas Cobb, 104–112. New York: Wiley-Blackwell.

McEnery, Tony. 2006. The Moral Panic about Bad Language in England 1691–1745. *Journal of Historical Pragmatics* 7 (1): 89–113.

McEnery, Tony, and Andrew Wilson. 1996. *Corpus Linguistics*. Edinburgh: Edinburgh University Press.

McHale, Brian. 1978. Free Indirect Discourse: A Survey of Recent Accounts. *PTL: A Journal for Descriptive Poetics and Theory of Literature* 3: 249–287.

McIntyre, Dan. 2006. *Point of View in Plays: A Cognitive Stylistic Approach to Viewpoint in Drama and Other Text-Types*. Amsterdam: John Benjamins.

McIntyre, Dan. 2007. Trusting the Text: Corpus Linguistics and Stylistics. *International Journal of Corpus Linguistics* 12 (4): 565–577.

McIntyre, Dan. 2008. Integrating Multimodal Analysis and the Stylistics of Drama: A Multimodal Perspective on Ian McKellen's *Richard III*. *Language and Literature* 17 (4): 309–334.

McIntyre, Dan. 2013. Context, Cognition, Discourse, History: Peter Verdonk's Stylistics of Poetry. In *The Stylistics of Poetry: Context, Cognition, Discourse, History*, ed. Peter Verdonk, 1–9. London: Bloomsbury.

McIntyre, Dan. 2014. Characterisation. In *The Cambridge Handbook of Stylistics*, ed. Peter Stockwell and Sara Whiteley, 149–154. Cambridge: Cambridge University Press.

McIntyre, Dan, and Brian Walker. 2011. Discourse Presentation in Early Modern English Writing: A Preliminary Corpus-Based Investigation. *International Journal of Corpus Linguistics* 16 (1): 101–130.

McKenzie, Malcolm. 1987. Free Indirect Speech in a Fettered Insecure Society. *Language and Communication* 7 (2): 153–159.

McKeon, Michael. 1987. *The Origins of the English Novel, 1600–1740*. Baltimore, MD: John Hopkins University Press.

Melis, Daniela. 2011. Creation and (Re)Presentation of Historical Discourse in Isle of Passion by Laura Restrepo. *Studies in 20th & 21st Century Literature* 35 (2): 250–267.

Meyer, Susan. 2003. From "Your Father Was Emperor of China, and Your Mother an Indian Queen": Reverse Imperialism in Wuthering Heights. In *Wuthering Heights*, 2nd ed., ed. Linda H. Peterson, 96–125. Boston and New York: Bedford/St. Martin's.

Meyersohn, Marylea. 1991. A Habermas Speech-Act Model: Modes of Rationality in Jane Austen. *Language and Style* 24 (3): 271–288.

Michael, Ian. 1987. *The Teaching of English: From the Sixteenth Century to 1870*. Cambridge: Cambridge University Press.

Minnis, Alastair. 2010. *Medieval Theory of Authorship: Scholastic Literary Attitudes in the Later Middle Ages*, 2nd ed. Philadelphia: University of Pennsylvania Press.

Mitchell, Philip. 2014. The Ethics of Speech and Thought Representation in Literary Journalism. *Journalism* 15 (5): 533–547.

Möhlig-Falke, Ruth. 2012. *The Early English Impersonal Construction: An Analysis of Verbal and Constructional Meaning*. New York and Oxford: Oxford University Press.

Montoro, Rocío. 2012. *Chick Lit: The Stylistics of Cappuccino Fiction*. London: Bloomsbury.

Moore, Colette. 2011. *Quoting Speech in Early English*. Cambridge: Cambridge University Press.

Myers, Greg. 1999. Functions of Reported Speech in Group Discussions. *Applied Linguistics* 20 (3): 376–401.

Nash, Walter. 1990. *Language in Popular Fiction*. London: Routledge.

Nevalainen, Terttu, and Helena Raumolin-Brunberg. 2004. *Historical Sociolinguistics: Language Change in Tudor and Stuart England*. London: Longman.

Nørgaard, Nina. 2007. Disordered Collarettes and Uncovered Tables: Negative Polarity as a Stylistic Device in James Joyce's "Two Gallants." *Journal of Literary Semantics* 36: 35–52.

Nørgaard, Nina, Beatrix Busse, and Rocío Montoro. 2010. *Key Terms in Stylistics*. London: Continuum.

Nünning, Ansgar, ed. 1998. *Literaturwissenschaftliche Theorien, Modelle und Methoden*. Trier: WVT.

Nünning, Ansgar, and Vera Nünning, eds. 2002. *Neue Ansätze in der Erzähltheorie*. Trier: WVT.

Nünning, Vera, and Ansgar Nünning, eds. 2004. *Erzähltextanalyse und Gender Studies*. Stuttgart: Metzler.

Oatley, Keith. 2001. Shakespeare's Invention of Theatre as Simulation That Runs on Minds. *Empirical Studies of the Arts* 19: 27–45.

Oatley, Keith. 2009. Such Stuff as Dreams: The Psychology of Fiction. In *Plenary Lecture to the Poetics and Linguistics Association, Wednesday 29 July*. Middleburg, Holland.

OED = Oxford English Dictionary. Available at <http://www.oed.com>

Oostdijk, Nelleke. 1990. The Language of Dialogue in Fiction. *Literary and Linguistic Computing* 5 (3): 235–241.

Page, Norman. 1973. *Speech in the English Novel*. London: Longman.

Palander-Collin, Minna, and Minna Nevala. 2010. Reporting and Social Role Construction in Eighteenth-Century Personal Correspondence. In *Social Roles and Language Practices in Late Modern English*, ed. Päivi Pahta, Minna Nevala, Arja Nurmi, and Minna Palander-Collin, 111–133. Amsterdam: John Benjamins.

Palmer, Alan. 2004. *Fictional Minds*. Lincoln and London: University of Nebraska Press.

Palmer, Alan. 2010. *Social Minds in the Novel*. Columbus, OH: Ohio State University Press.

Pascal, Roy. 1977. *The Dual Voice: Free Indirect Speech and Its Functioning in the Nineteenth-Century European Novel*. Manchester: Manchester University Press.

Pavel, Thomas G. 1986. *Fictional Worlds*. London and Cambridge, MA: Harvard University Press.

Peer, Willie van. 1986. *Stylistics and Psychology: Investigations of Foregrounding*. London: Croom Helm.

Peer, Willie van. 2007. Introduction to Foregrounding: A State of the Art. *Language and Literature* 16 (2): 99–104.

Peer, Willie van, and Seymour Chatman. 2001. *New Perspectives on Narrative Perspective*. Albany: State University of New York Press.

Person, Raymond F. 1999. *Structure and Meaning in Conversation and Literature*. Lanham, MD, New York, and Oxford: University Press of America.

Phillipps, Kenneth C. 1970. *Jane Austen's English*. London: André Deutsch.

Phillipps, Kenneth C. 1984. *Language and Class in Victorian England*. Oxford: Basil Blackwell.

Poutsma, Hendrik. 1914–1929. *A Grammar of Late Modern English*, 2nd ed. Groningen: P. Noordhoff.

Quirk, Randolph. 1961a. *The Study of the Mother Tongue: An Inaugural Lecture Delivered at University College London, 21 February 1961*. London: H. K. Lewis.

Quirk, Randolph. 1961b. Some Observations on the Language of Dickens. *A Review of English Literature* 2: 19–28.

Quirk, Randolph. 1974. *The Linguist and the English Language*. London: Edward Arnold.

Quirk, Randolph, Sidney Greenbaum, Geoffrey Leech, and Jan Svartvik. 1985. *A Comprehensive Grammar of the English Language*. London: Longman.

Radway, Janice. 1984. *A Phenomenological Theory of Popular and Elite Literature*. Ann Arbor: University of Michigan.

Ramazani, Vaheed K. 1987. Emma Bovary and the Free Indirect Si(g)ns of Romance. *Nineteenth-Century French Studies* 15 (3): 274–284.

Raumolin-Brunberg, Helena. 2002. Stable Variation and Historical Linguistics. In *Variation Past and Present: VARIENG Studies on English for Terttu Nevalainen*, ed. Helena Raumolin-Brunberg, Minna Nevala, Arja Nurmi, and Matti Rissanen, 101–116. Helsinki: Société Neophilologique.

Ravotas, Doris, and Carol Berkenkötter. 1998. Voices in the Text: The Uses of Reported Speech in a Psychotherapist's Notes and Initial Assessments. *Text* 18 (2): 211–239.

Rayson, Paul. 2018. *Wmatrix: A Web-Based Corpus Processing Environment*. Computing Department, Lancaster University. Software available at http://ucrel.lancs.ac.uk/wmatrix.

Rayson, Paul, and Roger Garside. 2000. Comparing Corpora Using Frequency Profiling. *CompareCorpora '00: Proceedings of the Workshop on Comparing Corpora* 9: 1–6.

Rhee, Seongha. 2013. "I know I'm shameless to say this": Grammaticalization of the Mitigating Discourse Marker Makilay in Korean. *Procedia- Social and Behavioural Sciences* 97: 480–486.

Rhee, Seongha. 2014. "I know you are not, but if you were asking me": On Emergence of Discourse Markers of Topic Presentation from Hypothetical Questions. *Journal of Pragmatics* 60: 1–16.

Richter, Virginia. 2009. Die große Erzählung vom Zufall: Charles Darwin hat Spuren auch in der Englischen Literatur hinterlassen. In *Neue Zürcher Zeitung*, Feb. 7. Accessed May 8, 2017. <https://www.nzz.ch/die_grosse_erzaehlung_vom_zufall-1.1925985>

Rimmon-Kenan, Shlomith. 2002 [1983]. *Narrative Fiction: Contemporary Poetics*, 2nd ed. London: Methuen.

Roeh, Itzhak, and Raphael Nir. 1990. Speech Presentation in the Israel Radio News: Ideological Constraints and Rhetorical Strategies. *Text* 10 (3): 225–244.

Roget, Peter Mark. 1992 [1852]. *Thesaurus of English Words and Phrases, Classified and Arranged so as to Facilitate the Expression of Ideas and Assist in Literary Composition*. London: Longman.

Romaine, Suzanne. 1982a. *On the Problem of Syntactic Variation and Pragmatic Meaning in Sociolinguistic Theory*. Cambridge: Cambridge University Press.

Romaine, Suzanne. 1982b. *Socio-Historical Linguistics: Its Status and Methodology*. Cambridge: Cambridge University Press.

Romaine, Suzanne. 1984. On the Problem of Syntactic Variation and Pragmatic Meaning in Sociolinguistic Theory. *Folia Linguistica* 8 (3–4): 409–437.

Romaine, Suzanne. 1998a. Introduction. In *The Cambridge History of the English Language*, Vol. 4: *1776–1997*, ed. Suzanne Romaine, 1–56. Cambridge: Cambridge University Press.

Romaine, Suzanne, ed. 1998b. *The Cambridge History of the English Language*, Vol. 4: *1776–1997*. Cambridge: Cambridge University Press.

Romaine, Suzanne. 1999. *Communicating Gender*. Mahwah, NJ: Lawrence Erlbaum.

Ronen, Ruth. 1994. *Possible Worlds in Literary Theory*. Cambridge: Cambridge University Press.

Ruano San Segundo, Pablo. 2016. A Corpus-Stylistic Approach to Dickens' Use of Speech Verbs: Beyond Mere Reporting. *Language and Literature* 25 (2): 113–129.

Rudanko, Juhani. 2006. The -ing Construction in British English, 1800–2000. In *Nineteenth-Century English: Stability and Change*, ed. Merja Kytö, Mats Rydén, and Erik Smitterberg, 229–241. Cambridge: Cambridge University Press.

Rudzka-Ostyn, Brygida. 1988. Semantic Extensions into the Domain of Verbal Communication. In *Topics in Cognitive Linguistics*, ed. Brygida Rudzka-Ostyn, 507–553. Amsterdam and Philadelphia: John Benjamins.

Ryan, Marie-Laure. 1986. Embedded Narratives and Tellability. *Style* 20: 319–340.

Ryan, Marie-Laure. 1991. *Possible Worlds, Artificial Intelligence and Narrative Theory*. Bloomington: Indiana University Press.

Ryan, Marie-Laure. 2006. From Parallel Universes to Possible Worlds: Ontological Pluralism in Physics, Narratology, and Narrative. *Poetics Today* 27 (4): 633–674.

Sacks, Harvey, Emanuel Schegloff, and Gail Jefferson. 1978. A Simplest Systematics for the Organization of Turn-Taking for Conversation. *In Studies in the Organization of Conversational Interaction*, ed. Jim Schenkein, 7–55. New York: Academic.

Sampson, Geoffrey. 1995. *English for the Computer: The SUSANNE Corpus and Analytic Scheme*. Oxford: Clarendon.

Sampson, Geoffrey. 1996. From Central Embedding to Corpus Linguistics. In *Using Corpora for Language Research: Studies in Honour of Geoffrey Leech*, ed. Jenny Thomas and Mick Short, 14–26. London: Longman.

Sampson, Geoffrey. 2001. *Empirical Linguistics*. London and New York: Continuum.

Sanders, José, and Gisela Redeker. 1996. Perspective and the Representation of Speech and Thought in Narrative Discourse. In *Space, Grammar, and Discourse*, ed. Gilles Fauconnier and Eve Sweetser, 290–317. Chicago: Chicago University Press.

Schuelke, Gertrude L. 1958. "Slipping" in Indirect Discourse. *American Speech* 33: 90–98.

Scott. Mike 2009. In Search of a Bad Reference Corpus. In *What's in a Word-List? Investigating Word Frequency and Keyword Extraction*, ed. Dawn Archer, 79–92. Oxford: Ashgate.

Scott, Mike. 2017. *Wordsmith Tools*. Oxford: Oxford University Press.

Searle, John R. 1969. *Speech Acts: An Essay in the Philosophy of Language*. Cambridge: Cambridge University Press.

Searle, John R. 1976. A Classification of Illocutionary Acts. *Language in Society* 5: 1–23.

Searle, John R. 1979. *Expression and Meaning: Studies in the Theory of Speech Acts*. Cambridge: Cambridge University Press.

Searle, John R. 1992. *The Rediscovery of the Mind*. Cambridge: MIT Press.

Searle, John R. 2010. *Making the Social World*. Oxford: Oxford University Press.

Segal, Erwin M. 1995. Narrative Comprehension and the Role of the Deictic Shift. In *Deixis in Narrative: A Cognitive Science Perspective*, ed. Judith F. Duchan, Gail A. Bruder, and Lynne E. Hewitt, 3–17. Hillsdale, NJ: Lawrence Erlbaum Associates.

Semino, Elena. 2001. Stylistics and Linguistic Variation in Poetry. *Journal of English Linguistics* 30 (1): 28–50.

Semino, Elena. 2002. A Cognitive Approach to Mind Style in Narrative Fiction. *In Cognitive Stylistics: Language and Cognition in Text Analysis*, ed. Elena Semino and Jonathan Culpeper, 95–122. Amsterdam: John Benjamins.

Semino, Elena. 2007. Mind Style Twenty-Five Years On. *Style* 41 (2): 153–173.

Semino, Elena, and Mick Short. 2004. *Corpus Stylistics: Speech, Writing and Thought Presentation in a Corpus of English Writing*. London and New York: Routledge.

Semino, Elena, Mick Short, and Jonathan Culpeper. 1997. Using a Computer Corpus to Test a Model of Speech and Thought Presentation. *Poetics* 25: 17–43.

Semino, Elena, Mick Short, and Martin Wynne. 1999. Hypothetical Words and Thoughts in Contemporary British Narratives. *Narrative* 7 (3): 307–334.

Serner, Gunnar. 1910. *On the Language of Swinburne's Lyrics and Epics: A Study*. Lund and Cambridge: Hjalmar Möller and W. Heffer and Sons.

Short, Mick. 1988. Speech Presentation, the Novel and the Press. In *The Taming of the Text*, ed. Willie van Peer, 61–81. London: Routledge.

Short, Mick. 1994. Understanding Texts: Point of View. In *Language and Understanding*, ed. Gillian Brown, Kirsten Malmkjaer, Alastair Pollitt, and John Williams, 170–190. Oxford: Oxford University Press.

Short, Mick. 1996. *Exploring the Language of Poems, Plays and Prose*. London: Longman.

Short, Mick. 2003. A Corpus-Based Approach to Speech, Thought and Writing Presentation. In *Corpus Linguistics by the Lune: A Festschrift for Geoffrey Leech*, ed. Andrew Wilson, Paul Rayson, and Tony McEnery, 241–271. Frankfurt am Main: Peter Lang.

Short, Mick. 2007. Thought Presentation Twenty-Five Years On. *Style* 42 (2): 227–243.

Short, Mick. 2012. Discourse Presentation and Speech (and Writing, but Not Thought) Summary. *Language and Literature* 21 (1): 18–32.

Short, Mick. Forthcoming. *The Stylistic Analysis of Drama and Film*. London: Longman

Short, Mick, Elena Semino, and Jonathan Culpeper. 1996. Using a Corpus for Stylistics Research: Speech and Thought Presentation. In *Using Corpora in Language Research*, ed. Jenny Thomas and Mick Short, 110–131. London: Longman.

Short, Mick, Elena Semino, and Martin Wynne. 1997. A (Free Direct) Reply to Paul Simpson's Discourse. *Journal of Literary Semantics* 26 (3): 219–228.

Short, Mick, Elena Semino, and Martin Wynne. 2002. Revisiting the Notion of Faithfulness in Discourse Presentation Using a Corpus Approach. *Language and Literature* 11 (4): 325–355.

Short, Mick, Martin Wynne, and Elena Semino. 1999. Reading Reports: Discourse Presentation in a Corpus of Narratives, with Special Reference to News Reports. In *English via Various Media*, ed. Hans J. Diller and Erwin O.-G. Stratmann, 39–65. Heidelberg: Winter.

Simpson, Donald P. 1975. *Cassell's New Latin-English, English-Latin Dictionary*, 5th ed. London: Cassell.

Simpson, Paul. 1993. *Language, Ideology and Point of View*. London: Routledge.

Simpson, Paul. 1997. *Language through Literature: An Introduction*. London and New York: Routledge.

Simpson, Paul. 2014. *Stylistics A Resource Book for Students*, 2nd ed. London and New York: Routledge.

Simpson, Paul. 2003. *On the Discourse of Satire: Towards a Stylistic Model of Satirical Humor*. Amsterdam and Philadelphia: John Benjamins.

Sinclair, John. 1991. *Corpus, Concordance, Collocation*. London: Oxford University Press.

Sinclair, John. 2004. *Trust the Text: Language, Corpus and Discourse*, ed. John Sinclair and Ronald Carter. London and New York: Routledge.

Skaffari, Janne, Matti Peikola, Ruth Carroll, Risto Hiltunen, and Britta Warvik, eds. 2005. *Opening Windows on Texts and Discourses of the Past*. Amsterdam and Philadelphia: John Benjamins.

Slembrouck, Stef. 1992. The Parliamentary Hansard "Verbatim" Report: The Written Construction of Spoken Discourse. *Language and Literature* 1 (2): 101–119.

Smith, Nicholas. 2003. Changes in the Modals and Semi-Modals of Strong Obligation and Epistemic Necessity in Recent British English. In *Modality in Contemporary English*, ed. Roberta Facchinetti, Manfred Krug, and Frank Palmer, 241–266. Topics in English Linguistics 44. Berlin and New York: Mouton de Gruyter.

Smitterberg, Erik. 2003. Multal Quantifiers in Nineteenth-Century English. *24th ICAME Conference*, April 23–27, 2003, Guernsey.

Smitterberg, Erik. 2005. *The Progressive in 19th-Century English: A Process of Integration.* Amsterdam and New York. Rodopi.

Smitterberg, Erik. 2006. Partitive Constructions in Nineteenth-Century English. In *Nineteenth-Century English: Stability and Changes*, ed. Merja Kytö, Mats Rydén, and Erik Smitterberg, 242–271. Cambridge: Cambridge University Press.

Sørensen, Knud. 1985. *Charles Dickens: Linguistic Innovator.* Aarhus: Arkona.

Sørensen, Knud. 1989. Dickens on the Use of English. *English Studies* 70: 551–559.

Sotirova, Violeta. 2007. Historical Transformations of Free Indirect Style. In *Stylistics: Prospect and Retrospect 3*, ed. David L. Hoover and Sharon Lattig, 129–142. Amsterdam: Rodopi.

Späth, Eberhard. 1987. Das Private and das Öffentliche Tagebuch: Zum Verhältnis von Fiktion und Journalismus in Englischen Roman. *Poetica* 19 (1/2): 32–55.

Spiegel, Gabrielle M. 1990. History, Historicism and the Social Logic of the Text in the Middle Ages. *Speculum* 65: 59–86.

Spiegel, Gabrielle M. 1993. *Romancing the Past: The Rise of Vernacular Prose Historiography in Thirteenth-Century France.* Berkeley and Los Angeles: University of California Press.

Stanzel, Franz K. 1981. *Theorie des Erzählens.* Göttingen: Vandenhoeck and Ruprecht.

Stanzel, Franz K. 2002. *Unterwegs: Erzähltheorie für Leser.* Göttingen: Vandenhoek and Ruprecht.

Stein, Dieter. 1985. Perspectives on Historical Pragmatics. *Folia Linguistica Historica* 6: 347–355.

Stephens, William B. 1987. *Education, Literacy and Society, 1830–1870: The Geography of Diversity in Provincial England.* Manchester: Manchester University Press.

Sternberg, Meir. 1982a. Point of View and the Indirections of Direct Speech. *Language and Style* 15 (2): 67–117.

Sternberg, Meir. 1982b. Proteus in Quotation-land: Mimesis and the Forms of Reported Speech. *Poetics Today* 3 (2): 107–56.

Stitt, Megan Perigoe. 1998. *Metaphors of Change in the Language of Nineteenth-Century Fiction: Scott, Gaskell, and Kingsley.* Oxford: Clarendon Press.

Stockwell, Peter. 2002. *Cognitive Poetics: An Introduction.* London: Routledge.

Stokes, Myra. 1991. *The Language of Jane Austen: A Study of Some Aspects of Her Vocabulary.* London: Macmillan.

Stubbs, Michael. 1996. *Text and Corpus Analysis: Computer-Assisted Studies of Language and Culture.* Oxford: Blackwell.

Stubbs, Michael. 2001. *Words and Phrases: Corpus Studies of Lexical Semantics.* Oxford: Blackwell.

Stubbs, Michael. 2002. On Text and Corpus Analysis: A Reply to Borsley and Ingham. *Lingua* 112: 7–11.

Stubbs, Michael. 2005. Conrad in the Computer: Examples of Quantitative Stylistics Methods. *Language and Literature* 14 (1): 5–24.

Sullet-Nylander, Francoise. 2001. Reported Speech in French Media Discourse. In *New Directions in Nordic Text Linguistics Discourse Analysis: Methodological Issues*, ed. Wenche Vagle and Kay Wikberg, 123–136. Oslo: Novus Förlag.

Sweet, Henry. 1925 [1891–1898]. *A New English Grammar, Logical and Historical.* Oxford: Clarendon Press.

Sweetser, Eve E. 1990. From Etymology to Pragmatics: Metaphorical and Cultural Aspects of Semantic Structure. Cambridge: Cambridge University Press.

Taavitsainen, Irma. 1993. Genre/Subgenre Styles in Late Middle English. In *Early English in the Computer Age: Explorations through the Helsinki Corpus*, ed. Matti Rissanen, Merja Kytö, and Minna Palander-Collin, 171–200. Berlin and New York: Mouton de Gruyter.

Taavitsainen, Irma. 1994. Subjectivity as a Text-Type Marker in Historical Stylistics. *Language and Literature* 3 (3): 197–212.

Taavitsainen, Irma, and Andreas H. Jucker. 2007b. Speech Act Verbs and Speech Acts in the History of English. In *Methods in Historical Pragmatics*, ed. Susan Fitzmaurice and Irma Taavitsainen, 107–138. Berlin: Mouton de Gruyter, 2007.

Taavitsainen, Irma, and Andreas H. Jucker. 2008. *Speech Acts in the History of English.* Amsterdam: John Benjamins.

Tagliamonte, Sali, and Rachel Hudson. 1999. *Be Like* et al. Beyond America: The Quotative System in British and Canadian Youth. *Journal of Sociolinguistics* 3: 147–172.

Tamir, Nomi. 1976. Personal Narrative and Its Linguistic Foundation. *Poetics and Theory of Literature* 1: 403–429.

Tannen, Deborah. 1982a. Oral and Literate Strategies in Spoken and Written Narratives. *Language* 58: 1–21.

Tannen, Deborah. 1982b. The Oral/Literate Continuum in Discourse. In *Spoken and Written Language: Exploring Orality and Literacy*, ed. Deborah Tannen, 1–16. Norwood, NJ: Ablex.

Tannen, Deborah. 1985. Relative Focus on Involvement in Oral and Written Discourse. In *Literacy, Language, and Learning: The Nature and Consequences of Reading and Writing*, ed. David Olson, Nancy Torrance, and Angela Hildyard, 124–147. Cambridge: Cambridge University Press.

Tannen, Deborah. 1986. Introducing Constructed Dialogue in Greek and American Conversational and Literary Narrative. In *Direct and Indirect Speech*, ed. Florian Coulmas, 311–332. Berlin and New York: Mouton de Gruyter.

Tannen, Deborah. 1989. *Talking Voices: Repetition, Dialogue, and Imagery in Conversational Discourse.* Cambridge: Cambridge University Press.

Tannen, Deborah. 2007. *Talking Voices.* Cambridge: Cambridge University Press.

Taylor, Mary Vaiana. 1978. The Grammar of Conduct: Speech Act Theory and the Education of Emma Woodhouse. *Style* 12 (4): 357–371.

Teubert, Wolfgang. 2005. My Version of Corpus Linguistics. *International Journal of Corpus Linguistics* 10 (1): 1–13.

Thompson, Geoff. 1994. *Reporting: Collins Cobuild English Guides 5*. London: Harper Collins.

Thompson, Geoff. 1996. Voices in the Text: Discourse Perspectives on Language Reports. *Applied Linguistics* 17 (4): 501–530.

Tognini-Bonelli, Elena. 2001. *Corpus Linguistics at Work*. Amsterdam and Philadelphia: John Benjamins.

Toolan, Michael. 2000. "What Makes You Exist?": A Speech Move Schematic and Its Application to Pinter's *The Birthday Party*. *Journal of Pragmatics* 32: 177–201.

Toolan, Michael. 2001. *Narrative: A Critical Linguistic Introduction*. 2nd ed. London: Routledge.

Toolan, Michael. 2006a. Narrative: Linguistic and Structural Theories. In *Encyclopedia of Language and Linguistics*, ed. Keith Brown, vol. 8: 459–473. Amsterdam: Elsevier.

Toolan, Michael. 2006b. Speech and Thought: Representation. In *Encyclopedia of Language and Linguistics*, ed. Keith Brown, vol. 11: 698–710. Amsterdam: Elsevier.

Toolan, Michael. 2007. Trust and Text, Text as Trust. In *Words, Grammar, Text: Revisiting the Work of John Sinclair*, ed. Rosamund Moon. Special issue of *International Journal of Corpus Linguistics* 12 (2): 269–288.

Toolan, Michael. 2009. *Narrative Progression in the Short Story: A Corpus Stylistic Approach*. Amsterdam and New York: John Benjamins.

Toolan, Michael. 2010. Foreword: Lost and Found in the Reading Machine. In *Literary Education and Digital Learning: Methods and Technologies for Humanities Studies*, ed. Willie van Peer, Sonia Zyngier, and Vander Viana, x–xxiv. Hershey, PA: IGI Global.

Toolan, Michael. 2016. *Making Sense of Narrative Text: Situation, Repetition, and Picturing in the Reading of Short Stories*. London: Routledge.

Traugott, Elizabeth C. 2004a. A Critique of Levinson's View of Q- and M-inferences in Historical Pragmatics. *Journal of Historical Pragmatics* 5: 1–26.

Traugott, Elizabeth C. 2004b. Historical Pragmatics. In *The Handbook of Pragmatics*, ed. Laurence R. Horn and Gregory Ward, 538–561. Oxford: Blackwell.

Trudgill, Peter, and Richard Watts, eds. 2002. *Alternative Histories of English*. London: Routledge.

Ungerer, Friedrich, and Hans-Jörg Schmid. 2006. *An Introduction to Cognitive Linguistics*. Harlow: Pearson.

Uspensky, Boris A. 1973. *A Poetics of Composition*. Berkeley: University of California Press.

Urban, Margaret, and Josef Ruppenhofer. 2001. Shouting and Screaming: Manner and Noise Verbs in Communication. *Literary and Linguistic Computing* 16 (1): 73–94.

Vandelanotte, Lieven. 2004. Deixis and Grounding in Speech and Thought Representation. *Journal of Pragmatics* 36: 489–520.

Vandelanotte, Lieven. 2009. *Speech and Thought Representation in English: A Cognitive-Functional Approach*. Berlin: Mouton de Gruyter.

Vandelanotte, Lieven, and Kristin Davidse. 2011. Tense Use in Direct and Indirect Speech in English. *Journal of Pragmatics* 43: 236–250.

Verschueren, Jef. 1999. *Understanding Pragmatics*. London: Arnold.

Vološinov, Valentin N. 1973 [1929]. *Marxism and the Philosophy of Language*. New York: Seminar Press.

Wales, Katie. 2001. *A Dictionary of Stylistics*. Harlow: Longman.

Walker, Brian. 2010. Wmatrix, Key Concepts and the Narrators in Julian Barnes's "Talking It Over." In *Language and Style*, ed. Dan McIntyre and Beatrix Busse, 364–387. Basingstoke: Palgrave Macmillan.

Walker, Brian, and Dan McIntyre. 2015. Thinking about the News: Thought Presentation in Early Modern English News Writing. In *Corpora and Discourse Studies*, ed. Tony McEnery and Paul Baker, 175–191. London: Palgrave Macmillan.

Walker, Terry, and Peter J. Grund. 2017. "Speaking Base Approbious Words": Speech Representation in Early Modern English Witness Depositions. *Journal of Historical Pragmatics* 18 (1): 1–29.

Watts, Richard. 2002. From Polite Language to Educated Language: The Re-Emergence of an Ideology. In *Alternative Histories of English*, ed. Richard Watts and Peter Trudgill, 155–172. London: Routledge.

Watts, Richard, and Peter Trudgill, eds. 2002. *Alternative Histories of English*. London: Routledge.

Waugh, Linda R. 1995. Reported Speech Journalistic Discourse: The Relation of Function and Text. *Text* 15 (1): 129–173.

Werth, Paul. 1999. *Text Worlds: Representing Conceptual Space in Discourse*. London: Longman.

Weste, Linda. 2014. "Country" in Australian Contemporary Verse Novels. *Journal of the Association for the Study of Australian Literature* 14 (3): 1–15.

Widdowson, Henry G. 2000. On the Limitations of Linguistics Applied. *Applied Linguistics* 21 (1): 3–25.

Wilson, John, and Heather Walker. 2015. Pragmatic Markers as Implicit Emotive Anchoring: Modality as Evidence of Trauma in the 1641 Depositions. In *Pragmatic Markers in Irish English*, ed. Carolina Amador-Moreno, Kevin McCafferty, and Elaine Vaughan, 248–269. Amsterdam: John Benjamins.

Wittgenstein, Ludwig. 1958. *Philosophical Investigations*. Oxford: Blackwell.

Włodarczyk, Matylda. 2007. *Pragmatic Aspects of Reported Speech: The Case of Early Modern English Courtroom Discourse*. Frankfurt: Peter Lang.

Wood, Joseph. 1880. Sight and Insight. *Modern Review* I: 224–234.

Wooffitt, Robin F. 2001. Raising the Dead: Reported Speech in Medium-Sitter Interaction. *Discourse Studies* 3 (3): 351–374.

Wright, Laura. 2000. On the Construction of Some Early Modern English Courtroom Narratives. In *English Diachronic Pragmatics*, ed. Gabriella di Martino and Maria Lima, 79–102. Naples: CUEN.

Wynne, Martin, Michael Short, and Elena Semino. 1998. A Corpus-Based Investigation of Speech, Thought and Writing Presentation in English Narrative Texts. In *Explorations in Corpus Linguistics*, ed. Antoinette Renouf, 231–245. Amsterdam: Rodopi.

Young, Tory. 2014. Brooklyn as the "Untold Story" of "Eveline": Reading Joyce and Tóibín with Ricoeur. *Journal of Modern Literature* 37 (2): 123–140.

Zwicky, Arnold. 1971. In a Manner of Speaking. *Linguistic Inquiry* 2 (2): 223–233.

Zwierlein, Anne-Julia, ed. 2005. *Unmapped Countries: Biological Visions in Nineteenth-Century Literature*. London: Anthem Press.

INDEX